BUT
WILL THE
PLANET
NOTICE?

BUT WILL THE PLANET NOTICE?

HOW SMART ECONOMICS CAN SAVE THE WORLD

GERNOT WAGNER

HILL AND WANG
A DIVISION OF FARRAR, STRAUS AND GIROUX   NEW YORK

Hill and Wang
A division of Farrar, Straus and Giroux
18 West 18th Street, New York 10011

Distributed in Canada by D&M Publishers, Inc.
Printed in the United States of America
First edition, 2011

Library of Congress Cataloging-in-Publication Data
Wagner, Gernot, 1980–
    But will the planet notice? : how smart economics can save the world / Gernot
Wagner. — 1st ed.
        p.   cm.
    Includes bibliographical references and index.
    ISBN 978-0-8090-5207-3 (cloth : alk. paper)
    1. Environmental policy.   2. Conservation of natural resources—Government
policy.   3. Conservation of natural resources—Citizen participation.   I. Title.

GE170.W34 2011
333.72—dc22

2011010743

Designed by Abby Kagan

www.fsgbooks.com

1   3   5   7   9   10   8   6   4   2

FOR KIWI

CONTENTS

BUT
WILL THE
PLANET
NOTICE?

DOING GOOD

"Paper or plastic?"

After all these years I still feel just a little bit smug saying "Neither." But does it really matter that I've lugged around my worn-out cotton bag all day? Should I feel less smug because it contains fruit trucked in from Florida? What about the lady behind me who has passed up oranges in favor of local apples?

Local is good. Fine. But when can I eat my daily apple? Local New York apples in the summer, after ten months in an upstate cool house, may well have a larger carbon footprint than apples flown in from Chile, harvested during the Southern Hemisphere's growing season. It's a global conundrum. Say you're a Londoner. Dutch flowers raised in a greenhouse lose out against roses grown under the Kenyan sun and packed into a 747 before reaching your neighborhood florist.[1]

I'm no No Impact Man, but I try to minimize my environmental footprint wherever possible. My wife and I live in a one-bedroom

apartment in New York without air-conditioning, much to the conster-
nation of our superintendent, who has offered to install a unit for free.
No way. We want to keep our combined monthly electricity and cooking gas bill under $30. That's less than a third of the U.S. national aver-
age. We have taken our super up on the offer to install efficient compact
fluorescent lightbulbs throughout our apartment, and I continue to
stare in amazement at our low-water, high-intensity toilet. Which
Ph.D. got to spend time testing that patent?

Why do I do all this? Is it pride, conviction, delusion? Yes, I enjoy
the self-affirmation of my "neither" at the grocery store and my warm
July apartment. Look at me! I understand what is going on around this
planet and am trying to relate to it in a constructive way. But do I really
think having an *über*efficient toilet flush will make a scintilla of difference in the final outcome? What if I have to flush twice? Even if I
convince my parents, my in-laws, my relatives, my friends, everyone
who ever passes through our home, and everyone who reads this book
to take the exact same steps, *will the planet notice*?

I may not drive, but I fly. I fly a lot. Almost every vacation my wife and
I go on is sealed by stamps in at least two of our four passports. I saw
my family in Austria six times last year, mostly on the way to and from
United Nations–sponsored climate meetings. So much for worrying
about three-ply toilet paper and the occasional out-of-season grape.
Whatever you and I do on a daily basis is dwarfed by a single cross-
Atlantic flight. However much you recycle or turn off lights, it will be
canceled out many times over by your driving a car. Driving ten thousand miles in even the most fuel-efficient Prius produces four tons of
carbon dioxide. That matches annual emissions for the average human
on the planet. It also equals two transatlantic round-trips on a commercial jet. Little wonder then that the average European emits around
ten tons per year; the average American tops even that at twenty.[2]

Transport choices raise real questions. Flying from Washington to

New York or from Salzburg to Vienna is nuts—environmentally and as a matter of personal comfort, cost, and speed. Flying from New York to Vienna is a different matter altogether.

How to balance the benefits of seeing my brothers, parents, and grandparents—or simply of roaming around a Moroccan souk or lounging on a Caribbean beach during vacation—against the environmental impact of the inevitable plane ride needed to do so? How do any of us balance our responsibility to the planet and to each other? Is Epcot the only environmentally sensible way for Floridians to see Paris, and Euro Disney the only way for Parisians to experience life on Main Street, U.S.A.? What good are the (dwindling) snows of Kilimanjaro if we can't experience them with a clear conscience? What are we—individually and as a society—prepared to give up to keep the snowcap and a million other aspects of life as we know it today?

NO VOLUNTEERS, PLEASE

One answer is to forgo modern comforts and opt for a modest, sedentary life. Good luck with that. Abandoned farmhouses and empty monasteries point to how well that goes over in our age. Two weeks of silence in a Buddhist yoga retreat in the Himalayas with BlackBerrys checked at the door? Sure. An entire life voluntarily lived off the grid? Not so much.

More important, what you and I do individually does not make the least bit of difference on its own. For every environmentalist voluntarily living in a Mongolian yurt in Alaska, there are plenty of Mongolians, Chinese, Americans, and many others who gladly would—and do—make up for the missing environmental footprint. Worse, many of the perceived environmental improvements in the United States, Europe, and other wealthy parts of the globe are a sleight of hand, achieved by shuttering factories producing energy-intensive products. We still use the same stuff; we just don't produce it ourselves. The planet doesn't care that it's now made in China and elsewhere with cheaper labor and resources. All else being equal, the planet would prefer products to be produced closer to where they are consumed to cut down on shipping.[3]

Short of the occasional rounding error or the off chance that your personal action will start a social movement, the small things you and I do in our daily lives, taken by themselves, have no effect. Not driving might keep me sane, safe, and save quite a bit of money, but it has virtually no global environmental impact. Going vegetarian? Zero. Wearing organic, natural fibers? Zip. Flying less, or offsetting emissions from flights? Zilch.

Worse, all these steps may well be counterproductive. Just think of the rain forest that needs to be cleared to grow the soy for my tofu or the additional land that gets converted to agriculture to produce pesticide-free cotton. Even buying carbon offset credits may backfire, if buying them makes me feel better about flying and as a result I do more of it. If the money is used to subsidize a wind farm, your offset dollars help decrease the cost of energy overall, which in turn may well motivate others to use more.

Most do-gooders encounter a "rebound" effect of sorts: now that I'm offsetting my carbon footprint by spending a few bucks to plant trees, I get to drive and fly more. The same goes for spending money on buying green energy.[4] Volunteering to spend a bit extra on my electricity bill ensures that my utility spends a bit extra on wind rather than on coal energy, but purchasing green electricity makes me think I can keep the air conditioner running without guilt, canceling some of the benefits.

In truth, broad-based studies of the rebound effect have shown that it hovers around 10 percent to 30 percent, most certainly less than a hundred.[5] A more fuel-efficient car makes you visit Grandma a bit more often; it doesn't void all of the environmental benefits. But that says little about offsets as marketing ploys and the ways individuals react to them. Why else would some airlines draw attention to their carbon footprint on their booking sites, if not for the hope that you would fly more often—or at least choose them over their rivals?

Even the warm and fuzzy feeling these actions create may come with negative side effects. Psychologists talk about the "single-action bias." I refuse to grab a plastic bag at the take-out place and falsely imagine that my token gesture somehow makes a difference that compensates for other environmental sins throughout the day. That bias can result in phenomenal mass delusion. Significantly more Democrats thought the environment was getting better after President Barack Obama took office than only a year earlier, as if the mere act of voting by itself made everything just dandy.[6] Thus go the unintended effects of a well-meant climate absolution. In the end, of course, the atmosphere notices neither the tiny positive nor the tiny negative effect of individual actions.

The question is how to get to a critical mass that does make a difference. When is one plus one no longer zero or even just two?

One way is to start a movement. The Nobel laureate Wangari Maathai and her followers have planted millions of trees in sub-Saharan Africa. "Slow food" is quickly spreading beyond foodie enclaves and college campuses and changing the way more and more of us look at what we eat. The Earth Day movement in the United States has had profound effects since its inception over forty years ago. The very first Earth Day drew twenty million people, a tenth of the U.S. population at the time, and rang in the environmental decade. It turned Richard Nixon into an environmental president and led him to sign some of the most significant pieces of environmental legislation, such as the U.S. Clean Air and Water Acts. Still, the environmental movement has yet to garner enough momentum to fix many of the crucial problems we are facing now.

Bill McKibben's 350.org is trying to rekindle that spirit and then some for a global climate movement. It has managed to mobilize some of the most widespread political protests in history, and it may yet end up pushing the needle. But the crucial point is that it's not up to the thousands or millions coming to the streets with "350" signs demanding that greenhouse gas concentrations in the atmosphere return to that level. It will be up to a handful of politicians to pass laws that will make the difference. That, of course, is exactly the point of these protests, and McKibben is the first to say as much.

The facts are brutally clear. The collective will and drive of billions voids most if not all feel-good efforts of freelance environmental heroism. It's the tremendous power of channeling those billions of individual decisions through markets that has provided Americans, Europeans, and a few lucky others with unprecedented levels of personal wealth. It has pulled hundreds of millions of Chinese out of poverty, and it is increasingly doing so for millions of others. Markets are the primary mechanism that produces modern growth and dynamism. They open up the playing field for innovators and entrepreneurs to create the creature comforts most of us can't imagine living without.

Yet this book is not an argument for market fundamentalism, shrinking government into oblivion and leaving everything to its own devices. Markets require property rights, a framework for legal institutions, and well-functioning enforcement mechanisms: no market without government.

Market forces unfettered by smart regulatory guidance have led to entire peoples being left behind, burst housing bubbles, and other assorted market crashes—the latest driving six million Americans to live off food stamps and pushing nations into the capitalist abyss.[7]

Despite these real and serious problems, whenever I get carried away deriding market inefficiencies and castigating capitalism, I am reminded of the brilliant *New Yorker* cartoon of two cavemen contemplating their short lives: "Something's just not right—our air is clean, our water is pure, we all get plenty of exercise, everything we eat is organic and free-range, and yet nobody lives past thirty."

Americans may live slightly shorter lives than many Europeans and the centenarian-producing Japanese. Recent gains in life expectancy may have stalled, and the leaky social net and obesity epidemic might even mean we're creeping backward, but people in the United States still live twice as long as much less fortunate ones in dirt-poor

Zambia, Angola, and Swaziland, which grace the bottom of the global ranking.[8]

Wealth is not everything in this calculus. Cuba's life expectancy famously rivals that of the United States without much free-market ideology. And of course, you won't be able to eat money when the last tree has been cut, the last river poisoned, and the last fish caught. But at least up to a point, having it sure seems to help.

SOME GROUND RULES

Money makes the world go 'round. I take this statement as my starting point. Whether we like it or not, our values and priorities have made this true. The nearly ubiquitous pursuit of wealth and status makes it a practical guide for both studying and nudging human behavior. After all is said and done, that pursuit is how most people behave on average. The question of whether or not this should be true is significant, profound, and pressing. It's also not one I attempt to answer. I leave that to theologians, philosophers, poets, and new-age yogis searching for a deeper meaning in life.

With money making the world go 'round, it's also no doubt true that free markets left to themselves are destroying our environment. We are eating raw, mercury-laced endangered species from ever-less-populated seas while cooking the planet under a blanket of greenhouse gas pollution. It's no longer a question of *if* New York City will be underwater if we don't turn things around soon. It's a question of *when*. No continent will be unaffected, with up to a billion people on the move.[9] Talk about extreme events. And that—without action—is what *will* happen.

That's a starting point as well. I am not setting out to prove and reprove the science. Plenty of volumes have been written on the topic that do so admirably. I do not pretend to know more than entire National Academies of Science or to be able to recount the facts of global warming more persuasively than award-winning science writers from

Heidi Cullen to Tim Flannery, Ross Gelbspan, Mark Hertsgaard, Elizabeth Kolbert, Mark Lynas, Bill McKibben, Carl Safina, the late Steve Schneider, and, yes, Al Gore.[10] The recent politicization of basic chemistry and physics is unfortunate, but it does not change the facts—nor is it a matter of "belief." As astrophysicist Neil deGrasse Tyson says, "The good thing about science is that it's true, whether you believe in it or not." Climate change is a serious threat to our planet and human welfare. Case closed.[11]

To be sure, there are many aspects of an increasingly unstable climate that have yet to be clarified. Most of them make things more urgent, not less so. There is indeed a teeny, tiny chance that the vast scientific consensus is missing something crucial and that the planet will somehow cope with greenhouse gas concentrations at twice their preindustrial levels, and growing. Yet the chance is much greater that the notoriously conservative scientific community is lagging behind the latest trends.

The North Pole seems to be turning free from summer sea ice fifty years ahead of schedule—within this decade rather than the latter half of the century, as predicted in consensus documents as late as 2007.[12] That even has effects on the length of days. The melting poles act like an ice skater stretching out her arms while spinning. More weight farther from the axis slows her down. The same happens when ice melts on the poles and more water accumulates near the equator. Dumping carbon into the atmosphere is literally slowing the rotation of the planet. Things are bad and getting worse, and behind the remaining uncertainties is the strong possibility that they are much worse than we understand.

Moreover, climate may be the defining environmental issue of our time, but it's not all that's out of whack and getting worse because of misguided market forces. The global carbon cycle is only one of many we as humans are now dominating and changing beyond recognition. Our influence on the nitrogen cycle is arguably much worse, and we have long taken over the oceans and changed entire ecosystems irreversibly.

Science begone. This book is about both more personal and much larger questions: What about the energy-saving lightbulb? Or passing on the beef?—questions that haunt us every day. To which we should always add, does the planet notice what you and I do personally? That, if anything, is *the* question we need to ask ourselves, and it turns all these personal questions on their heads.

If you are hung up on whether or not you should order the skirt steak, you are missing the mark by several orders of magnitude. The question is whether society at large should—and not in a paternalistic red-meat-is-bad-for-you kind of way.

Let's imagine everyone suddenly started ordering steak. If that happens in a single restaurant, the kitchen would run out soon enough, and the waiter would have to start apologizing profusely. Of course, you are free to leave the restaurant in search of your meat fix. On the planet, that's impossible. At that scale, we are indeed facing real limits. Moreover, we can't influence these limits—and the way we are coping with them—by ourselves.

The fundamental forces guiding the behavior of billions are much larger than any one of us. It's about changing our system, creating a new business as usual. And to do that we need to think about what makes our system run. In the end, it comes down to markets, and the rules of the game that govern what we chase and how we chase it.

Scientists can tell us how bad it will get. Activists can make us pay attention to the ensuing instabilities and make politicians take note. When the task comes to formulating policy, only economists can help guide us out of this morass and save the planet.

In an earlier time with simpler problems, environmentalists took direct action against the market's brutal forces by erecting roadblocks or chaining themselves to trees. That works if the opposing force is a lumberjack with a chain saw. It might even work for an entire industry when the task is to ban a particular chemical or scrub a pollutant out of

shelter, water
energy,

smokestacks. But that model breaks down when the opposing force is ourselves: each and every one of us demanding that the globalized market provide us with cheaper and better food, clothes, and vacations.

There is no blocking the full, collective desires of the billions who are now part of the market economy and the billions more who want to—and ought to—be part of it. The only solution is to guide all-powerful market forces in the right direction and create incentives for each of us to make choices that work for all of us.

The guideposts we have today for market forces evolved helter-skelter from a historical process that gave almost no weight to the survival of the planet, largely because the survival of the planet was not at stake. Now it is. Since we can't live without market forces, we need to guide them to help us keep the human adventure going in workable ways, rather than continue on the present path right off the edge of a cliff.

Presidential candidate Barack Obama said it most succinctly: "Well, the truth is, Brian, we can't solve global warming because I f——ing changed light bulbs in my house. It's because of something collective."[13] He was cautious enough to say this after the debate moderated by Brian Williams and not in front of rolling cameras, or he might not have been elected. But the spirit of his remark is absolutely right.

It's not that everyone shouldn't be insulating homes, carrying around cotton canvas bags, and taking public transport. The point is exactly that *everyone* should do these things, and not from the desire for smugness or personal satisfaction, but because it's the cheapest, easiest thing to do.

As much as this issue has been politicized, this is not about right versus left, Republicans versus Democrats, conservatives versus conservationists, or markets versus the environment. This is about liberating markets and consequently turning each and every one of us into a force for good; it's about making sure that increasing GDP, gross domestic product, does not decrease collective well-being.

It's about taking personal responsibility for costs we now socialize and impose on society and the planet as a whole. Our choices are already being influenced by forces much larger than ourselves. They always have been and will be. The question is whether the nudging we submit to is guiding us where we want to go, preserving life and the rotation of the planet as we know it.

This equation has no neutral ground. It's not a clear-cut moral issue, nor is it a personal question that has a simple answer based on one's belief system. This isn't as easy as the decision to go vegetarian, as much as I would have liked to write a book like Jonathan Safran Foer's *Eating Animals*, a gripping essay that convinced Natalie Portman, a lifelong vegetarian, to turn vegan and one that convinced my wife, a lifelong seafood lover, and me, a lifelong Austrian, to give up meat once and for all. The conclusion is simple: Don't eat animals. Saving the planet is in a different league altogether. It's not something that can be resolved by yourself, or in a personal conversation between you and your God. It's between you and the seven billion people breathing the same air, drinking from the same interconnected water system, and looking to the same sun for light, energy, and heat.

Foer had an additional benefit: fuzzy animals, most of whom are cute. Alas, my argument means keeping company with economists. Some of these encounters will be pleasant, friendly exchanges of ideas. Some will be like bitter pills. It's easy to like economists when they work on cutesy topics from baby names to sumo wrestlers. It's tougher to like them when they prescribe trillion-dollar bailouts of loathed financial companies, or when they work on ensuring that we will never find ourselves in a situation where we wished we could bail out the planet. But in the spirit of remaining on a livable Earth, here goes.

GAME PLAN

right) .

Many of the questions in this book are at the very heart of human survival. How can we guide market forces in the right direction, away from the earth-shattering, planet-destroying ways of the past into a low-carbon, high-efficiency, low-impact future? Or, most simply, how the heck do we get out of this mess?

There will be lots of questions, some data, fewer firm conclusions. One conclusion, though, is already clear: pick your battles wisely, don't sweat the small stuff, live the 80-20 rule, and generally follow whichever cliché prompts you to avoid missing the biodiversity of an entire carbon-sequestering, life-giving forest for a single tree.

This is not about recycling the battery or putting your milk carton into the right receptacle. (Which one is it anyway? It's not just paper. It's not plastic either. And what about the thin film of sour milk inside? Is it worth the water or perhaps even dish soap to get it all out?) It's about freeing ourselves from those worries and instead fretting about the big issues.

It doesn't get much bigger than a near-total collapse of the financial system and a planet on life support. That's where we will start.

1

CUE THE ECONOMISTS

ECONOMICS 101

Ask around what caused the financial crisis, and the answer, absent expletives, will be some version of "wrong incentives." The road signs guiding market forces pointed in the wrong direction. Wall Street wasn't doing what was in everyone's best interests. What's good for Goldman Sachs turned out not to be all that good for America.

Shift your focus on what ails the planet, and the answer will be very much the same. "Wrong incentives" are as important here as they were in the financial crisis. Replace "Goldman" with "Exxon," and you have everyone's favorite environmental villain. They ravage the planet for their own gains, without regard for anyone else around them. Greedy bastards.

There is something to this idea, as knee-jerk as it might be. By now, "privatizing profits and socializing losses" has its own *Wikipedia* page. On Wall Street, that translates into "too big to fail." If my bets pay off,

I will get the fat year-end bonus. If they don't, I will be on a one-way (business-class) flight back from the craps table in Vegas, and everyone else—you, government, society—is left with cleaning up the mess. Heads I win, tails you lose; or, the dirty underside of capitalism for the masses, and the gentle safety net of socialism for the corporate echelons.

The environment is in the same situation, caused by the same misguided incentives. Exxon, BP, and the like rake in record profits while enjoying dubious tax loopholes and special subsidies.[1] When an oil platform in the Gulf explodes and entire fishing grounds go belly-up, everyone faces the consequences. And that says nothing about global warming, where literally everyone—all seven billion of us—is affected, the poor and disenfranchised most of all.

The risk calculus that capitalism was supposed to force risk takers to make, it turned out, was a hoax. It became instead a one-way street where those who controlled the wealth stood to make the gains, and those who carried the liability side of the planet's balance sheet were expected to clean up after them.

Waiting in the hope that corporate executives will be shamed or enlightened into giving up loopholes, forgoing subsidies, and turning corporations into charities is a fool's game. Greed—capitalism—is not the problem, and vilifying any company that turns a profit is ludicrous. That's its appointed purpose, and, like it or not, it's the single most effective organizing principle of modern society. I am not saying capitalists are doing God's work; they just work to feed their families and bank accounts, like the rest of us.

You and I are rich and can enjoy the pleasures of reading and writing books because of it. If you read this in any kind of electronic form, or aren't afraid of losing loved ones to typhoid, cholera, or the plague, or have ever sat in a car, train, or plane, you will certainly appreciate the fact that capitalism didn't stop its ascendancy around the time Gutenberg printed his first Bibles. We don't want to stop market forces, even if we could. We want to work with—not against—them.

The solution is clear: *put the right incentives in place.* Or, if you care for more sophisticated academic parlance: *internalize the externalities.*

Measure how much damage each and every action does, put a dollar value on it, and set the appropriate price. Don't like trillions of dollars being sent around the globe every day at the stroke of a button? Introduce financial transaction taxes.[2] Don't like treating the atmosphere like a free sewer? Put a price on carbon.

That's a wrap, people. Two problems solved at once. Future financial crises averted; environmental crises gone. I'll save myself the trouble of writing the rest of the book, and you can get back to worrying about whatever occupied you before the recession and an increasingly unstable planet crowded those worries out. We even save a few trees or iPad charges in the process. Win-win-win.

If only it were that simple.

POLITICAL ECONOMICS 101

In 1990, Congress, in its finite wisdom, capped total economic damage payments for any one offshore oil spill at $75 million.[3] This despite the fact that no one in either chamber apparently knew what it meant to link these kinds of limits to ever-rising prices—a.k.a. inflation—or that $75 million wasn't all that much even then. Worse, perhaps they all did and still voted for the final bill 99–0 in the Senate and 360–0 in the House. Talk about a slam dunk. When it comes to contradicting Economics 101, bipartisanship, apparently, is all the rage.

It's not hard to concoct conspiracy theories on how Big Oil controls the political machine. Yes, politicians do what voters want them to do. If not, they get voted out of office. That would be Democracy 101. But vested interests clearly have a stake in the status quo, and it doesn't get much bigger than Big Oil, which comprises some of the most profitable companies in history.

Surprise, political "leaders" aren't always driven by deeply held convictions. Reaching the masses requires having a megaphone, and megaphones cost money. Lots of it. By now, U.S. national and even some state-level elections run in the hundreds of millions of dollars. Little wonder politicians say what big donors want them to say. Money speaks and votes. Politics 101.

During the 2008–10 congressional fight to enact a comprehensive climate law, Big Oil, King Coal, and climate deniers of all stripes spent around $500 million against sensible climate action, outspending environmental campaigners, renewable-energy interests, and the like to the tune of ten to one. Never mind that there is some reason to believe that even the United States may have a "climate majority."[4] Careful polling unearths three-quarters of Americans who say that the climate is changing and that humans are the cause of it. Over 85 percent say they want limits on how much air pollution businesses are allowed to emit. Still, recent poll results show clear trends toward increased polarization and politicization of century-old scientific facts. When Al Gore says global warming is happening, you no longer care what basic physics and chemistry say. You care about whether or not you would vote for Gore for other reasons. One key factor in all of this is money. Those who have it can sway the malleable masses. Those who don't can't. By the time the Senate all but killed climate legislation in the summer of 2010, dirty money had prevailed.

Amazingly, that's not always the case. The same Congress that voted 99–0 and 360–0 to cap damages for offshore oil spills also voted 89–10 and 401–25 to cap sulfur dioxide pollutants that cause acid rain. That's small potatoes compared with capping carbon dioxide emissions, but it has shown how unusual coalitions between environmental activists and business interests can form to pass a strong market-based law. More recently, in 2010, venture capitalists and others with stakes in a greener future outspent and out-campaigned opponents of a comprehensive climate bill in California to the tune of three to one. Thirty million dollars for keeping a climate bill on the books; $10 million to suspend it.[5] In the end proponents of the bill prevailed. It's not the first time that Sacramento showed Washington the way on environmental issues. Perhaps there's some hope after all.

There are other ways to change minds. How about a global campaign to right the wrongs? Let's put "Internalize Externalities" on bumper stickers. Stage teach-ins at the local parish. Organize the Million Internalizers March on Washington. I can see Madonna lining up for the London concert and Nepalese Sherpas spelling out those two all-important words on the dwindling snows of the Himalayas, in biodegradable paint. Activism 101.

That's clearly a crucial component: raise awareness, start a movement. Convince everyone around you to eat locally grown food— slowly—and quickly plant a million trees in the Sahel. Concerts help, too. Madonna even wrote a new song for Live Earth in 2007. And we have seen Sherpas in action as well. A group of them joined thousands of others in holding up "350" signs all over the world as part of a campaign to limit greenhouse gas concentrations to 350 parts per million in the atmosphere, what's required to stabilize the climate and stop sea levels from rising too far. (We are now at above 390 and counting.)

Activism is important—I'm in one of those "350" pictures—and lots of crucial things are happening on the ground: from American teens being miles ahead of their parents in their awareness of how they are changing the planet, to a new generation of Indian youth leaders realizing that environment and development ought to go hand in hand. There's hope, lots of it. Sadly, we don't have another decade or two until those young leaders come of age. And even once they do, and this is the crucial point, the solution will be very much the same as what we have on deck.

That answer is clear: get comfortable with the idea that we ought to be using markets and market forces, and use the very people—you, me, all of us—whose greed and everyday behavior got us into the mess in the first place to get us out of it. It's time to substitute the right incentives for the wrong ones and set a new default path for the planet.

ACCOUNTING 101

Sadly, we have known about this fundamental problem of misguided incentives at least since Madonna was dancing circles around her fellow third graders—and the problem didn't just appear in obscure academic writings. Robert F. Kennedy lamented on March 18, 1968, in the first major speech of his presidential campaign, that gross domestic product "measures everything . . . except that which makes life worthwhile."[6]

Consider the Christmas tree.

When I put on my water-repellent Birkenstock hiking boots and trudge through the snow to a Christmas tree farm to get my Norway spruce for the most idyllic of family fests, I pay the farmer for his trouble of growing the tree with organic fertilizers, keeping it pest-free without pesticides, and packing it in a biodegradable mesh bag. Mainly, though, I pay for the tree itself, the wood. I don't pay for the roots' sophisticated water filtration services, nor for the needles' equally sophisticated system for cleansing the air. No one does.

These essential arboreal functions and the cleaner water and air they provide are worth a big fat zero in our corporate and societal balance sheets. Most trees only become valuable once dead. A standing tree may be valued for its future timber but little else. Put that tree forever beyond the saw of man, and its effective value in our official statistics falls to zero.

GDP is our main economic yardstick of how well we are doing as a society.[7] It determines the fortunes of entire peoples, not least those of the people in power at any given time. Two consecutive quarters of declining GDP, and the bean counters at the National Bureau of Economic Research, the official scorekeepers of such things for the United States, declare a recession. Have that announcement coincide with the election cycle, and the president can start packing. Ask Gerald Ford, Jimmy Carter, or George H. W. Bush. Or ask John McCain why he thinks he didn't make it into the White House in 2008.[8]

Long-term trends are even more important. When Hong Kong,

Singapore, South Korea, and Taiwan—the Asian Tigers—roared into the global consumerism super-league within a few decades, GDP was the scorecard that put them there. China is now following suit in the most far-reaching transition ever.

It would be comforting to say that more GDP is always a good thing, and to a point that's clearly the case. Living on a dollar a day is miserable no matter how you look at it.

But RFK had it exactly right. GDP reflects a lot of destructive and nonproductive activity, and all but ignores everything other than material wealth, money. The work of leaves and tree roots is just one such contribution left to the wayside. Indonesia's GDP growth figures throughout the 1970s and 1980s would have been cut in half had the official number crunchers bothered to consider that extracting a tree trunk or a barrel of oil from the ground today means it's no longer there for the taking tomorrow.[9] The same recalculation could be done the world over, for Madoff-style, fairy-tale accounting has been the norm for a long time. It's like running a business and reporting only your revenue, not the costs of raw materials. Now those costs are galloping forward, and it's time to audit the books honestly.

If the game is to maximize GDP as currently constructed, protecting the planet is not in the cards. Every ton of coal taken out of West Virginia mines adds over $30 to GDP, but no one accounts for the fact that the ton is no longer in the ground. Imposing that simple act of honest bookkeeping would decrease the value to half, around $15.[10] And that still doesn't account for the larger human and environmental costs: black-lung disease in miners, destruction of ecosystems from mountaintop removal, coal sludge runoffs polluting rivers near mines, or the impacts on public health and the world's climate of burning the coal.

Oil is just like coal: everything gets added, nothing subtracted. Every barrel of oil pumped out of the ground, whether it ends up in your gas tank or on our shorelines, increases GDP. The barrel that gets burned in your car adds to GDP because you pay for it at the pump. The barrel that washes up onshore adds to GDP because someone pays for the cleanup costs.

What's true for countries is also true for companies. They gladly add gains from selling oil to their corporate balance sheets. The ensuing pollution is someone else's problem. And you can't blame Exxon's management for making sure this is the case. They have to. It's not just the nature of the game; it's the law. Managers have fiduciary responsibilities to the company's shareholders to maximize profits. The current road signs, as it were, all point them in that one direction. And without that incentive, capitalism as we know it could not function. If managers don't manage in the interest of a company's owners, the model of corporations will fall apart. If depleting natural resources comes at zero charge and the planet doesn't count, exploiting it isn't just good business. It's the only business.

There are plenty of case studies of companies that do well by doing good. But that's the point. These are case studies. Many others are hunkering down in their respective industries and going about doing business as usual. BP might want to claim it's moving "beyond petroleum," but a million rebranding campaigns can't hide the fact that its core business is oil. The economy as a whole isn't changing gears voluntarily.

Let's look back to the financial sector for a particularly poignant example. In the lead-up to the latest economic crisis, everyone up and down the financial-sector food chain had been facing the wrong incentives, and in many instances they still are. Whether you are the poor mortgage broker reduced to cold-calling renters in graduate student housing (one tried to convince my wife and me in 2005 that we could afford to get a $400,000 interest-only mortgage: "You're still in school now, but you are graduating soon, right?" "Well, yes, but she will be a medical resident, barely making enough to pay back her student loans." "Oh, hmm, we can work something out"), whether you are a credit-rating agency hired by the issuer of an overly complicated financial instrument to rubber-stamp that it is indeed secure, or whether you are Chuck Prince, the CEO and chairman of what was once the world's largest bank, in the end you are responding to the incentives presented to you. There were plenty of crooks and even more who checked their moral compasses at the door, but most were only following orders.

This is not the Nuremberg defense: I know my actions were illegal, but I was just following orders. Actually, it's the opposite. The orders followed didn't lead to illegal actions. Just as fiduciary responsibility compels Exxon managers to extract ever more oil, it also requires everyone in the finance sector to keep on dancing. Shortly before collecting his own $40 million golden parachute, Chuck Prince uttered his famous last words: "As long as the music is playing, you've got to get up and dance." Emphasis on "you've got to." And the fact that legislators had erased many of the existing checks and restrictions—those few road signs that had been pointing in different directions—only lit fire under Prince's and other bankers' feet.

Don't vilify Prince. He had it right. Bankers ought to be dancing to the music. That's what we are paying them for, and the task isn't to stop them or to turn off the music entirely. Regulators need to make sure that everyone faces the full consequences of his or her actions. The goal may be to slow down the dance a bit, but mainly it's to change the beat.

The same goes for environmental problems. No one wants entrepreneurs and businesses to stop dancing. Well, let me amend that. I'm sure there are some environmentalists who would rather have all business grind to a halt. That can't be the goal, though. Explain to a poor Indian living on a dollar a day—who watches his infants die because of preventable diseases and poor sanitation—that now that we are rich and he is not, the world must stop all development for the sake of preserving unspoiled nature. Beyond being immoral, it is utopian to imagine it possible.

We know that there are strong forces compelling us to dance. But we also know that we can't keep dancing the way we have been so far, not while the planet is burning. The big question is how to change the dance beat. Why now? And how quickly can we do it? Time to seek counsel from a higher power.

ECONOMICS 102

Sitting through one of Martin L. Weitzman's lectures is a transformative experience. Not because he is the clearest and most organized lecturer. He isn't, and he concedes as much. It's because every once in a while Weitzman takes command of the blackboard and doesn't stop writing for the next eighty minutes. A Wednesday in November 2005 was one of these days.

"Mathematically advanced." Those are the first two words on the class syllabus. You bet. "I think he just derived a new theory," said one puzzled student confiding his confusion to me. I know that spells trouble. As the teaching assistant, I had to take the math and translate it into (German-accented) English by the next day's review class.

Weitzman is fond of saying that the best way to learn is a couple of No. 2 pencils, a blank notebook, and a few hours alone on a hard, wooden chair: "Make your own mistakes. It's the only way you will learn." The reason most students diligently come to the review even if they sometimes skip the actual lectures isn't because they've taken him up on the suggestion. Most of the time they want translations, or better yet answers. That day they just wanted to understand what in the world had happened in class the day before.

Weitzman hadn't derived a new theory. Not quite. He had presented results from his latest research, the culmination of several months of painstaking work, into a problem that has vexed economists for generations: Why don't people invest more money in the stock market?

The answer, it turns out, has as much to do with stocks and the financial crisis that would haunt the world later that very decade as it does with the climate crisis facing our planet. The direct link between them: ten-foot women.

IT'S NOT OVER TILL THE FAT TAIL ZINGS

Weitzman showed impeccable timing in the lead-up to the financial crisis. While most everyone else was getting ready to ride the latest stock market bubble, he started worrying about a problem that has stumped economists for over two decades: the equity premium puzzle.

Equities, stocks in companies, seem to be paying premium returns to investors. If you invested $100 in stocks in an average year over the past several decades, you would, on average, have $107 a year later—a 7 percent return. Contrast that to the so-called risk-free rate of return of close to 1 percent. This is what investors get when they put their money in the investment equivalent of "under the mattress": short-term Treasury bills backed by the U.S. government, (still) considered one of the safest investments in the world. The difference, the risk premium to make up for your sleepless nights fretting about the stock market, is 6 percent.

That's reality. It also happens to be "real" in the economic sense of the word. That's what's left over after everything is said and done. Not a bad return on your money, if you can get it. It means your investments double once a decade.

Except economic theory doesn't seem to agree. It says that under rather reasonable and widely used assumptions for U.S. economic growth (2 percent per year) and a somewhat opaque but well-established factor depicting the inclination of individuals to accept risk (commonly measured to equal 2 as well), the risk premium should be closer to 0.08 percent. If $100 invested the safest way imaginable gives you $101 next year, putting those $100 into stocks, says standard economics, should give you $101.08. That paltry 0.08 percent is almost a hundred times less than the 6 percent difference we see in the real world.

I would be lying if I said that I didn't consider switching majors when I first heard about this "theoretical discrepancy" in college. Calling this failure of economic theory "embarrassing" is to put it mildly. I wasn't expecting Newtonian physics–style accuracy, but this borders on the obscene. Economists nowadays use their craft to explain everything from cheating in sumo wrestling to primate mating patterns. What we do not seem to have a handle on is how the stock market works.

One interpretation of these results is that investors just don't get it. They don't put nearly enough money into stocks. Instead, they put their money under a mattress and lose out on reaping otherworldly returns in the stock market. Some kind of bias, myopia, or simple ignorance, the argument would run, is at work here. The former White House and World Bank chief economist Larry Summers, during his early days in academia, once began a draft paper with the line "There are idiots. Look around."[11]

The solution? Let's just tell the misguided masses about this finding. Or even better: keep it to yourself at first, and put all your money into stocks. Other people will realize the error of their ways soon enough. Investors will put more money into stocks, their risk premium will decline, and economic theory will turn out to be right after all. By then you will have made out like a bandit.

Not quite. This strategy of trying to game the market for your own benefit might work for an insignificant theoretic quirk here or there, but it will fail if the theory is supposed to describe most human investment behavior, about which we have data spanning decades and reflecting millions or billions of observations. There must be another reason why people don't invest more in the stock market, something economic theory doesn't quite capture, something every professor of financial economics and generations of graduate students have missed—the perfect setup for Weitzman.

Weitzman is known for his razor-sharp writing and his intellect, which towers above his students and many of his fellow economists, even at Harvard. In his first book, *The Share Economy*, written in 1984, he foreshadowed the rise in stock options and employee ownership models. He laid out how both could help fight stagflation, the dreaded combination of economic stagnation and high inflation, and break the link between employment and the business cycle. A *New York Times* editorial hailed it as the "best idea since [John Maynard] Keynes."[12]

Weitzman has never been one to shy away from controversial topics. He single-handedly developed an economic theory of biodiversity—which species to save when you can't save them all, what he called the "Noah's Ark Problem"—and worked on ways to measure sustainability and the relative worth of future generations. Now he had a different problem on his hands: fixing the way economists look at the stock market.

He had a hunch but not much more. Statisticians, investment analysts, economists, physicians, and many other members of the wonk set tend to look at the world and see "normal distributions." Many everyday phenomena can be put neatly into this shape, not unlike a bell. Hence, the name "bell curve": a fat body, and thin tails on either end.

Take height. The average American woman in her twenties is five feet four inches tall.[13] Out of one hundred randomly chosen women, ninety will be between five feet and five feet eight inches, the large body of the bell. Really short or really tall women are rare. Only five of the hundred, on average, will be taller than five feet eight inches. Despite their preponderance on the runway, six-foot women are oddities, at least statistically. Only one woman in recorded medical history was taller than eight feet. Zeng Jinlian grew to 8 feet 1.75 inches before she died at the age of seventeen. No one, woman or man, ever grew to twice the average height.

Yet in other parts of life we do see ten-foot women. Stock market crashes are one example. On any given day, the stock market moves a couple of percentage points up or down. Sometimes it even jumps up 5 percent or down 5 percent. Large movements are rare, but unlike living, breathing ten-foot women, they are possible.

Such possibilities defy our powers of imagination, so, sadly, we tend to ignore them—as it turns out, at our peril. October 19, 1987, entered the history books as Black Monday when the Dow Jones Industrial Average crashed 22.6 percent in a single day. In the Black Week beginning with October 6, 2008, the Dow fell 18 percent—a weeklong runway of one unlikely creature after another. On May 6, 2010, the Dow lost almost a thousand points within minutes before it regained its

footing and jumped back up.[14] It shouldn't happen. It must not happen. It does happen.

If, instead of women's heights, we draw stock market movements on a piece of paper, the bodies of the bells become smaller. Their tails are thicker. Some of these tails are outright obese, "fat" in technical statistical jargon.[15]

Ten-foot women do not register on the radar of ordinary statistics and economics. They are anomalies, outliers, something to be ignored lest the analysis get too messy. "Statisticians have known about fat tails for a while," Weitzman explains, "but we simply haven't known how to deal with them. So we just assume them away." That's often an okay strategy. No model can explain reality fully. No map is a complete replica of the geographical area it tries to show. There are always some phenomena left unexplained. Trouble is, here the phenomena left out are crucial to the outcome. I can't say I like the idea of ten-foot women. I am intimidated by them as much as the next guy, but we can't just assume them away. As rare as they may be, ten-foot women rule the world.

So what's a risk manager to do? Let's imagine that he fully under-

stands that he is ignoring ten-foot women at his peril. He has read Nassim Nicholas Taleb's *The Black Swan* and grasped its argument around surprises waiting at every turn, but even so he can't just call all economic modelers ignorant dweebs. Taleb might get away with it, but the risk manager can't. His boss demands advice based on real data, a model.

"You have to capture reality in a tractable model," Weitzman likes to say. "Tractable" seems to be Weitzman's favorite word. Too complicated, and the model won't help anyone. Too simple, and you end up ignoring the details that really matter. Modeling is as much art as science, akin to mapmaking—and you always need to keep your audience in mind. A tourist in Paris needs a way to find the most direct path from the Louvre to the Arc de Triomphe with nods to Montmartre and Notre Dame, preferably with sights and street names in spellings he recognizes. The local plumber cares more about every side-street apartment address, and building maps with even more detail. Even the plumber's map, though, requires abstractions. A city map capturing *every* detail would be an impressive feat. It would also be entirely useless.

Weitzman is a master modeler—part artist, part scientist—and is always looking for that sweet spot, the model in which theory no longer ignores reality and no one living in reality can afford to ignore the theory.

His next step was clear: move from reality back to theory and find a way to represent ten-foot women in an equation any risk manager can understand. Weitzman retreated to his seaside home and spent months poring over papers and textbooks—immersing himself in a parallel statistical universe, an alternative and underused way of looking at numbers: Bayesian statistics.

The Reverend Thomas Bayes first developed these ideas in eighteenth-century England, but others have managed to sideline them for the most part ever since. Ordinary statistics assumes that life operates like a card game. There are fifty-two cards in a deck. The only mystery is which of these cards you will draw next. Bayes figured life was more complicated. He argued that in addition to not knowing which card in the deck would come next, we didn't know how many cards the deck had to begin with. That seems to be a fair assumption about life. There are "unknown unknowns," as the former secretary of defense Donald Rumsfeld might say. Stuff happens.

Mainstream economics wanted little to do with Bayes for over two centuries. The formulas that arose from this kind of thinking weren't nearly as elegant or easily taught as classical statistics. No kidding. Weitzman would emerge every once in a while to present some Bayesian insights at research seminars. When he did, the faces on most of the economists in those rooms looked as puzzled as his students'.

In the end, he wrote a paper that explained the full equity premium puzzle—and then some. It's not that we can't explain why stocks command a premium. Once we take these "unknown unknowns" seriously, "the puzzles even reverse." As he tried to argue to the group of a dozen students attending his class with me, "It's no longer a question of why people aren't buying more stocks." Now it's a question of why, given the occasional ten-foot woman delivering a surprise, they are buying them at all. The models that economists have used for decades do not take into account the actual risks faced by consumers. They ignore ten-foot women. In Weitzman's model, that's no longer the case. Economic theory reflects these past crashes perfectly. Investors are now the ones who forget, as is indeed the case in reality. Consequently, the 6 percent risk premium may actually be too low given all the risks involved.

It took another two years and several revisions for Weitzman's paper to make its way through the labyrinth that is the academic peer-review process. The final paper, modestly and just a tad cryptically titled "Subjective Expectations and Asset-Return Puzzles," appeared not a moment too soon. It was published in the summer of 2007, at the same time that Bear Stearns became the first victim of the mortgage meltdown and the financial crisis slowly started to take shape.

This tends to be the moment when even the most hermit-like academic steps out of theory land and goes to the airwaves, explaining how his insights could have saved the global financial system. Or at least he starts to rake in lucrative consulting and speaking fees for brief appearances in high-powered boardrooms and at corporate retreats. Four Seasons Jackson Hole, anyone? Successful consulting firms have been founded on much less of an insight.

Weitzman, however, was never one to preach to the masses or to rest on his intellectual laurels. He soon moved on to a much bigger target: the climate crisis.

A PLANETARY GAMBLE

Only it wasn't much of a move. It doesn't take much to shift gears from the financial to the climate crisis. It's the same problem, and as it turns out, it has a similar solution. Protect yourself against ten-foot women. It's the extreme events that define the outcome.

Weitzman owns a home barely above sea level near Gloucester, Massachusetts, a beautiful little fishing town just under an hour north of Boston. I might be a bit biased; I proposed to my wife there. The place is any nature lover's dream. Weitzman certainly is one of them. He is also an avid gardener who apparently requires quite a bit of fertilizer. He landed a mention in a Jay Leno monologue after being charged with stealing a truckload of manure from a horse farmer near his home in 2005, on April 1, his birthday. Weitzman pleaded not guilty at the time and has since settled the case, although he maintains that he had permission to take the manure. Some of his friends and colleagues have had their fair share of fun with it. One colleague sent him an e-mail saying, "Congratulations. Most economists I know are net exporters of horse shit. And you are, it seems, a net importer."

Global warming is not simply a topic of personal interest for Weitzman; it's "one of the largest intellectual challenges" of his, and indeed our, lifetime. He certainly treats it as such. In classic Weitzman fashion, he spent months reading through stacks of scientific reports and dove into the atmospheric science and assorted other literature to reevaluate firsthand some of the conclusions found by the Intergovernmental Panel on Climate Change, the authoritative scientific body usually given the last word on all things climate.

The fun paid off. He has since written a handful of papers applying insights from his work on stock markets to climate change and draws the clearest parallel yet between the two.[16] Once again, it's the ten-foot women that matter most. It's Bayes's deck-of-cards problem—when you draw the next card, you don't know how large the deck is. It's Rumsfeld's "unknown unknowns"—the unforeseen events that derailed the U.S.-led occupation of Iraq. It's Nassim Nicholas Taleb's "black swan"—unimaginable for someone who has only ever seen white ones. It's a Frenchman's "c'est la vie," Forrest Gump's box of chocolates. Put all of the above together in a way statisticians can understand and you get "fat tails."

If nothing were done to limit greenhouse gas emissions into the atmosphere, expected average effects would be bad enough. The current IPCC consensus view says that global average temperatures would rise by another 3.5°F to 7°F by the end of the century, on top of the roughly 2-degree rise since we humans started to burn up fossil fuels at the beginning of the Industrial Revolution. (The IPCC, of course, speaks in centigrade. That makes 2°C to 4°C of warming on top of the 1°C since the Industrial Revolution.)

A rise of 3.5 to 7°F and the Greenland ice sheet would be in real danger; the West Antarctic ice sheet would begin to melt. The two combined hold enough water to raise global sea levels by forty feet. Of course, we don't know exactly when they are going to melt. It may already be too late to save either. We may still have time to reverse course. We do know that they will melt, if we don't change course. Moreover, that's the average effect, and it does not yet include increased extreme weather events from droughts and famines on one end to more intense hurricanes, typhoons, and monsoons on the other, to say nothing of large-scale species extinction or the disappearance of coral reefs.

It's impossible to emphasize this enough: *not if, when.* If we don't change course, these things will happen, and some are already happening.

Still with me? If not, I'll blame it on what psychologists gallantly describe as "cognitive dissonance."[17] It's akin to shutting out bad news when that news doesn't correspond to the accepted hypothesis in one's brain. We are pumping billions of tons of greenhouse gas pollution into the atmosphere each year, and every scientist worth his or her Ph.D. tells us that these gases trap heat. But look, it's snowing! How can the planet possibly be getting warmer? That click in your brain was your cognitive dissonance kicking in. (Never mind that, scientifically, more snow in winter is what we should see with a more unstable climate.)

There is a lot to this psychological phenomenon, but let's first stick close to the underlying climate science and Weitzman's take on it. There is more bad news: 3.5°F to 7°F is the average in two senses of the word. It's the expected warming around the globe. Some parts of the planet will warm by less, and might even become cooler. Others will warm more. The poles with their surrounding ice sheets are particularly prone to greater-than-average warming—not a good sign for your beachfront property, or for much of human civilization, for that matter.

Worse, 3.5°F to 7°F is average in another sense: it's the range of temperature increases across six different scenarios commissioned by the IPCC. Each of these scenarios comes with uncertainties. The range for the most optimistic scenario with the 3.5°F average is 2°F to 5.5°F. The range for the most pessimistic scenario is 3.5°F to 11°F. So really, we are in for "likely" warming somewhere between 2°F and 11°F. With 2°F, things may turn out to be fine after all; 11°F would be catastrophic. The British science writer and centigrade afficionado Mark Lynas's *Six Degrees* painstakingly lists climate impacts degree centigrade by degree centigrade. He ends with 6°C (11°F). Any increase beyond that is an unknown *nightmare* land, and 11°F itself isn't all that comforting. Lynas's first citation in that chapter: Dante's *Inferno* and the sixth circle of hell.

So far, recorded trends have not been very encouraging. The growth rate in emissions over the past two decades has been greater than the worst-case scenario modeled by the IPCC. That puts us a lot closer to 11°F than to 2°F. And none of what we have done so far takes into account the vaunted ten-foot women.

Climate science is a messy business. In the end, we care about temperature changes, sea-level rise, and the many other direct and indirect effects. Consequences like sea-level rise are a function of temperature. Temperature changes, in turn, are a function of the concentration of greenhouse gases in the atmosphere. Concentrations are a function of emissions. Every one of these steps has uncertainties surrounding it. Things vary, sometimes a lot.

We are reasonably sure about the connection between emissions and concentrations, although even there we can only talk about ranges, not exact links. (One big unknown is sinks, the amount of carbon that gets sucked out of the air through natural sources like forests and uptake by oceans.)

A much larger uncertainty surrounds "climate sensitivity," the step between concentrations and temperatures. It's the crucial link between tiny amounts of carbon dioxide—an odorless, colorless gas humans can't detect—and what we read off a thermometer every day, what we can all feel: temperatures.

Carbon dioxide is measured in ppm, short for "parts per million." One ppm is about the equivalent of one drop of water in a thirteen-gallon tank. Before 1750, the concentration of carbon dioxide in the atmosphere was 280 such drops in the tank, or 280 ppm. By now we are at 390, and things are pointing up to 450, 550, and beyond. Climate sensitivity is shorthand for what happens to temperatures when concentrations double.

The range of possibilities is disconcerting. The IPCC's latest comprehensive review, its *Fourth Assessment Report*, lists twenty-two recent attempts to measure climate sensitivity. Taken together, these studies say that a grand planetary experiment of doubling carbon dioxide concentrations could yield higher temperatures anywhere between 3.5°F and 8°F with a best guess of about 5.5°F. That's what the IPCC calls the "likely" range for climate sensitivity, what would happen roughly two-thirds of the time.

If we had a hundred planets at our disposal and could run this experiment of doubling carbon dioxide concentrations on each of them, sixty-seven would have temperature increases of between 3.5°F and 8°F. What happens on the other thirty-three, on the tails of this bell curve? That's where we are back in the wondrous and disconcerting world of fat tails, black swans, ten-foot women, and other scary creatures.

Weitzman has calculated the chance of extreme climate sensitivity, the thickness of these tails, and has come up with disturbing results: the IPCC's tails, much like the financial-sector models that got us into so much trouble, are too thin.

The IPCC's own interpretation of the numbers says that there is a 5 percent chance of a doubling of carbon dioxide concentrations leading to temperature changes of greater than 12.5°F and a 1 percent chance of climate sensitivity greater than 18°F—the difference between a balmy 72°F spring day and a 90°F scorcher.

Weitzman looks at the same data and concludes that the IPCC cut off its tails too quickly: "I did my own calculations. I ran it by at least fifteen geophysicists—from the poor assistant professor at Harvard, who I cornered, to world-class scientists." If you consider all uncertainties and don't disregard extreme events, the results are more like a 5 percent chance of warming greater than 18°F and a 1 percent chance of warming greater than 36°F. Five out of a hundred planets would see temperatures rise 18°F by the end of the century at the rate we are spewing out pollution right now. Life as we know it would already be very different with warming of 2°F, 3°F, or 5°F. With 10°F or 18°F, we might want to pack up now and look for another planet.

We might as well do that before it's too late. Weitzman's latest draft paper focuses on 21.5°F (or 12°C, if you are keeping score in centigrade):

> For me, [21.5°F] is iconic because of a recent study, which estimated that global average temperature increases of [around 20–21.5°F] would cause conditions under which more than half of today's human population would be living in places where, at least once a year, there would be periods when death from heat stress would likely ensue after about six hours of exposure.

Full disclosure: my name is in the acknowledgments of Weitzman's latest paper, but I had nothing to do with that passage, except for pointing out that his first draft included it twice. That may not have been such a bad thing. The authors of the original study add a dry warning: "This likely overestimates what could practically be tolerated: Our limit applies to a person out of the sun, in gale-force winds, doused with water, wearing no clothing, and not working."[18]

Six hours on a planet like that would lead to death, if you are wet, naked, out of the sun, being buffeted by "gale-force winds," resting, and presumably otherwise healthy. If not, you might die sooner. That paper is brought to you by the throwaway rumor rag commonly found in every supermarket checkout lane: the *Proceedings of the National Academy of Sciences*. Per Weitzman, following his analysis of IPCC data, there is almost a 5 percent chance that we will be on a planet like this. Welcome to the planetary edition of Russian roulette.

We don't have to wait until this nightmare scenario before we see the life-changing effects of an unstable and increasingly warming climate. Some of the earliest studies of climate change and agriculture have concluded that warmer climates may actually be beneficial. But don't give out that sigh of relief quite yet: beneficial up to a point, and not for long at that. Again, the *Proceedings of the National Academy of Sciences*:

> We find that yields increase with temperature up to [84°F] for corn, [86°F] for soybeans, and [89.5°F] for cotton but that temperatures above these thresholds are very harmful . . . Holding current growing regions fixed, area-weighted average yields are predicted to decrease by 30–46% before the end of the century under the slowest (B1) warming scenario and decrease by 63–82% under the most rapid warming scenario (A1FI) under the Hadley III model.[19]

Translated into English, entirely without exclamation marks and other emphases added: holy cannoli.

The production of some of our most fundamental agricultural staples—corn, soy, and cotton—will decrease by between a third and a half by the end of this century per this analysis, and that's under the best possible scenario, which no one believes any longer will, in fact, happen. The most rapid warming scenarios, which by now are already conservative, show decreased production by two-thirds or more.

Full effects go much beyond food production alone. Our society is well-adjusted to current climates. Increase temperatures and tempers flare. Drivers honk more on hotter days. In general, productivity goes down as heat goes up, and the overall effect may be even larger for those in office buildings than for growing food outdoors. The latest study looking at effects in the Caribbean finds that as temperatures rise, productivity drops more than twenty times faster off the farm than on it.[20]

Remember my quick reference to "cognitive dissonance," which allows us to forget all of this at the sight of the first snowfall? I wish I could taste some of that right about now. This is the world we are heading toward at full speed.

It comes down to a simple insurance question. There's a small chance that everything will be fine and that Weitzman, the IPCC, Al Gore, insert-your-climate-change-Cassandra-here, and I are wasting your time. But, sadly, there's a much better chance that things will not be all that pleasant—the wide body of the bell curve. And on the opposite end of the curve, there's a chance that even nude, in the shade, stationary, and whipped by gale-force winds, we won't make it.

Amazingly, we've been here before. One recent headline: "Death Toll Exceeded 70,000 in Europe During the Summer of 2003."[21] Slowly, the lines between supermarket-checkout-lane publication and scientific journal begin to blur. The tally of dead Europeans, sadly, comes from the latter.

Acting now to prevent an even greater death toll is the prudent thing to do. It's the rational thing to do. In many ways, it's the only option we've got. The gods were even kind enough to give us a parallel lesson in our failure to deal with risk during the latest financial crisis and ensuing multitrillion-dollar morass: Don't be in denial about your fat tails. Put them on a diet. Stop feeding the beast.

The solution is still the same—right the wrong incentives, internalize externalities, privatize the socialized costs—and the case now is stronger than ever. We better nudge ourselves in the right direction, or await the nudging—more like a beating—from the ten-foot women.

I encouraged Weitzman to make the case in his paper a bit stronger. Academic clarity isn't enough here. We need a cri de coeur, a clarion call, and it would be good if it came from someone like him. His response: "I am reluctant to pound home the message even harder. I've learned the hard way over many years that if you have a good case, it speaks best for itself."[22]

Alas, no.

Sadly, a good case all too often doesn't speak for itself. We wouldn't be where we are today if it weren't for the fact that we, as a society, have systematically chosen not to listen to the best science and to take appropriate action. We can always wait for more scientific results to come in. We can always hope that Weitzman, the authors of the "heat stress" study, the ones looking at crop failures, the ones reviewing the 2003 European heat wave, and lots and lots of others are proven wrong. Perhaps there's a first-grade math error somewhere, and one of these studies is overstating things by a factor of a thousand. It happens to the best. One or the other individual study may well be proven wrong in subsequent research. But wishing all are simply wrong, or wishing all of them away, is not a strategy.

TOLD YOU SO

Weitzman was not the first to point out the importance of fat tails and extreme events—far from it.[23] To get to the bottom of this question, we need to take the ten-minute walk from Littauer 313 to Littauer 312. One is in the Littauer Center, which houses the economics department; the other is in the eponymous building at the Harvard Kennedy School of Government. Same Littauer, entirely different vibe.

Littauer 312 has been Richard J. Zeckhauser's office for as long as anyone at the Kennedy School can remember. He used to have a joint appointment in the economics department, but he is not one smitten by extraneous titles (nor the extra teaching and advising requirements): "It got to be a real pain to handle the logistics of it and the paperwork." That's just as well. He clearly fits in better at a place that teaches and values practical thinking over mathematical prowess.

Practical does not mean nonrigorous, and he has elevated logical reasoning to an art form. Zeckhauser won the mixed-pairs contest at the 2007 North American Bridge Championships forty-one years after winning the U.S. pairs title. In between he wrote some 250 economics papers, with no sign of slowing down. He collaborates on most of his papers and is not shy to admit that he defers to his coauthors for formalizing equations as well as mundane number crunching. Zeckhauser provides the ideas.

One idea that has been a constant throughout his research is that uncertainty matters. Zeckhauser goes one step further and talks about risk, uncertainty, and ignorance. Risk is the deck of fifty-two cards. Uncertainty is not knowing the number of cards or how many decks are in play. That's Bayesian statistical land, which Weitzman has mastered to the joy of mathematically minded economists everywhere. Ignorance is when all math goes out the window. No one knows the possible outcomes or how likely they would be.

Nassim Nicholas Taleb obsesses about these types of situations in *Black Swan*. He accuses anyone conflating real-world situations with games of chance of committing a "ludic fallacy," from Latin *ludus*, "play." Case in point: the highest-impact losses faced by casinos do not occur on the card tables à la *Bringing Down the House*. They occur much closer to *Ocean's Eleven* fashion: when an angry contractor tries to blow up the building, when the owner's daughter gets kidnapped, or when the star performer Roy Horn of Siegfried & Roy gets maimed by one of the team's signature white tigers. That last tragedy cost the Mirage $100 million, more than any legitimate gambler had ever cost the casino or likely ever will.

Zeckhauser disagrees with Taleb about the value of games. Real-world contract bridge, by Zeckhauser's reasoning, is somewhere between uncertainty and ignorance. There are fifty-two cards, and "it is a game with clearly laid-out rules. But there are also four players and too many possible scenarios for anyone to compute sensibly in an actual game situation." That's particularly true at 2:00 a.m. after dozens of rounds spent trying to interpret your own and your partner's hands, those of your opponents, all of their faces, body cues, and everything else that might give a clue as to what is going on. Smarts help. So does the ability to make decisions in the face of unknown and unknowable situations. No wonder Bill Gates and Warren Buffett excel at bridge, or at least enjoy playing it.

Zeckhauser, in turn, is eager to dole out advice to would-be investors and practices what he preaches. He doesn't shy from talking about his investments. His own, apparently wildly successful real estate investment venture has been returning 23 percent on its—his—money per year. "During the height of the crisis, it only returned 14 percent." Not bad for a year when virtually everyone else lost money.

His article "Investing in the Unknown and Unknowable" stands out for both its timeliness and its timelessness: it's the uncertainty, stupid. There is little to be gained through mathematical sophistry—"when your math whiz finance Ph.D. tells you that he and his peers have been hired to work in the XYZ field, the spectacular returns in XYZ field have probably vanished forever"—and much more by analyzing politics, balancing inherently uncertain outcomes, looking for the right partners, and constantly being on the lookout for new opportunities. That's where the big bucks are, in the realm of the "triple U": unknown, unknowable, and unique.

Some forms of insurance look like the U trifecta. Zeckhauser tells the tale of the California Earthquake Authority trying to buy reinsurance for catastrophic losses back in 1996. The Authority provides insurance to Californians. That may well be a fool's game: the bigger the earthquake, the more needed the insurance; but a really big earthquake may bankrupt the insurance itself. The obvious solution is to spread the risk even more widely. Not many earthquakes affect both California and New York simultaneously, and if they did, we'd have bigger problems anyway. So the California Earthquake Authority decided to reinsure the insurance it provides.

Reinsurance is a big business. Munich Re and Swiss Re are among the largest insurance companies in the world. In this case, though, neither of them bit. And some of the most sophisticated financiers—loaded with finance Ph.D.'s and heavy on risk-modeling wizardry—took a pass as well.

None other than the bridge enthusiast Warren Buffett jumped in and bought the entire lot. He took the opportunity to justify his decision to go into the reinsurance business in the 1996 Berkshire Hathaway annual report: "We don't know—nor do we think computer models will help us, since we believe the precision they project is a chimera. In fact, such models can lull decision-makers into a false sense of security and thereby increase their chances of making a really huge mistake."[24]

Buffett goes a step further than most would dare to go in their annual reports: "We've already seen such debacles in both insurance and investments. Witness 'portfolio insurance,' whose destructive effects in the 1987 market crash led one wag to observe that it was the computers that should have been jumping out of windows."

It didn't take long for Buffett's warning to come true once again. The year 1998 saw the spectacular implosion of Long-Term Capital Management, which lost billions over the course of a few months and required a government-engineered $3.6 billion bailout to avoid taking down the wider financial system.[25]

Remember when $3.6 billion was a big number?

More important, remember what happened after? Neither do I. That's because nothing much happened. We all went back to business, and then some. The LTCM bailout might have required emergency meetings of top bankers and some arm-twisting by the New York Fed. The damage was contained, LTCM died, a few were left with scars, and the wild-and-crazy overleveraged, underregulated ride continued and picked up significant speed. We spent the following decade building many more potential LTCMs. Regulators missed the boat completely.

In 1999, the Federal Reserve chairman, Alan Greenspan, warned that large financial institutions created the potential for "unusually large systemic risks"—code for taking down the entire financial system. Greenspan ten years later: "Regrettably, we did little to address the problem." Regrettable, indeed. In the latest crisis, $3.6 billion is a rounding error. Global bailouts and government guarantees from 2007 through 2009 add up to between $3 trillion and $13 trillion, depending on who's counting what.[26] Europe added another $1 trillion in 2010, when everyone already thought the storm had passed.

Never mind the sums, these kinds of financial bailouts are at least possible. We might be throwing good money after bad, but it's all money. Bailing out the planet is in a different league altogether. For starters, bankruptcy—declaring it quits and beginning from scratch—is not an option.

I attended M. Scott Taylor's keynote address at the annual meeting of the European Association of Environmental and Resource Economists in Amsterdam. Taylor is a star theoretical economist, with the uncanny Weitzman-like ability of turning simple English statements into math. As far as these conferences go, the title was as sexy as can be: "Environmental Crises: Past, Present, and Future." Taylor began with the demise of Easter Island, made famous by the Pulitzer winner Jared Diamond in his bestselling *Collapse*. Easter Island is home to hundreds of giant stone figures, *moai*. It's no longer home to many trees. Destruction of the local environment led to dramatic climate changes and several near-total collapses of Easter Island's population.

The most vexing question of this story has always been, who cut down the last tree? Somebody must have seen how devastating that would be. Where were Easter Island's tree huggers chaining themselves to the last tree, the last five, or fifty?

Diamond shows in English, and Taylor in math, that by the time the last tree was standing, the island's ecology had been pushed well beyond its tipping point of certain demise. Little could have been done once the forces leading to the eventual collapse had been set in motion. No human would have had to cut down the last remaining trees. By that point nature was capable of felling them all by itself.

The problem with tipping points is that they come unannounced. And on Easter Island, once that point was reached, there was no time or reason to found the Easter Island Conservationist Society. By then it was too late.

It doesn't take much to connect the dots to climate. There are three ingredients: tipping points, strong feedback, and weak governance. Climate change, Taylor argued in carefully couched academic language, had all three. Plus there's the "potential precipitating event" of rapidly rising greenhouse gas pollution. Does he think a climate crisis is "likely"? "No, I don't. But then again, no crisis ever is." Cold comfort. It isn't "likely" that your house is going to burn down next year or that you will get into a car crash. Still, most home owners insure themselves against fires, and law often mandates car insurance. Weitzman's one-in-twenty chance of certain death isn't exactly "likely," either, that's true. His own home is on the seashore. But it's hard to conclude it's a planetary game of chance worth playing.

I sat next to Michael Toman during Taylor's talk. Little of what Taylor had to say was news to him. He manages the World Bank's energy and environment team in its Development Research Group and spends his professional life worrying about an unstable climate. He spent a good part of the speech hunched over his laptop, finishing up some last edits on a paper he had been co-authoring with Zeckhauser. The title makes clear where they stand: "Responding to Threats of Climate Change Mega-catastrophes." Plural. Not "if," but "when" and "how."

In the broadest sense, most think of two types of responses to catastrophic climate change: mitigation, climatespeak for reducing pollution that is causing the problem in the first place; and adaptation, rolling with the punches and adjusting to live with rising temperatures, rising sea levels, and extreme events.

This paper added a third: geoengineering, messing with the planet's thermostat in ways other than addressing the direct cause.[27] That's how far we have come. Some of the same scientists who first warned about global warming twenty or more years ago are now cooking up schemes to hack the planet: mimic volcanoes and pump dust into the upper atmosphere, create artificial clouds, or deliberately change the environment in other ways to counteract the havoc that burning fossil fuels has been and still is creating. David Keith, a respected climate scientist, colleague of Taylor's at the University of Calgary, and one of the leading geoengineers, calls it "chemotherapy" for the planet. "You are repulsed? Good. No one should like it. It's a terrible option." Another similarly fitting term would be "planetary tracheostomy." Sadly, if we can't get our obscene levels of pollution under control soon, it may still be better than letting the planet fry by itself.

I would add a fourth category: suffering. The rich will adapt. The poor will suffer. The ultimate policy question is which combination of the four we will choose, or, more likely, which combination will be forced on us given our reluctance to act on mitigating the problem to begin with.

Before you try to digest all of this and wish you could simply dismiss it instead, remind yourself once again of our very natural human tendency to do just that. You don't even have to be thinking about snowfall to want to disavow any knowledge of an increasingly warming planet. Almost anything sounds better than thinking about a planetary-scale catastrophe—and the thought of ten-foot women marching through your dreams doesn't help.

Call it "cognitive dissonance," "cognitive dismissal," call it what you will. By far the most simple, economically rational, laboratory-tested psychological response is to just do nothing. Time to stare nothing in the face.

2

DOING NOTHING

Turning on the lights in my apartment causes a chain reaction with seemingly disastrous consequences. The simple act of flicking the switch, repeated thousands of times in other homes, tells someone somewhere to increase the number of electrons sent over the grid. Those electrons need heat to get them excited enough to do as told, and that heat is, more often than not, provided by burning coal. Polluting coal. Given the overwhelming evidence that taking coal, oil, and gas out of the ground and burning them doesn't just pollute rivers, lungs, and entire communities but also overheats the planet, the only responsible reaction is to leave the switch alone.

Of course, you shouldn't stop there. Don't turn on the heat. Don't turn on the air-conditioning. Don't drive. Don't fly. Don't move. Your metabolism at night is 15 percent slower than during the day; your pulse can decrease by more. Stay in bed. Breathe and eat if you must, but only in moderation. In short: do nothing.

Even No Impact Man of *No Impact Man* fame doesn't decrease his pollution to zero. He conserves energy wherever possible yet doesn't stay in bed all day. But let's imagine you're prepared to go as far as you can to become Lowest-Impact-Possible Man. Your atmospheric footprint just went to somewhere around one ton of carbon dioxide per year, or a quarter of the global average. That's down from twenty tons for the average oil-gobbling American or ten tons for the average compact-car-driving-yet-still-driving European. That one ton corresponds to the subsistence level of someone living with the bare necessities.[1]

Congratulations. The world might be proud of your achievement if only anyone knew. Alas, you're proscribed from typing on your computer or going on the radio or television or taking off on a promotional tour—No Impact Man's example to the contrary notwithstanding.

LESS THAN A DROP

The atmosphere, however, doesn't care. It will not notice your actions. Not because you aren't trying hard enough to decrease your personal impact. It's the trying that will go unnoticed. Your own actions are less than a rounding error in our planetary pollution accounting. No Impact Man did, in fact, have no impact on the world.

Sure, the 300 million Americans each emitting twenty tons and the 500 million Europeans each emitting ten tons are a large reason for the mess we are in. But that's the point: it's the average that matters—and the sheer number of people emitting that many tons.

Let's say you are one of the fortunate 300 million Americans, and you have done your homework. You know your gigantic carbon footprint, you know it's a problem, and you are doing all you can to reduce it. In fact, you are going to the max and decreasing your impact from twenty tons to zero overnight. You can't actually do that all by yourself, but you could pay someone else to decrease his or her emissions on your behalf. TerraPass will send you a sticker in return that you get to display prominently declaring your carbon neutrality to the world, right in the windshield of your electric car.

That sticker is for your neighbors' admiration. The atmosphere wouldn't notice the difference. The average across all Americans would still be a solid 20 tons. (If you feel compelled to work out the math, you decreasing your emissions from 20 to 0 overnight would bring the average down to 19.9999999. That's 20.000000, rounded to the nearest gram of carbon dioxide pollution. In other words: 20 tons.)

Buckets are even better to demonstrate this than decimal points. Hold one under a dripping faucet and start counting. A highly scientific experiment reveals around 300,000 drops in a standard five-gallon bucket. I hate to break it to you: you are but one in seven billion on this planet. Your portion of global emissions is much less than a drop in that bucket—almost five thousand times less, even for an American.

No Impact Man has no impact on the world—if he acts alone. It takes all of us acting together for the planet to notice. Far from needing no-impact men, the situation screams out for seven billion *impact* men and women.

• • •

Why not turn to corralling the masses? Gandhi did it. Wangari Maathai did it. Bill McKibben did it. All were or are extremely successful in their own right. But their successes pale in comparison with religion.

Christianity has around two billion followers; the Catholic Church alone has around a billion members. (Full disclosure: I believe somewhere in the Vatican, I am listed as one in that billion. In Austria, membership practically comes with citizenship, although I have yet to make it to any of the U.S.-based meetings. Needless to say, people like me may well inflate the Church's numbers.)

Let's give the Church the benefit of the doubt and stick to the billion figure. It's impressive, to say the least. One out of seven billion may not have much of an impact. One billion out of seven is a different story. Even that number, though, won't be enough to save the planet.

Let's say the pope decided to not get out of bed in the morning and instead bring his emissions down to the bare minimum, the one ton per person per year given current technologies. And let's say all one billion Catholics followed his example and did the same. That would remove a sizable chunk of pollution, on average around three billion tons of carbon dioxide emissions per year.[2] Even if all two billion Christians suddenly found common cause in following the pope's example, we would still be left with over twice the amount of yearly carbon emissions that the atmosphere can bear.[3] And that's not all.

It took the Catholic Church two thousand years to get to a billion followers. We don't have another thousand years. We have much closer to ten years, at most. That's ten years to effect real political action that brings emissions down, globally. Yes, Facebook had a half billion members in less than a decade, but sadly, joining a Facebook group is not quite the same as actually leaving a mark. Getting a billion people to do something that makes a difference is a tall order.

THE OTHER WAY OF DOING NOTHING

All of this assumes that we can indeed convince billions of people to make steep sacrifices. It seems highly unlikely for a billion Catholics to suddenly follow the pope's lead in moving to a life of simple pleasures: off the grid, off the roads, and out of the skies. And that assumes the pope could be convinced to do just that to begin with. The much more likely outcome is that most of us will just go about living our lives, perhaps turning off an extra light once in a while or refusing to take that plastic bag in the checkout lane.

We are preprogrammed to tune out inconvenient facts. Our minds can only keep so many worries front and center at any given time, and something as seemingly distant, remote, and uncertain as an unstable climate tends not to make the cut. We would much rather think happy thoughts, and we go to great lengths to do just that.

It's also much easier to follow the herd than to stick out and be brandished an oddball. That's a well-documented psychological phenomenon as much as it's a necessity in light of everyone else dancing around you, and it goes for wild beasts on the African plains as much as for those on Wall Street trading floors. If you follow the herd, and the herd turns out to be wrong, you are no worse than everyone else. If you speak up, you run the risk of being wrong and falling prey to a predator. Many people saw that housing prices were inflated long before the crash that began in 2007. It was in plain sight on the front pages of newspapers. *The Economist* identified the bubble as early as September 2002. But anyone betting against the thundering herd for the intervening five years would have lost a great deal of money.

The same goes for saving the planet. We will be shifting to sources other than oil eventually. That's not a secret. Oil is a finite resource, after all. But as long as there is money to be had pumping oil out of the ground and pollution into the atmosphere, the herd will continue to do so. Unless you have found a way to make a living in a niche somewhere as a do-gooder or feel content leaving the race altogether, you will, too. Your best bet—for your own sake and even that of your children—is simply to say nothing and follow everyone else.

I might be carrying my groceries home in a cloth bag in New York, where, for the most part, it's convenient and socially accepted, but I have never refused a single plastic bag offered to me when buying breakfast on the side of the road in Bangkok. There, regardless of whether you buy cut fruit, a jug of freshly squeezed orange juice, or a simple bun, it comes with at least one plastic bag, if not two or more—and anything warm comes in a Styrofoam container wrapped in a plastic bag, with a plastic spoon or fork, individually wrapped in plastic.

Plastic bags are shorthand for cleanliness and progress. No Thai refuses them, even for something eaten on the spot, where not having the bag would be more convenient. And few foreigners would refuse them either. When in Bangkok, do as the Thais do.

You don't have to go as far as Bangkok to witness herd behavior in action. Plastic bags may have turned into the latest green scourge for

Whole Foods shoppers, but if the drugstore across the street still hands them out like free candy, you will end up with one in your hand someday regardless of how green and well intentioned you are. Herd behavior wins the day, and it's what the herd does that the planet notices.

Usually.

WHEN DOING SOMETHING DOES BARELY ANYTHING

Plastic bags come with real costs—as well as with real benefits. Convenience is prized for a reason. Regardless of what your environmental attitudes are, you've got to admit they do their job well. Instead of you having to lug old bags to the store, they are right there when you need them most. They are clean. They are convenient. They work.

That convenience comes at a price. I don't need to see pictures of seagulls ensnared by decade-old plastic bags to realize that disposal is an issue. The slogan "Reduce, reuse, recycle" has practically been invented for them. Yet beyond an individual tragedy, an economist eyeing that seagull sees a larger cause. The benefits of plastic bags are most often privatized, their costs socialized. That has been the perfect recipe for the financial crisis as much as it is for galloping environmental problems.

In the case of plastic bags, it's me who benefits when I get one on my way out of the store; it's everyone who has to look at it tangled around the poor seagull. That bird pays the ultimate price. It doesn't get to vote or have an opinion in court, but we can easily project the price from seagull world back into our own. I'd chip in a penny or two per bag to know that the seagull and her friends live happily ever after, and so would many others.[4] Admittedly, I'd be hard-pressed to want to contribute much more than that. A fairly general result from a number of studies establishes that people are willing to spend as much money— commonly a few dollars—to save one bird as they are to save a great many. That complicates matters a bit.

I have yet to come across the authoritative economic study of the full cost of plastic bags (and pity the grad student, somewhere, working on it as we speak), but a good guess for the socialized cost of each plastic bag would be on the order of a few cents, give or take. It's more than zero, certainly. But it's not all that much, either. There is that small percent of bags that manage to kill the beloved seagull, but billions of other bags end up in, and remain in, landfills for hundreds of years. That also comes at a price, which is likewise currently ignored, but average it out, and it can't be more than a fraction of a penny. For argument's sake, let's run with a few pennies, which, in fact, is what Ireland and cities like Washington, D.C., have done, charging initial prices of fifteen euro cents and five cents per plastic bag, respectively.

Ireland introduced its PlasTax in 2002, becoming the first country to do so. The effect? Plastic bag demand declined by no less than 90 percent, or about one billion bags, a year. That's a huge shift for a tiny fee. (Ireland has since raised its PlasTax from fifteen to twenty-two euro cents to ensure inflation doesn't make it even tinier.)

Washington's five-cent fee on all disposable bags, paper or plastic, became law on January 1, 2010, and early signs point to similarly large shifts in consumer behavior. When you stand at the register paying for a $50 purchase, a five-cent fee per bag, 0.1 percent of your total bill, makes less difference than the extra ounce of lunch meat the butcher added after you had already said "Thanks, that's good."

The added cost doesn't make the difference. It's the principle that counts. Suddenly not receiving a free bag at the register became the new norm. And consumer behavior changed.

PlasTaxes achieve their goal at little cost and with little intrusion. If you insist on getting your plastic bags to use as trash bags at home or to pick up after your dog, ask for them and thou shalt receive. People might judge you, but you can buy them without (m)any questions asked. They are just no longer a free birthright. Not getting a plastic bag has become the new normal.

• • •

San Francisco didn't quite trust the switch to a new status quo. It chose an approach very much unlike Washington or Ireland and banned plastic bags outright. That ban may well keep even more seagulls safe, but of course it's also more coercive. Now you no longer have the chance to make a conscious choice: pay for a bag or don't. In effect, San Francisco's plastic bags carry an infinite price tag. No money in the world can buy them, legally. Plastic bag peddlers get pushed out on the street, start an underground economy, and charge exorbitant amounts of money for bags of dubious quality. Cartels and illegal bag gangs form. Conflicts ensue, tearing at the very fabric of our society.

Perhaps. But let's remember we are talking about plastic bags here. Even if the world embraced the smartest possible plastic bag policy, an Ireland-style small fee, and a fundamental global shift in norms, the planet would notice, at best, a baby step.

China, in fact, has started to adopt a similar policy mirroring Ireland's small fee. If done correctly, that may well prove a turning point in the global fight against plastic waste, but the real value comes with getting the Chinese used to thinking about environmental taxes. On the scale of culprits, plastic bags are small-fry.

Don't get me wrong. I love seagulls and applaud dramatically cutting down on the unchecked proliferation of plastic bags. Focusing on how to check their spread, however, is at best a first step in our thinking about larger, more threatening problems.

WHEN DOING NOTHING IS NOT AN OPTION

Appendixes tend to be of little use other than as places for writers to dump the dullest of background materials in an effort to show that they ought to be taken seriously. Leave it to the government to hide some of the most important official words written on climate policy in a long time in an obscure appendix.

Look up, if you are so inclined, the final rule on test procedures and rule-making activities for small electric motors in the United States. Skip to the riveting technical support document, and then go straight to appendix 15A of said support document. That's where the goodies are hidden, although you wouldn't necessarily know it from the title: "Social Cost of Carbon for Regulatory Impact Analysis Under Executive Order 12866."

Appendix 15A puts a price on carbon pollution. The cost: $20 per ton in 2010.

Every ton of carbon dioxide we release into the atmosphere does around $20 worth of damage. Multiply that times twenty, and we are at $400 per year for the typical American. That won't break the bank, but it's not nothing either. Your wallet would certainly notice. Multiply by all Americans, and the planet most certainly does.[5]

Twenty dollars per ton is not the first nor final word, but unlike for plastic bags here it actually pays to get things right.[6] Appendix 15A represents the collective effort of a dozen government agencies and offices to survey the landscape of economic writings over the past decades—the bibliography cites seventy of the most relevant contributions by some of the most prominent academics in the field. The resulting $20 in turn represents the best estimate for the socialized cost of each ton of carbon dioxide pollution. It's far from an exact science, though. Twenty dollars is the middle value. It could be as high as $35 or as low as $5. So much for a definitive statement.

The range is not for a lack of trying. It's simply an inherently difficult problem that boils down to a question of how we as a society value our children, or more to the point: today versus tomorrow. We are already seeing signs of a planet out of whack all around us, but these are nothing compared with what could happen in ten, twenty, or, for that matter, seven billion or so years when our sun turns into a red giant and turns Earth into a cinder. We tend to discount that event. No environmentalist is up in arms about it. In any case, it will happen entirely without our own doing.

Our solar system burning up, of course, has nothing to do with the warming planet we are experiencing now. But there is one crucial connection: something that happens two or three hundred years from now might as well be happening seven billion years from now in terms of how much it matters to us right now financially. Discounting makes losing an entire planet's worth of wealth a billion years in the future not worth anything now. Discounting also makes losing vast amounts of wealth two or three hundred years from now worth, at best, a buck or two in today's money. The same logic applies, to a lesser extent, to anything happening in a hundred, twenty, or ten years—or tomorrow, for that matter. That's often the biggest discrete step. Why do today what could be shoved off until tomorrow? We discount the future, no matter how close.

Let's take it for granted that rising sea levels would require us to move New York City farther inland in a couple hundred years. The costs of that move—no doubt billions of dollars—would be eminently affordable today. All it takes is to put aside a million dollars, say, and watch it grow in the bank over the next two hundred years. If you earned 7 percent interest, you could expect your rainy-day stash to double every ten years. In two hundred years, that million will have multiplied to several billion dollars. Soon enough, moving New York will no longer seem that expensive. The beauty of compound interest: patient investing—Warren Buffett's wealth—is based on it.

The money question is how high these interest and discount rates are supposed to be. If you earn 10 percent a year, your investments double every seven years. That's Buffett territory. Buffett, of course, is Buffett because his wealth has outgrown everyone else's consistently for decades. That's clearly not a guide for social policy. You and I are closer to 6 percent, considering a combination of stocks and other investments. Now money doubles every twelve or so years. And the U.S. and global economy as a whole grow much closer to 3 percent, when wealth doubles every quarter century.

Three percent enjoys a relatively broad economic consensus as a middle-of-the-road estimate for discounting socialized costs like future damages incurred on a warming planet. There's no full agreement.

Some economists argue for rates of 2.5 percent and below. Others argue for 5 percent and above. Appendix 15A uses these same three values: 2.5, 3, and 5. Socialized costs of $20 per ton of carbon dioxide in 2010 correspond to the middle estimate.

The $20 per ton may well be revised up or down in future iterations, and sadly it seems as if up is the way it would go. None of the uncertainty around the discount rate talks about the ten-foot women and other creatures we have already encountered. After largely ignoring them for decades, economists are only beginning to incorporate the implications. For now, most of that thinking is still in the appendix to appendix 15A, and we only get a hint of what to expect once we do take uncertainty more seriously: a socialized cost closer to $65 for each ton of carbon dioxide in 2010.[7]

What we do know for sure is that the cost is significantly higher than $0. That's the price we attach at the moment, possibly even below that by giving tax credits and paying outright subsidies to encourage our addiction to fossil fuels.[8] Imagine public health officials trying to discourage cigarette smoking but giving tax breaks to everyone from teenagers on up to buy their daily pack. We could moralize all we want about how cigarette smoke is bad for the lungs, or we could stall and call for more studies to nail down even the last detail of just how bad it will be. But all of that distracts from the real issue at hand: we as a society are paying each of us to further our collective addiction while ignoring the enormous costs it entails.

My extra ton of carbon dioxide pollution adds fractions of pennies to everyone else's costs, and everyone else's tons do exactly the same. No one takes individual responsibility. We get all the downsides of socialism without any of the nanny-state benefits that make the French gloat whenever they see *ze workaholic Américains* sweat on the way to their offices on a perfectly nice August beach day.

We know the solution. Some cities and countries have already flirted with it in their efforts to reduce the number of disposable plastic bags. We even have one that has been proven to work without us having to pin down the exact cost of each ton of carbon before we get started. That solution is putting a firm limit on total pollution and putting in place a market for pollution reductions. But don't take my word for it quite yet. Let's first do a bit of due diligence and go back to the 1970s to get a better sense of what works and what doesn't when it comes to making the planet notice the difference.

3

ALL-OR-NOTHING CONSERVATION

Volunteerism alone won't do. So what's next? We know fundamental change has to be driven by guiding society as a whole in the right direction. There are known ways to do that. In fact, there are laws. Lots of them.

Zoom back to the 1970s. On January 1, President Richard Nixon signed the National Environmental Policy Act. Its full title is the National Environmental Policy Act of 1969, but Nixon knew better than to sign it before the New Year and jinx the possibility of calling the 1970s the "environmental decade." He soon formed the Environmental Protection Agency—a Nixon creation housed in part in the Ronald Reagan Building in Washington, D.C. And having avoided the jinx, he didn't stop there.

The 1970s also saw passage of the Clean Air Act (1970), the Federal Water Pollution Control Act (1972), the Federal Insecticide, Fungicide, and Rodenticide Act (1972), the Noise Control Act (1972), the Coastal

Zone Management Act (1972), the Endangered Species Act (1973), the Safe Drinking Water Act (1974), the Forest and Rangeland Renewable Resources Planning Act (1974), the Federal Coal Leasing Act (1976), the Toxic Substances Control Act (1976), the Resource Conservation and Recovery Act (1976), the National Forest Management Act (1976), the Federal Land Policy and Management Act (1976), the Fishery Conservation and Management Act (1976), the Clean Air Act Amendments (1977), the Clean Water Act (1977) amending the 1972 version, the Surface Mining Control and Reclamation Act (1977), the Are You Still with Me Only One More to Go Control Act (1977½), and the Outer Continental Shelf Lands Act (1978).[1]

These twentysome laws didn't appear out of the blue. It took decades of gray skies and years of increasingly stark awareness that burning rivers, foul-smelling air, and disappearing birds and bees were no way to live.

ENVIRONMENT VERSUS BUSINESS: 1–0 (IN OVERTIME)

Take DDT. It's shorthand for dichlorodiphenyltrichloroethane. It could just as easily be shorthand for the nascent U.S. environmental movement throughout the 1960s.[2]

No one won a Nobel Peace Prize for ending World War II. However, the Swiss chemist Paul Müller won a Nobel Prize in Medicine for discovering the properties of DDT. Müller made his discovery in 1939, just in time for DDT to gain war-hero status. The United States and its allies used it as their main weapon against typhus in Europe and malaria in Southeast Asia. DDT saved lives and helped win the war.

Fast-forward a few years to 1948. When Müller picks up his Nobel Prize, it's already apparent that DDT may not be the kind of precision weapon it had been made out to be. It does indeed kill insects and rodents we don't want. Sadly, it also kills animals we'd like to keep around. Not only are they cute to look at, but we often depend on them for a functioning food chain and ecosystem. Applying DDT to control the gypsy moth, it turns out, also decimates forest birds. That might be a small price to pay during a war. Collateral murders during peacetime are a different matter altogether.

The *Journal of Economic Entomology*, where some of the early research on the problems of DDT had been published, proved no match against a Nobel Prize citation and the full might of the chemical and agricultural industry lobby. With no environmental agency to appeal to, mounting evidence of DDT's baleful effects meant little. The first Federal Insecticide, Fungicide, and Rodenticide Act had been on the books since 1947, but it was the U.S. Department of Agriculture that administered the act, with predictable results. The USDA represented farmers and the farmed environment, not the natural one. In the first twenty-four years of the act, not one pesticide had been banned without the consent of its manufacturer.

Fifteen years later, in 1962, Rachel Carson warned of a birdless "silent spring." Hearings followed. Reports were written. Recommendations were given—some at the highest level of government. In 1963, the President's Science Advisory Committee argued that the "elimination of the use of persistent toxic pesticides should be the goal." The environment was poised to notice, but the USDA was still in charge and, not surprisingly, still beholden to industry and farm interests.

It took a handful of bird enthusiasts—scientists, high school teachers, and lawyers—from Long Island, just outside New York City, to band together under the slogan "Sue the bastards." That's what they did.

First they sued a local mosquito control commission and its eccentric commissioner known for occasionally swallowing a dab of DDT to "prove" that it was harmless. The commission stopped using DDT in 1966. Next came Michigan, and finally Wisconsin, which banned it in 1970. The group of scientists and lawyers had since founded the Environmental Defense Fund—gracious source of my biweekly paychecks—and set their sights on the USDA the same year. Rather than swallowing dabs of DDT, the USDA balked, stalled, and stonewalled until the issue moved over to the newly created Environmental Protection Agency, where DDT finally met its match. The EPA prohibited its use in the United States in 1972, a ban later upheld by the Supreme Court. Environmental costs, the justices determined, far outweighed public health benefits in the United States. To a chorus of birds, the planet noticed. So, too, did industry.

Suing the bastards worked. It also cemented the view that business and the environment were mortal enemies. It's one or the other. Pick your side; then pick your lawyers.

The Endangered Species Act was perhaps the strongest and most sweeping law coming out of the environmental decade. It was also the one law that contributed most to reinforcing the illusion of the environment-business dichotomy. The law professor Jonathan Adler describes it as a pit bull: "short, compact, has sharp teeth and a strong grip."

It's the kind of bill that should make politicians proud: identify a problem; put in place a strong, bipartisan law. That, of course, assumes it works.

$10 MILLION FOR A DEAD BIRD

Birders have few hard-and-fast rules. Some of my bird-watching friends swear by *The Sibley Guide to Birds*, some by a particular set of binoculars, some by their ears alone. One facet most birders agree on, though, is that they ought not to cry out the name of the bird, lest they scare it off into the woods, never to be seen again. Alas, that's precisely what Tim Gallagher and Bobby Harrison, two expert birders, allegedly did on February 27, 2004, when they thought they spotted an ivory-billed woodpecker.

I might have screamed, too.

The last confirmed ivory-billed woodpecker died sometime in the 1940s. Ever since, every few years someone has stepped forward claiming that he had either heard or seen the bird. These people aren't crackpots—at least not all of them, and certainly not Gallagher and Harrison. One has been the editor of the Cornell University Laboratory of Ornithology's *Living Bird* magazine since 1990. The other may be one of the most renowned ivorybill experts alive.

That's more than you can say about the bird.

The 2004 "sightings" were the most promising to date. Within a year, they resulted in a grainy videotape of a woodpecker, a handful of independent reports, and an article in the reputable journal *Science*.[3] The news triggered a $10 million search and conservation effort, including dozens of bird enthusiasts, robotic video equipment, and a call by the interior secretary, Gale Norton, for a "Corridor of Hope Cooperative Conservation Plan," referring to a large area of land, 120 by 20 miles, in eastern Arkansas where the purported sightings occurred. To no avail. Cameras picked up dozens of images of woodpeckers, but all of more common varieties. The ivory-billed woodpecker remains on the Endangered Species List without a confirmed sighting in over sixty years.

The bird may yet turn up somewhere. It would be terrific if it did, if we rediscovered it, nursed the population back to viability, and allowed ivory-billed woodpeckers to roam freely in their natural habitat. Condors and whooping cranes have been nursed back from the brink of extinction. Perhaps we could do the same for a rare woodpecker variety.

But should we bother? What price are we prepared to pay for it?

Instead of spending $10 million on searching for a dead bird or nursing a species back to viability, we could use the same money to build a children's hospital and buy malaria bed nets for the poorest of the poor. These are clearly worthwhile causes, too. Or let's say the money has already been allocated for conservation efforts. It might have been better spent still on the Colorado River watershed or on floodplain restoration near New Orleans, rather than on an Arkansas bayou. Or perhaps we could have focused on a different species. What makes woodpeckers more worthy than snail darters? We have only so much money to do good. Let's spend it wisely.

The ivory-billed woodpecker has a close genetic cousin, the pileated woodpecker. Indeed it's close enough to apparently dupe experienced ornithologists into announcing fantasy sightings and run the risk of ruining their reputations. Perhaps we should conclude that the pileated variety sufficiently fills in for the ivory-billed woodpecker. That might seem like heresy, but it gets to the heart of the problem.

NOAH'S ARK LTD.

We can't save all species from extinction. Never have, never will. We have discovered and named somewhere on the order of a million species. Total estimates range in the ten or even hundred millions, the overwhelming majority of them insects.[4] We are surely killing undiscovered species every day. Halting all human activity, globally, is not an option. And we simply can't build an ark big enough for everyone. How should we prioritize?

Enter Martin Weitzman, whom we have already encountered via his ten-foot women. He started to worry about this exact problem—which species to save if you can't save them all—in the early 1990s, long before I met him.[5] My first encounter with his way of thinking about conservation came during an undergraduate lecture. It was the kind of eye-opener every economist in training and certainly every environmentalist should experience.

The setting was rather intimate, sadly typical for Weitzman's courses. Thirty students show up the first day, twenty the next; ten end up enrolling. It's not the kind of class you take if you are out to boost your grade point average. It's also not the kind of class you would want to take if you are in it for the inspiring stories. Weitzman ends the lecture exactly where he starts it and where he spends most of the time outside class: with pure logic.

Some may let their thinking be guided by cute, fuzzy creatures or impressive-looking birds—"charismatic megafauna." Not Weitzman. He breaks the question down into its most elemental parts. The goal ought to be to maximize biological diversity, which makes perfectly logical sense for a number of reasons. Diversity is a good to be cherished. Monocultures are susceptible to disease and generally aren't the way nature organizes itself.

In proven Weitzman fashion, he takes that idea and translates it into math, in this case the genetic distance across species. His numbers come from DNA hybridization experiments, where the units happen to be in "degrees centigrade." (No relationship to climate change, at least not this way.) Two birds that are so similar that even seasoned ornithologists can't tell them apart would be separated by a short line. If you tried to plot a hummingbird and an ostrich, they would presumably show up on different ends of the notepad.

Weitzman looks to cranes to make his map come to life, numerically speaking. The genetic distance between the common Eurasian crane and the East Asian hooded variety shows up with a score of 0.07. That makes them so close they could be brothers from another mother. The Central African black-crowned and the Central Asian demoiselle crane come in at 4.17 degrees—distant cousins at best. The North American whooping crane and the ubiquitous Eurasian crane are much more like true family again. Their genetic distance is a mere 0.29 degrees.

These numbers by themselves say little other than who should recognize each other at the family reunion. The all-important next step is to figure out who would actually show up.

The European crane would likely play host. It is so common its probability of extinction is close to zero. The North American whooping crane isn't quite as lucky. Its probability of complete extinction within the next fifty years is 35 percent. That's shockingly high, although the situation is a lot better than it was not too long ago. In 1941, around twenty whooping cranes were left in the wild. By 2010, the entire population was up to a few hundred. Which begs the question: Should we spend all our crane conservation money on making sure the whooping crane recovers from its critically endangered status?

That may well be the conclusion if you just looked at the probability of extinction. It's also what the Endangered Species Act says we ought to do.

Once we combine extinction probabilities with the diversity map, things look very different. It ought to matter that the whooping crane has several extremely close cousins, none nearly as threatened as it is. That changes the entire story of which cranes to protect.

It's also the story of the ivory-billed woodpecker. Losing the bird—or, most likely, having lost it—is tragic. But given that the pileated woodpecker is alive and well and, apparently, almost as impressive to impressionable birders, it may not be that much of a loss to the ecosystem or to biological diversity. The $10 million earmarked for the ivory-billed woodpecker might be better spent on preserving species that are truly unique in their genetic makeup, perhaps even if they aren't as threatened as the ivorybill or the whooping crane.

Weitzman is no anticonservationist. He likes the outdoors as much as the next tenured Harvard professor with a secure enough job to enjoy them while contemplating his mathematical derivations. The goal is not to gut the Endangered Species Act. It's to make conservation more effective. Conventional wisdom (and the Act itself) says that we ought to do everything possible to save an endangered species. Weitzman and his math say that, instead, we should focus on diversity and on keeping the most valuable species off the endangered lists to begin with.

That shouldn't be particularly controversial. It would imply more aggressive conservation sooner. Why not, argues Weitzman, "spend scarce biodiversity conservation dollars to prevent truly unique species from becoming endangered in the first place"?

This entirely joyless approach to conservation has plenty of caveats. Protecting species is not a clean trade-off. Some actions, motivated by the desire to help one endangered bird, may well help others. Or not. More important, you can't go out and pick and choose the most valuable species based on DNA alone. Some endangered varieties may be key players in their respective ecosystems, while others with possibly more unique genes play no such role in the wider web of life. And what about their often unquantifiable value in popular culture or mythology?

If the Nature Conservancy wants to spend its members' money on buying and protecting swamps in which an ivory-billed woodpecker might reside, let them. If some crazed bird enthusiasts like to wade through waist-deep swamps for days, crying at the purported sight of their beloved ivory-billed woodpecker, good for them. Weitzman would be the first to approve of them showing up at the crack of dawn for their excursion. That simple act alone shows that some people put enormous value on the bird's existence. That's their private choice, and conservation policy ought to take some of that into account—though it probably shouldn't be the only criterion.

We may not want to move to a mathematical conservation formula overnight, but at least we shouldn't act diametrically opposed to its counsel—which, by and large, is what's happening now. We wait until a species makes it onto the endangered list. Once it's there, we spend as much money as we can scrape together to protect it, paying almost no attention to the fundamental trade-offs involved. In other words: *too much, much too late.*

Sadly, American environmental policy at large follows that dogma. It even holds true for climate policy, except that there is no "too much"— yet. But we are clearly heading in that direction, mirroring our approach to species conservation all along the way. We wait and wait until the ivory-billed woodpecker or the planet as a whole is in such dire straits that we then need to pull out all the stops to avert disaster—a silent spring, a submerged Manhattan, a final six hours of life spent naked, wet, and buffeted.

For the woodpecker, it's $10 million to set aside a piece of land in the hope of finding another bird after thinking it dead for over half a century. For the planet, it will be billions and billions in defensive measures to protect us and the life we hold dear and some truly scary planet-hacking geoengineering methods few scientists can even imagine. The longer we wait, the more it will cost in money and lives.

But we are not quite ready to leave birds altogether—especially the kinds that are already endangered. There's another twist to the Endangered Species Act that screams out why this kind of approach to environmental law simply won't do for a problem like climate change.

Spoiler alert: we not only start our conservation efforts too late; there are good reasons to believe that the approach itself doesn't work. In the end, all the last-minute emergency measures may not add up to much of anything: *too little, much too late.*

THE ENDANGERED SPECIES ACT KILLS BIRDS

Meet the red-cockaded woodpecker, which you are indeed able to do, at least in some pine forests in the southeastern United States. It's not quite as rare as its ivory-billed brethren, but people may still cry at its sight—in this case not birders but landowners. They stand to lose up to $200,000 in annual timber harvest income if a single colony of the endangered species is found on their property.[6] Their reaction: "Shoot, shovel, and shut up."

Shooting birds outright may not be the wisest option: once they are officially endangered, one successful hit could land you a $100,000 fine or a year in jail. But shoveling is very much on the table.

Landowners use those shovels, chain saws, and other often perfectly legal means to avoid finding birds on their properties in the first place. Red-cockaded woodpeckers like to nest in older southern pine trees. The strategy for landowners is clear: be one step ahead, and cut down the bird's favorite old trees before the first woodpecker pair starts building its nest.

Cutting down these trees has an impeccable logic. People respond to incentives, and landowners are no different. They have good models of when they ought to be cutting down trees to maximize their profits. Once woodpeckers move in, they move in for good, and all timber revenue is gone. Woodpeckers happen to prefer older trees. Knowing this, landowners opt to cut the trees when they have barely hit forty to foreclose on woodpeckers ever building their first lodging.

It's not just about cutting down trees early. Landowners can be much sneakier than that and drive out the birds without sacrificing their older pine trees. Woodpeckers prefer forests with clear understory: large trees—no bushes, shrubs, or young pine tree saplings. Before humans came along, these shrubs would be kept at bay by frequent, natural fires. That's no longer the case. We now fight forest fires, mostly to protect nearby developments. It would be profitable for landowners to mimic these natural fires by removing and selling pine straw, which is used to cover roofs in some areas of North Carolina. The straw can net more income over the life of a forest than the trees themselves.

Yet once again, figure in the woodpecker, and the equation changes. Landowners opt not to cut the understory because they know that leaving it drives out the woodpecker. For private profits, having your forest "infested" by an endangered species is the worst of all possible outcomes. No surprise, in the fight of man versus bird, man comes out ahead—even though the bird has the spirit, if not the letter, of the law on its side.

Sadly, the red-cockaded woodpecker is not alone. Economists haven't gotten to many other species yet, but there is at least one other similar case of an endangered bird that's now even more endangered because of quirks in the Endangered Species Act. The pygmy owl is being driven out of its homes because landowners develop properties earlier than they otherwise would to avoid having their land be designated as critical habitat worthy of protection.[7]

Dean Lueck and Jeffrey Michael, two economists who pinpointed the landowner behavior in the woodpecker case, have also unearthed a copy of the 1996 *Developer's Guide to Endangered Species Regulation*. In it the National Association of Home Builders lays out in no uncertain

terms the best strategy for landowners: the "scorched earth" technique—
"maintain the property in a condition such that protected species cannot
occupy the property."

You can't really blame landowners for their behavior. They only
stand to lose once a woodpecker moves in. We may not like what they
do, but saying "pretty please" and wishing it were so will not make
it so.

Though perhaps the problem rests with the woodpecker and the
diminutive pygmy owl, not the Endangered Species Act itself. Let's go
a size bigger.

BALD EAGLE MURDER MYSTERY

Not too long ago things didn't look all that good for the bird on the
presidential seal. The lower forty-eight states were once home to a half
million bald eagles. By 1963, that number had shrunk to four hundred
nesting pairs, and all indications pointed to zero in the near future.
The bald eagle found its way onto the Endangered Species List in 1967,
under the Act's first incarnation, thereby becoming a member of the
"Class of '67."[8] Membership is a dubious honor, and reunions would
be sad affairs. Of the seventy-eight species on the list, only a handful
made it off because they recovered. More were removed because they
disappeared forever.

That's hardly unique to the Class of '67. Since then two thousand
species have been listed as endangered or threatened to become endangered in the United States. Of those, fewer than fifty have ever made it
off the list. Recovery has been the exception.[9]

The bald eagle can count itself among the lucky few that recovered.
One reason may be the minor point that this is the bald eagle, not a woodpecker or some pitifully unappealing insect. People like to look at bald
eagles. They are the epitome of "charismatic megafauna." Eagles, along
with sea otters, bison, bears, lions, and tigers, feature prominently in

children's books. It's easy to see why grown-ups would like to protect them and easy to see why green groups rely on pandas and polar bears, not snail darters, as their mascots.

Environmentalists and government officials from the Fish and Wildlife Service went all out in trying to pull the bald eagle back from the brink. They transplanted birds from Alaska and Canada, bred them in captivity, and released them in forested areas suitable as habitats. They created four National Wildlife Refuges. They mobilized one of the largest conservation efforts, most often with the backing of the Endangered Species Act.

Even private landowners ought to be proud to find a pair nesting on their property. Maybe. But the nudging of landowners is not what brought the majestic bird back from four hundred to over ten thousand nesting pairs in the lower forty-eight states within forty years and led to its ceremonious removal from the Endangered Species List in 2007. Nor was it the length of time Americans worried about eagles. True, they had been under special protection well before 1967. The Bald and Golden Eagle Protection Act of 1940 fined $100,000 or threatened a year in jail to anyone caught trying to "pursue, shoot, shoot at, poison, wound, kill, capture, trap, collect, molest or disturb" a bald eagle, its nests, or its eggs. No loud talking lest you end up with a criminal record.

The law mattered little. Bald eagle populations declined precipitously despite the early and seemingly watertight protection.

The culprit: DDT.

Even otherwise undisturbed eagles couldn't hatch offspring, because DDT caused birds to crush their own eggs. Versions of the chemical found their way into the birds' reproductive systems and prevented them from forming shells with enough calcium. The result was thin-shelled eggs that cracked under the weight of their own moms trying to keep their future offspring warm. Out of over ten thousand pages of expert testimony from 125 witnesses collected over the course of eight months, these facts were easily the most convincing piece of evidence that led to the U.S.-wide ban on DDT in 1972. That ban, not the Endangered Species Act, is the primary reason why the bald eagle population recovered.[10]

DDT spurred the kind of ban that should make economists proud as well.

First, there's the pollution side of the ledger. It's a small step between DDT in the reproductive system of the bald eagle and in the human uterus. Never mind that the evidence suggesting that DDT is a carcinogen is not as solid as the evidence for it causing thinner eggshells. Call me a purist, but I like my amniotic fluid to be toxin-free.

Then there are the benefits, or lack thereof. By 1972, there was little to no human health benefit to using DDT in a country like the United States. Malaria had ceased to be a public health problem by the 1950s.[11] Few benefits, high costs: the perfect recipe for making sure DDT got phased out in the United States except for specific uses under a public health exemption granted by the EPA.

The story is different elsewhere. DDT is used to this day in some developing countries to combat malaria, and often for good reason. There are few effective alternatives. Yes, birds in developing countries face the same, thinner eggshells as birds in the United States, but if forced to choose between a human and a bird life, most would understandably choose the human any day of the week. It's tough to cast an absolute verdict that proves universally applicable around the world.

DDT kills. Sometimes it also saves lives. Swallow dabs of DDT at your own peril, but banning it outright everywhere would be a similarly foolish decision. Keep it flexible. Stay nimble. Not all pollution is bad. If what we get on the plus side far outweighs the negatives, it makes a lot of sense to tolerate a bit of DDT. The thought of DDT in the amniotic fluid surrounding my child makes my stomach turn inside out, but the thought of my wife dying of malaria is far worse.

The same logic goes for almost everything we do to protect the planet. We need to prioritize what must get noticed—whether it's saving a species from extinction or reducing infant mortality—and put our scarce resources toward figuring out how to effect real, noticeable change. Stabilizing the global climate is one such area. When the entire planet looks endangered, a woodpecker here or there doesn't feel all that important. The rigors and absolutes of the Endangered Species Act are at best an instructive example of what not to do to stabilize the climate. Perhaps, though, we could make it a bit more flexible to at least save a few birds in the process.

KEEP IT NIMBLE

Money is at the root of all environmental problems. Endangered species are no different. Misguided greed causes threats to wildlife in the first place. Lack of money means we can't protect them all. When limited money runs up against infinite ambition to save all species, many die. (And the ones that are saved do not necessarily contribute the most to biodiversity.)

One solution is more money. The more federally protected habitats we have, the more species can survive the onslaught of development, but that, too, soon runs into real limits. We can't protect them all, no matter how hard we try. Every time you step on a piece of land that hasn't already been covered with lifeless concrete and fake marble by a mall developer—you know, actual soil—you might be stepping on a unique critter. Since paralysis is not an option, protecting every species on the planet isn't one either.

That leads directly to a Weitzman-style reform of our approach to conservation: acknowledge trade-offs explicitly.[12] Realize that we can't save every species. Target biodiversity hotspots rather than species one by one. Aim to maximize "ecosystem services"—that is, direct human benefits from nature like clean air and water, space to enjoy in our free time, and greenery to look at while we work. Make finite conservation dollars go further. Prioritize, prioritize, prioritize. Economize, economize, economize. In econospeak, make conservation more efficient.

Look to its benefits; look to its costs; aim to get as many benefits at the least cost.

Sadly, it isn't happening quite yet. "Exploring ideas like that would exaggerate what we are doing," acknowledges Michael Bean, a senior attorney at the Department of the Interior charged with making the Endangered Species Act work better. He speaks eloquently about the problems facing the act. Still, it's the law of the land and the cornerstone of species protection in the United States. Bean doesn't lose a beat while sticking to his well-balanced, lawyerly words: "Part of my role is to make the law more effective for species protection and cheaper for land managers." One such approach is trading land for species protection.

You and your neighbor both have land that houses the golden-cheeked warbler. You happen to be in the habit of actively encouraging people to shell your land with multiple rounds of ammunition every day and can't guarantee anyone's safety on that property, let alone the bird's. And you certainly can't afford to have every offender of the Endangered Species Act on your property pay $100,000 or spend a year in jail. Your shooters are training to defend the United States in case of war.

The Fort Hood military base in Texas was in this situation. Giving up basic training for soldiers was not an option. Giving up the base wasn't either. Instead, the army entered into agreements with surrounding landowners and paid them to conserve their land in return for being able to use its own. Landowners received money for conservation, the military was able to continue fulfilling its training mission, and the golden-cheeked warbler found protected territory down the road from the army base.[13] Everybody won.

Adam Smith looked at specialization in a pin factory. Michael Bean talks about specialization in land conservation and "turning endangered species into assets, not liabilities." This type of trading system got its start in California in the 1980s, yet it's still only used on thousands of acres.[14] It takes a while for all parties involved to wrap their minds around trading land for species protection and then actually make it happen.

Flexibility pays. "Business versus the environment" may be a convenient straw man for both sides, a cry to rally their respective bases, but for the most part it helps no one, except perhaps the lawyers each retains. That becomes particularly apparent when we scale things up from warblers, woodpeckers, and the occasional eagle to protecting the globe as a whole.

WHAT WOULD THE FLINTSTONES CHOOSE TO PROTECT?

Major General Lachlan Macquarie's grave acknowledges him as the "Father of Australia." He has islands, rivers, and cities named after him. Sydney has a Macquarie Street, a Macquarie Place, a Macquarie Lighthouse, and Macquarie Fields. It no longer has Fort Macquarie.

The fort towered over Sydney harbor and managed to maintain a modicum of peace and security. Still, its useful life expired at the turn of the last century. It met the wrecking ball in 1901, when it made way for the Sydney tram depot.

The depot was nothing like your typical rail yard. It managed to look very fort-like and may have duped the casual onlooker. Its location was impressive, too—too impressive for a tram depot. Sydney's urban planners had other ideas for the site overlooking the harbor. The depot closed in 1955 to be replaced by the Sydney Opera House.

The opera house is easily one of the world's most recognizable buildings. Put it on a postcard next to a kangaroo, and you have many people's image of Australia. City planners won't be deploying another wrecking ball anytime soon for that reason alone. There is another: in 2007, UNESCO included the building on its list of World Heritage Sites. Thus ends the cycle of continuous, creative destruction and urban renewal.

UNESCO has been designating sites of cultural significance and natural beauty ever since the 1972 World Heritage Convention went into effect. The criteria are nothing to scoff at: successful places must "represent a masterpiece of human creative genius" or "contain superlative natural phenomena or areas of exceptional natural beauty and aesthetic importance." That's a tough hurdle to beat, with or without diplomatspeak. And the list goes on, adding a few more "unique" and "outstanding" qualifiers.

The ones that make it through read like anyone's bucket list: Angkor Wat, the Taj Mahal, Notre Dame, the Egyptian pyramids, Stonehenge, Machu Picchu, Brasília, the historic centers of Salzburg and Vienna, Robben Island, the Serengeti, Kilimanjaro, the Grand Canyon, the Everglades, Yellowstone, and some nine hundred others. Fifteen hundred hopefuls are waiting to be recognized as places of import. Among them are Frank Lloyd Wright buildings, Charles Darwin's home, and many more entire cities, national parks, and wildlife reservoirs.

With the UNESCO seal of approval comes recognition, protection, and—the hope goes—tourism dollars. For many of the places, that's well deserved, much needed, and often long overdue. Some cultural places may not be as well maintained were it not for UNESCO's spotlight and may not have withstood the wrecking ball of time and decay, or perhaps even the literal version.

For others, it's both a blessing and a curse. Ngorongoro—famous for its natural beauty and infamous as a Maasai refuge after their eviction from the Serengeti—made UNESCO's list in 1979. That attracted considerable attention. By now Ngorongoro is no longer just a refuge for wildlife and the occasional safari tourist. It's a site for mass tourism, traffic jams in and out of the crater, and proposed hotel developments. It would be unfair to blame UNESCO for this. Who knows, the crater might be in considerably worse shape had it never received the UN seal. But you can arguably blame UNESCO for worse.

Imagine what would have happened if UNESCO had been around five hundred years ago. Some of the cultural icons of our day may have been lost forever—or rather, UNESCO would have foreclosed the option of ever seeing them in the first place. There would be no Mozart's birthplace in Salzburg, no opera house in the historic center of Vienna, and no Sydney Opera House.

Had UNESCO been around five thousand years ago, we might have a well-protected natural heritage site in the form of the Nile floodplains between Giza and Dahshur, but in return there could be no Egyptian pyramids. It would have been hard to justify moving massive amounts of stone in front of the Bronze Age World Heritage Committee. If they played their cards right, we would have never made it into the Iron Age.

Thus is the lot of the conservationist. The Flintstones' UNESCO might well have frowned on the invention of the wheel: too dangerous; too much environmental impact; too disruptive to "physical and biological formations or groups of such formations, which are of outstanding universal value from the aesthetic or scientific point of view."

Are national parks bad? Of course not. I wish I could spend more time in them. We may have too few of them as it is. New York City's Central Park is a lovely refuge in any season, but it's no Grand Teton. There is a lot to be said for designating more land as national parks and growing the number and size of cities instead. Or in a less extreme version: grow high-density cities interspersed with unspoiled nature rather than the environmentally dubious in-between of detached, oversized single-family homes on manicured suburban lawns connected by barren residential roads.

President Teddy Roosevelt fully deserves his label as an environmental hero and his immortal association with the teddy bear. He established five national parks and laid the foundation for many more with the Antiquities Act of 1906. The Grand Canyon and many other spectacular wilderness areas became national monuments, forever freezing them in time. Teddy Roosevelt's birthplace, a nicely maintained town house a block from my office, is one of the many National Historic Sites in this category. Yet that's not the way to protect the planet at large.

Strict conservation is good—up to a point. It works for defined areas like the world's biological hotspots, home to most of our biodiversity. It doesn't work for large, indivisible, shared, essential resources. We can't set aside *all* land, water, or air. We can put bluefin tuna or polar bears on the Endangered Species List, but the list won't save them. We cannot solve overfishing or global warming through conservation efforts alone. Setting aside marine sanctuaries may protect entire ecosystems—the Great Barrier Reef is on the UNESCO list—but setting aside the entire ocean is out of the question. And the UNESCO designation renders itself meaningless when the reef's existential threat is outright bleaching due to an ever-warming atmosphere, aided by an increasingly acidic ocean.

Setting aside the entire protective layer around our planet is out; setting aside portions of it is pointless. We need different kinds of environmental laws to deal with these issues.

4

FEWER FISH, MORE DOUGH

"No fish by 2048."

There are lots of things wrong with this statement. For one, it's a stark reminder about how false accuracy is a real problem in science reporting, if not science. Why not 2050, or "within our lifetime"? What about uncertainties, let alone fat tails, ten-foot women, or other unpredictable outcomes that may put the date much closer or, if we are lucky, push it off further into the future? Many fisheries *are* declining at an alarming rate, but no one knows when zero hour will come. The authors of the 2006 *Science* article who first mentioned the year 2048 went to great lengths to explain that they were simply projecting from current trends, not predicting. Others, though, seized on that date as if it were carved into the seabed, using it as a means to focus public attention on an unfolding environmental disaster.[1]

That's the more disturbing aspect of the 2048 figure: the fact that scientists are indeed able to project current trends of seafood exploitation and come up with a year within our lifetime when we will be running out of viable seafood populations.

We are exploiting fish, ostensibly a "renewable resource," at such a rate as to prevent it from renewing itself. If we keep going the way we are going now, we will run out of fish long before we run out of oil, a non-renewable resource.

That's also where the date 2048, falsely accurate as it may be, serves a useful purpose. The specificity makes the crisis feel real and imminent. It would be good for the climate crisis to have a similar date. Polar bears? Gone after 2039.

The thought of zero fish hour is enough to turn any "pescitarian," the kind that eats fish, into a true meat-without-feet-is-still-meat vegetarian. Jonathan Safran Foer's *Eating Animals* doesn't mince words:

> The average shrimp-trawling operation throws 80 to 90 percent of the sea animals it captures overboard, dead or dying, as bycatch. (Endangered species amount to much of this bycatch.) Shrimp account for only 2 percent of global seafood by weight, but shrimp trawling accounts for 33 percent of global bycatch.

That's the good kind of shrimp.[2] Farmed shrimp, particularly in Southeast Asia, avoids bycatch but creates enormous pollution around mostly artificial, disease-prone shrimp lakes sewers.

All of that is a rather pointless plug for moral superiority and Foer's book. He doesn't need the publicity, and I don't need to remind you and me that what we do personally makes almost no difference. In the spirit of avoiding false accuracy of the kind that gave us 2048 rather than 2050 and worrying about decimal points, I'll be clear: it makes *zero* difference. Unless a majority of us, globally, turn away from eating fish—the probability of which is approximately zero as well—your giving up seafood benefits your health rather than the planet's. (Giving up mercury and the other concentrated pollutants that come with fish would likely be good for you and your IQ—assuming you make up for the missing nutrients by eating the right kinds of vegetables. Okay, really, that's it for my moralizing. Maintaining your IQ is wholly your personal decision.)

In reality, people the world over are doing the exact opposite: we consume more and more seafood. Shrimp is no longer a delicacy for the occasional hors d'oeuvre at fancy dinners; it's on the menu at most diners, preferably battered and fried, masking a taste that's anything but what shrimp is supposed to taste like. Salmon has turned into everyone's low-calorie favorite, not to say anything of all-you-can-eat sushi buffets and tuna rolls at the corner deli. Global average seafood consumption has increased by over half in the past half century. The increase was highest in developing countries, where it has more than doubled, but of course developed countries still come out ahead: the global rich consume almost exactly twice as much seafood per person as the global poor.[3]

Fish isn't a poor man's dish. The richer we all are, the poorer we can expect our oceans to become. And the problem won't solve itself. We're in serious need of some mutually beneficial coercion.

IT'S NOT WHO YOU KNOW, IT'S WHOM YOU KNOW—AND WHAT YOU OWN

James Acheson's *Lobster Gangs of Maine* at times reads like a mystery novel, rife with rough-and-tumble protagonists making their living on the sea, intrigue and backstabbing up to the point of the occasional burning outhouse, and plenty of allusions to the fact that lobstermen may organize themselves closer to Sicilian Mafia clans than independent outdoorsmen. There are family feuds, initiation rites, and stories of men—they are for the most part men[4]—with better "skill with the knife" than as fishermen. Knives, here, aren't used for literal backstabbing, but rather to cut traps of those who violate the boundaries of lobstering territory allocated to them by norms, tradition, and fellow lobstermen. That's exactly what makes lobster fishing a prime example of one of the most important lessons in what economic thinking can contribute to a healthier planet: *property rights matter.*

You own it, you protect it. Your family or community owns it, your family or community protects it. If it belongs to nobody, tender loving care goes out the window.

Lobsters are a peculiar type of seafood. They used to be fed to New England prisoners, but no more than once a week. More would have been cruel and unusual punishment. By now they top the menus of fine and not-so-fine dining establishments everywhere, regardless of how far they might be from the nearest ocean. That ubiquity could have equaled demise, and for a time it did.

Go back to the end of the nineteenth century, and you have a world confronting one of those projected dates: no more lobster by year X, except that year X was even closer back then for lobster than it's now for fish. Throughout the eighteenth century, New England lobsters were big—up to five pounds big—and there were a lot of them out at sea.[5] It took a while to develop the technology to transport live lobsters in large quantities to Boston and New York kitchens and beyond. (Another peculiarity of lobsters: they need to be transported alive and killed by the cook, accompanied by an occasional screech if done directly in boiling water. The sound is mere steam escaping the shell, not an actual cry in pain. Still, it sounds all too real. I forsook home-cooked lobsters after only one attempt, long before I turned vegetarian.) Real innovation came with the arrival of the first lobster canning factory in Gloucester, just north of Boston. Lobsters became cheaper; more diners demanded them, raising their price; more lobsters were caught; more canneries opened; lobsters became cheaper; more diners demanded them, raising their price; more lobsters were caught; more canneries opened; lobsters became cheaper; more diners demanded them—until suddenly fewer lobsters were caught.

That's not how markets are supposed to work. In your classic textbook factory, the more people want, the more people get. If factory owners can't keep up with production, prices rise, more factories open, and we are again in a happy equilibrium. Not so here. Lobsters aren't produced; they are plucked off the seabed. As long as the price is higher than what it costs to catch, can, and ship them, that's exactly what lobstermen will do. And why wouldn't they? A lobster not caught is a lobster not sold. Out in the wild it's worthless to this year's bottom line. Soon enough, though, that logic hits a wall.

Dwindling stocks and declining lobster size forced industrial lobster buyers to venture ever farther north up the coast of New England. Early in the nineteenth century, one of the most fertile lobster grounds was off the coast of Cape Cod. By the 1840s, buyers turned north to the Gulf of Maine. By the 1880s, Maine lobsters were getting smaller and scarcer, and buyers ventured into Canadian waters. That's when you know you are in trouble, when New England lobsters no longer come from New England.

Regulators in Maine started to put on the brakes. They decreed that only lobsters above a certain size could be caught and that fishermen couldn't catch any female lobsters bearing eggs. They put restrictions on who, how, and when: who could get lobster licenses (residents only), what gear could be used to catch lobsters (only particular types of traps), and when to do it. In 1874, lobster fishing was prohibited between August and October. Starting in 1875, lobster canning was banned for an equal amount of time. Industrial canning was on its way out. The last lobster canning factory closed up shop by 1895. Regulation worked up to a point, but it didn't work at its full potential before the arrival of lobster gangs. Soon things started to look up. Gangs aim for self-preservation: preserving their families, their way of life, their territories, and, as it turns out, the lobster stock out at sea. Yet gangs alone were not enough. They depended on a crucial ingredient that allowed them to translate the mantra that "property rights matter" into practice.

A crucial peculiarity of lobsters relative to most fish is that they hardly move. Bluefin tuna can swim dozens of miles a day and move thousands of miles between hemispheres in search of warmer waters during northern winters. Lobsters, at least the ones off the coast of Maine, have a much harder time getting around. Their typical annual mileage hovers in the single digits. That seeming handicap exerts huge influence over how they get treated. What makes lobsters easier targets for the humans out to catch them turns out to be the species' saving grace.

If lobsters left alone spawn and multiply on your very own territory, it makes a lot of sense to let some go today for a greater haul tomorrow and in years to come. That's what is happening in Maine—in part voluntarily, in part by local and state regulators stepping in and putting restrictions on catch sizes, the types of equipment used, how many traps each lobsterman can have, and how many licenses are handed out in the first place. Amazingly, sometimes lobstermen themselves ask government to step in with these types of restrictions.

Who can place traps where—who joins which gang—is the biggest decision of them all. It's not enough to be a resident and to have the drive and the equipment. Newbies need to jump through hoops to pass muster with the established powers that be. That means getting a formal license and joining the local Lobstermen's Association as much as being accepted by a particular harbor's gang and being able to tune your own two-way radio to your gang's frequency without running the danger of having your very first set of traps cut by overly protective rivals. Most often it also means being a local. James Acheson recalls a New Jersey man in his fifties: he "had another income and a large gang

of traps but also had plenty of unwanted advice to offer local fisher-men. He lasted approximately two weeks in the fishing business. Even-tually he was forced to leave town."

Tuna, sadly, is in the opposite situation. Local or not, everyone can join the fun. Catching tuna is a global scuffle with factory ships chasing increasingly dwindling stocks in international waters. Letting tuna go today does not mean you will catch more next year. It means your competitor will catch them tomorrow. No one owns the territory where tuna roam. It's in no one's interest to do unilaterally what would be needed to preserve the fish.

PRIVATE THOUGHTS

We can no longer afford to consider air and water common property, free to be abused by anyone without regard to the consequences. In-stead, we should begin now to treat them as scarce resources, which we are no more free to contaminate than we are free to throw garbage into our neighbor's yard.

These two sentences should have been in quotation marks. They come courtesy of Richard Nixon, spoken at his State of the Union address on January 22, 1970.

Even then, these observations weren't exactly new. Aristotle philosophized about them in 350 B.C.: "For that which is common to the greatest number has the least care bestowed upon it. Everyone thinks chiefly of his own, hardly at all of the common interest."[6] Translated into today's lingo: "In the history of the world, no one has ever washed a rented car."[7]

Owners protect their property better than renters, and what goes for renters applies much more so for fishermen, loggers, or general polluters in a global free-for-all. You can be sure that if someone actually owned the atmosphere, he or she would come knocking on your door if you continued spewing unchecked pollution into it day after day. (Or imagine if carbon pollution were color coded, every particle in the atmosphere traceable to its polluter.) Of course, no one does own the atmosphere. And no one owns the oceans, either, outside the relatively narrow two-hundred-nautical-mile territorial band countries claim for themselves.

Garrett Hardin has mustered a cult following for lamenting the "tragedy of the commons."[8] He looked to pastures as an example of how open access warps minds and ensures environmental catastrophe. Each ranger gains from adding that one extra cow to the pasture. He gets the full benefit of having one more animal graze for free while the additional cost is split among everyone—the perfect recipe for disaster: "A hundred and fifty years ago a plainsman could kill an American bison, cut out only the tongue for his dinner, and discard the rest of the animal. He was not in any important sense being wasteful. Today, with only a few thousand bison left, we would be appalled at such behavior."

Shift from bison to tuna and climate-destabilizing greenhouse gas pollution, and it's readily apparent why every environmental economist in training reads Hardin.

Or at least it's apparent why every environmental economist in training finds Hardin on her reading list. In truth, it's the kind of article that's eminently skippable. Everyone knows the story, and everyone knows what comes next: *privatize the commons*. Market forces, properly channeled, will do the rest. If only all fish in the sea or all air in the atmosphere were owned by someone, the planet would be okay.

The logic is compelling. Assume the most money-centric, hyper-rational, anti-environmental capitalist—that little guy from Monopoly—were given sole title to the entire Atlantic Ocean. To our surprise, Rich Uncle Pennybags might suddenly become Mr. Sustainability. That's where the money is. He'd want clean, healthy waters brimming with tuna, swordfish, cod, and lobster, because that would make his big, watery asset more valuable. If he couldn't harvest all the seafood himself, he'd get offers he couldn't refuse from fisherman—but as a shrewd capitalist, he'd make sure that this year's harvest would leave the ocean just as valuable next year, and the next. If he decided to allow anyone to drill for oil, he'd be damn sure that the blowout preventers had batteries that worked. And what works for the Atlantic also works for fishing, hunting, pumping oil, drawing water, and polluting air or land.

That at least is the caricature of Hardin's counsel followed to its logical conclusion: privatizing nature wins the day. Assign one capitalist to each natural asset and watch environmental problems disappear into thin (clean) air. It has also been my impression of Hardin's views for the longest time. I had not read his original five-page article when I was supposed to (and I know of few others who did). Why bother?

Turns out Hardin was making a much larger point, one about overpopulation. His conclusion: "The only way we can preserve and nurture other and more precious freedoms is by relinquishing the freedom to breed, and that very soon." Seeing the conclusion in this light—and in combination with Paul Ehrlich's *Population Bomb*, which appeared the very same year—I suspect many economists would be much more reluctant to point to Hardin's piece as a prime example of the need to privatize the commons. Yet he has somehow escaped the fate of Ehrlich, a fellow ecologist, who has been roundly criticized among economists for his Malthusian views that global mass starvation due to overpopulation was imminent. That counsel turned out to be as wrong in 1968 as it was when Thomas Malthus first made it in 1798.

I will not get into the population question now, even though it is, of course, an important debate to be had. (Fast-forward to chapter 6 for more on Ehrlich's gloom and how it stacks up against technological optimism, one of the most consequential debates for the future of civilization.)

Rather than shadowbox with what Hardin did not (and did) say, we need to wrestle with Ronald Coase.

NOBEL THOUGHTS

Hardin never won a Nobel Prize for his ideas. Another man whose writings are on everyone's reading list with few bothering to read them can claim the distinction: Ronald Coase won the Nobel for showing that all you need is well-defined property rights and environmental problems will sort themselves out. Give polluters the right to pollute and let everyone else buy their way to cleaner air. Or if you are so inclined, give children the right to breathe freely, and let polluters compensate them justly for being able to knock points off the children's IQs. As long as property rights are well defined, we'll get to the optimal level of pollution.

That's at least the caricature of what he said. Coase has been at the University of Chicago since the 1960s. Of course he would argue for government to get out of the way and let markets rule the day.

Not quite.

Coase actually picked up his Nobel "for his discovery and clarification of the significance of transaction costs and property rights for the institutional structure and functioning of the economy."

That's a mouthful. The two key ideas are transaction costs and property rights, and the Swedes might have put them in this order for a reason. Property rights are crucial, but we can't just assign those rights and ignore everything else, especially not when it comes to the costs of parties getting together and solving disputes among themselves—the transaction costs involved in any such encounters.

If there were no transaction costs, you could assign property rights at random. People who valued them more could readily buy them from whoever they were assigned to in the first place. You could assign drivers the right to plow through crosswalks, and then let pedestrians buy the right to safe passage. Where there are transaction costs, though—it can be challenging to negotiate with a speeding car as you try to cross the street with your toddler—things quickly get more complicated. Coase surely agrees, even if some of his ardent free-market disciples might wish it were as easy as putting property rights on everything and then letting individuals and courts figure out the rest. No need for government to step in. Sadly, that's often wishful thinking. Coase himself recognized as much and often disagrees with later interpretations of his thoughts. One of the better interpretations of Coase's writings has the promising title "Coase Versus the Coasians."

Having no government might work if there are only two parties involved: a polluting factory and the victim of that pollution downstream. As long as it's clear who owns which right—the factory to pollute, or the resident to clean water and air—everything should be fine. That's the classic Coasian situation. Who owns the property rights matters a lot for who will get compensated by whom, but the overall outcome will be efficient either way. Either the factory owner compensates the resident for the pollution damage or, ideally, cleans up the pollution in the first place, or the resident pays the factory to stop polluting. Problem solved.

Then there is the real world, where more often than not it costs something for the factory owner and the resident to get together and start negotiating. If there are only two of them and the dispute is small enough, it might be relatively cheap. If the pollution in question affects an entire city, or the planet, the transaction costs will be enormous.

Now the charge is for government to step in. That's, in fact, what government is for to begin with: solving problems where the costs for individuals to get together and do so won't lead to a desirable outcome.

The two extremes of full privatization of all of nature and full-out socialism leave another area in between. The Maine harbor gangs don't quite fit into either Hardin's or Coase's picture. Lobster territories are private up to a point, but not entirely.

Economists typically aren't known for being nuanced. They are known, though, for responding to incentives. So perhaps this should change things. In 2009, Elinor Ostrom shared a Nobel Prize in Economics for looking at exactly the question of what happens in between the two extremes: the tuna's global free-for-all and the straw man of all-private-all-the-time. The Nobel citation commended her "for her analysis of economic governance, especially the commons." Maine harbor gangs are a prime example.

What goes for Maine lobstermen goes for pastures in the Swiss Alps, small forests in India, irrigation rights in Spain and the Philippines, and umpteen other cases. Ostrom's librarian at Indiana University, Fenton Martin, established a comprehensive database of five thousand documents—and that by 1990, when Ostrom wrote her most important book, *Governing the Commons*. By 2010, that number had grown to over fifty thousand documents, including around a hundred detailed, distinct case studies. Ostrom set out to find patterns across these disparate cases. At first, she was looking to deduce a blueprint, a single rule. That turned out to be no small feat.

Bear with me. Ostrom won a Nobel for her nuance for a reason. She identified six common themes of what works and what doesn't.[9] First and foremost, avoiding the tragedy of the commons takes well-defined territories. Maine's harbor gangs definitely share that feature. People who violate the boundaries of their own lobstering ground might find their lobster traps cut or their outhouses burning. Even Hardin's pastures should have clear boundaries: fences, usually, or other, natural limits. Second, she found a rough link between the costs and the benefits of the rules of the game. If lobstermen found that cheating paid, gangs would quickly fall apart. Self-interest still rules the day. Similarly, and point number three, everyone wants a say in setting up the rules. Not everyone's advice will be heeded, but everyone at the very least will be heard. That's not just an act in futile pseudo-democracy; it's key for keeping everyone on board and committed. Fourth on Ostrom's list is monitoring. Someone ought to keep track of what's going on. That could be either the unelected gang kings or the duly elected head of the local Lobstermen's Association. In either case, he or she needs to draw authority by cultivating the respect of everyone involved, and also provide a forum for grievances, another one of Ostrom's points. Which leaves us with her sixth: there must be sanctions for violations of any kind. These can't be too exorbitant at first but ought to be increasingly stiff for repeat offenders. Three strikes and you are banished from the harbor.

Now, that's the kind of list that is deserving of a Nobel. But lest anyone conclude nuance was the path to simplicity—complete steps one through six, problem solved—Ostrom came up with a term that ought to make linguists *and* economists squirm: "polycentricity."

Preventing the tragedy of the commons turns out to be a messy business. Systems that combine private efforts, public governance, and communities of various shapes and sizes tend to manage resources best. And it's often the community function that has the biggest influence. Maine lobstermen don't just compete with each other once to catch as many lobsters as possible for themselves. They face each other not just out at sea but also at the 7-Eleven, at the school play, and at Sunday services.

The key word in all of this is "manage." Hardin has by now acknowledged as much. Thirty years after his article that caused the original stir, he wrote a follow-up for *Science* in 1998, in which he declared his "weightiest mistake" to be "the omission of the modifying adjective 'unmanaged.'" The tragedy of the unmanaged commons makes ruin inevitable. Although, here again, he manages to present the solution as an either-or: the choice is either "socialism or the privatism of free enterprise." If you like to describe Maine harbor gangs as "socialist," fine. I have a feeling that they would strongly disagree and may even back up their verbal disagreement with decidedly nonsocial behavior. The true system of checks and balances that keeps the system afloat is much more nuanced than that. It's "polycentric," to use Ostrom's awkward yet Nobel-winning word.

The crucial question now becomes which kinds of commons can be managed—whether Mafia-style as with Maine's harbor gangs or in slightly less dramatic settings like Alpine pastures or ancient irrigation systems that have been managed successfully for many centuries. The example of the factory upstream and the pollution victim downstream is on one end of the spectrum. That's Coase and Hardin's territory. Maine lobster grounds are somewhere in the middle. That's where Ostrom shines. But neither of these cases truly applies to problems so large they affect all seven billion of us. The Mafia might have global ambitions, but no gang is large enough to manage anything close to the global commons, like the entire ocean or atmosphere.

THE GLOBAL PRIZE

A few hundred Maine lobstermen divvy up the lobster grounds between Gloucester, Massachusetts, and the Canadian border. Washington may intervene on occasion, but for the most part the lobstermen manage to organize themselves in local harbor gangs, regional lobstermen's associations, and statewide regulatory agencies. Most of their self-policing actions—the unspoken shaming and shunning of violators of the unwritten rules—are hidden from the law.

Scaling that kind of arrangement up to the global level, tying in millions of fishermen or billions of polluters, isn't very promising. But there is a surprising twist to the comparison.

The world has fewer countries than there are Maine lobstermen. In 2010, there were fewer than 200 countries—192 to be exact. That's up from around 50 in 1900, and the number may well increase in the future. But for now it seems rather manageable. Let me rephrase that: there are plenty of problems, conflicts, and wars in the world, but the important point is that when it comes to solving global problems, more often than not, the conflict is among the 200-odd countries rather than seven billion individuals. The scale now is huge, but the scope is manageable— except that it's states we are dealing with rather than lobstermen.

These are the kinds of parallels used by Elinor Ostrom in a book she jointly edited with Robert O. Keohane, my former boss's dad.[10] Small world—which is, in fact, their point. The very same countries that try to hammer out environmental agreements don't just meet in Rio de Janeiro, Kyoto, or Copenhagen; they also meet for the Doha trade negotiations, nuclear disarmament talks, various sorts of war games (imagined and real), and so on. All these issues are what morph the United Nations into the illustrious talking shop it is, rendering it staggeringly frustrating yet immensely important.

The number of countries that really matter is even smaller. It's often up to Washington, Brussels, Beijing, Moscow, New Delhi, Tokyo, and a handful of others to maintain the global balance of power and keep the peace. Solving global commons problems then becomes a worldwide game of tit for tat, much like sorting out who gets to place which lobster traps when and where.

No parallel is perfect. For all their individualism, lobstermen look very much the same—or at least any two Maine lobstermen look and act more alike than, say, the United States and China, or possibly even the United States and some of its closest allies in Europe.

Being different is often a strength when it comes to cooperating on trade issues. That's why we trade in the first place, because others have what we don't. Being too different, however, isn't very conducive to solving commons problems. There it helps that lobstermen all talk the same language, use similar numbers of traps, and go to the same church. If your negotiating partner claims whaling to be part of its national heritage, negotiating a global whaling moratorium becomes tough. If China's economy depends on cheap, dirty coal, capping carbon emissions is similarly difficult. Then again, we did manage to negotiate a whaling moratorium—admittedly one with some loopholes for "scientific whaling"—and China is making strides toward decarbonizing its economy. (We will come back to that last point later. For now, let's just conclude that things are both simpler and more complex than they appear at first glance.)

Of course, it doesn't end with countries as perfectly formed individual entities. The trade or climate negotiator showing up at the UN talks may speak for her president or even her parliament, but that still doesn't mean that the outcome at home is a foregone conclusion. Being a dictatorship might come in handy in these kinds of situations. For democracies, the situation is different. Local voters could nix the best intentions of their political leaders. Even more important, solving any kind of global commons problem depends on local laws. Those laws sometimes go back centuries.

GLOBAL PROBLEMS, LOCAL SOLUTIONS

The Magna Carta may have limited the powers of the king, established the foundation for habeas corpus, and been a beacon of legal light in the otherwise dark Middle Ages. It was not quite as kind to fish.

Overfishing has been around since at least the Middle Ages, and regulation wasn't far behind. By 1200, the first fishing restrictions had been put in place, no doubt prompting the unenlightened paragraph in the Magna Carta that asks for fish to be set free. The document ordered the dismantling of all private fish weirs throughout England, effectively putting ponds back into the public domain.[11] That's a noble idea, if it weren't for the pesky inconvenience that humans like to exploit that to which they have free access.

Of course, most medieval approaches to fishery management were, well, medieval. It's easy to imagine boiling oil being spilled over who gets to fish where, and historians tell us there was a lot of that.

Flash forward a few hundred years, and the choice is much the same, just now much bigger and consequential for the planet: a free-for-all at sea or some type of oceanic order.[12] If you choose the former, fisheries would surely collapse, and everyone—fishermen, diners, and fish (not to mention the planet and everyone on it)—would lose. If you opt for the oceanic order, fisheries still might collapse, of course, unless it's done intelligently.

Let's start by eliminating the truly dumb ideas that have haunted us for too long.

One way of limiting fishing is to put a cap on the number of fishermen. That's a simple and obvious first step: hand out fishing licenses, perhaps to half the existing fishermen. The half with a license are good to go out on their boats. The rest are out of luck. Leaving equity aside, the solution turns out to be rather simplistic. The ones with licenses can just double down on their efforts, and they surely will. The result is half as many fishermen each catching twice as much fish, if not more. It would be easy to scoff at the thought of anyone seriously proposing this type of restriction for a commercial fishery, if it hadn't actually happened to tragic effects. Managers of the British Columbia salmon fishery reduced the number of licenses by a fifth. The result? Fishermen with licenses bought bigger and better boats. The entire fleet ended up with more capacity to catch salmon than before the license limit. Put that in the regulatory category of "nice try."

Yet there is one opportunity to make things even worse: announce beforehand your intention of eventually capping the number of fishermen allowed into a particular fishery. So it happened in the Alaska halibut fishery in the 1970s. Suddenly fishermen who had never before caught a halibut started catching them in anticipation of limited entry later. It's a perfectly sensible move by the individual fisherman. It's anything but sensible from the regulator's point of view, assuming she has any intention of regulating the industry to protect the fish.

If limiting the number of fishermen and their boats doesn't work, perhaps the regulatory lens should be focused on time? That's what Maine lobstermen faced when the lobstering season was severely limited starting in 1874, a move that drove out commercial canning factories and contributed to saving Maine lobsters. Perhaps so, but without additional measures and the tight-knit, self-regulatory harbor gang culture to support it, the move could easily have made things worse.

Once again, look no further than the Alaska halibut fishery, which is outcompeting itself for the most asinine attempt to bring a fishery back from the brink of extinction:

"Halibut catch is falling year after year."

"I've got it. Let's limit the days people can go out and fish."

"A hundred days?"

"No, too much."

"Fifty?"

"Halibut stocks are still disappearing."

"Five?"

"No."

"Two!"

"Genius."

In the early 1990s, the Alaska halibut season totaled forty-eight hours—for the entire year. Do I need to spell out the results?

Fishermen spent 363 days of the year tooling up their gear, putting together war strategies, and storing up sleep reserves before getting in starting positions ready to launch a full-blown assault on any living critter in sight. Thousands of boats competed for the same dwindling supplies of fish. The scene at the twenty-four-hour Le Mans race was relaxed and organized by comparison. Fishing boats became bigger and faster by the year. It proved a stunning example of how technology beat out regulation in a big way. Perhaps that's the answer?

Let's regulate technology directly! None of those satellite-guided factory ships with mile-long nets. Every fisherman gets a single rod. That should protect fish, and indeed it would. Combined with limiting licenses, such regulation should lead to the perfect recipe: who, when, and how all neatly tied up in one comprehensive regulatory package. The Magna Carta may have charted the course in that regard, outlawing fish weirs, the latest in net technology of thirteenth-century England.

In practice, technological limits do not take the form of "thou shalt" but of "thou shalt not." This isn't a car race where everyone sits in nearly identical vehicles to "test the skills" of the driver. Instead, regulators outlaw the newest bottom-trawling nets or limit nets to certain sizes.

This type of regulation comes with several problems. For one, enforcement is exceedingly difficult. Why not just own two types of nets: one to show the inspector, the other to fish? Add to that the fact that specific restrictions are relatively easy to evade—regulators can't possibly stay ahead of every conceivable technological innovation—and the business soon develops into a permanent race between the regulator and the regulated. Most important, direct technology restrictions are extremely intrusive. How else can you check on whether fishermen on hundreds of boats comply with ever-changing rules trying to keep up with the technological arms race?

Then there is the money question: Why not allow new technologies if they enable fishermen to do their job more cheaply, more safely, and generally better? One reason is that fish tend to lose out in this equation. The term of art is "overcapitalization." Allowing all new technologies means that too many of the latest gadgets are chasing too few fish. It's a race of who can locate the remaining fish fastest and claim them for themselves: the race for the commons. Outlawing all conceivable new technologies doesn't make things better. Now fishermen stock up on the old technologies and spend much too much money on them: too many outdated boats chasing too few fish.

The most damning critique of any such method of fisheries regulation—whether it's capping the number of fishermen, capping their days at sea, or restricting their gear—is that all of them manage to be too direct and too roundabout at the same time. They are very intrusive, top-down, command-and-control, I-know-better-than-thee approaches with government inspectors virtually breathing down fishermen's necks or, worse, barring them from fishing altogether. Yet they still miss the target.

They don't cap the actual number of fish caught. That's the goal, the only goal. The planet doesn't care how many fishermen are out there. It doesn't care how long they fish. It doesn't care how many boats or nets they use. We might care about any of these things for other reasons, but the fish in question clearly don't notice a difference.

If the goal is to limit how many fish can be caught in a given fishing season, do exactly that: *cap the total catch.*

That's the most scientifically sound, economically efficient, and politically expedient way of regulating fisheries. It's the only way. As difficult as it may be to determine the maximum sustainable catch, it's much easier than limiting the number of fishing licenses or regulating gear in the hope of capping total catch at a level low enough not to crash the fishery.

There are two ways to go about doing this. Let's start with the one that would be all too easy to dismiss, if it weren't used so frequently with disastrous consequences. Fishery managers determine the total number of fish that can be caught in any given season. That's difficult but far from impossible to do. It's also only the first step. Next managers announce that quota for the world to see. They might as well blow a whistle. Everything we have lamented before reappears, only now in its purest form: uninhibited by technological restrictions, each fisherman tries to catch as much fish in as short a time as possible to ensure that he gets his largest possible share under that total cap. Regulators step in and close the fishery once that cap is reached. We see the same kind of overcapitalization—too many boats chasing too few fish—and the effect the Alaska halibut fishery has made infamous: the fishing season gets ever shorter, until we do the nautical equivalent of sending a crowd of starving people to an all-you-can-eat buffet for exactly three minutes. But enough with making fun of Alaskans and their dismally performing halibut fishery and disturbing regulatory record.

Let's turn to a superbly performing fishery that uses caps on total catch the right way: Alaska's halibut fishery after 1995.[13] The trick that has made all the difference has been handing out ownership shares in the total catch to individual fishermen.

The logic is compelling. Fishery scientists determine the total sustainable catch, but instead of declaring it as the overall goal of the annual race to catch as many fish in as little time as possible, regulators print up individual shares in that total catch. Fishermen then get the guaranteed right to catch a predetermined amount of fish. That simple step makes all the difference. It's no longer a race. Much like with the Maine lobster, what you don't catch today will still be there for you tomorrow. You own the right to a certain number of fish. Period. Your neighbor can't take it away from you just because you went to a sonogram appointment today or watched your kid's football game. The motivation to treat fishing as if it were a competitive free-for-all is gone.

Bigger engines enable you to haul in your catch earlier, but the reason to go overboard in the technological arms race is gone. The fishery quite naturally settles into the optimal number of vessels. Fishing becomes safer, more sustainable, and more profitable. Overcapitalization is a thing of the past. Fishermen no longer use larger and larger boats to chase fewer and fewer fish. It's now in their interest to decrease costs. Things generally get much more relaxed. Alaska's halibut fishing season has increased from two to over two hundred days, all without additional restrictions or regulations.

Sounds like socialist nirvana with the guiding hand of regulators replacing the invisible hand of the market. In fact, it's anything but. This is much closer to the "privatism of free enterprise" Garrett Hardin described as the other solution to the commons problem, the exact opposite of socialism. Fishermen affected by the changes wax poetic, using terms like "liberty," "freedom," and "dignity." Increasing the fishing season from two to two hundred days doesn't just make fishing more relaxed; it also means that fishermen no longer bring in half their entire annual catch in one day. That avoids flooding the market with halibut all at once, crashing the price in the process.

With higher prices, lower costs, and more sustainable catches, revenues doubled and profits quadrupled in the first five years of the program. It doesn't get more free market than that—except it does: fishermen aren't just allowed to use their catch shares to fish themselves; they can also sell them to other fishermen. Properly regulated, such sales guarantee that catch shares ultimately go to those who want to fish and can do so most cheaply. It makes the market run smoother while keeping the total catch in the fishery constant.

Everyone does what he or she does best. The regulator determines total allowable catch in the fishery, something individual fishermen cannot and should not be trusted to do themselves. Fishermen determine who catches how much, something the regulator cannot and should not be trusted to do herself. Everyone wins, including the fish and the planet.

MARKETS FOR THE ENVIRONMENT

Out of over eleven thousand fisheries in the world, more than a quarter collapsed during the second half of the twentieth century.[14] In fact, following those numbers to their logical conclusion led to the overly precise projection that all fisheries will have collapsed by 2048, unless we change course. That's a damning verdict on the way we manage our oceans. Or rather, how we don't manage them.

Fortunately, the course to take instead is quite apparent. Had all fisheries applied individual catch shares by 1970, over 90 percent would still be alive and well today, and that's a conservative estimate. Using markets doesn't guarantee success. Trying to work against them, however, seems a sure recipe for disaster. If no one owns rights to a particular fishery or the ocean at large, no one will take care of it. The same goes for the atmosphere. *Property rights matter.* Simple as that.

Reality adds a few twists. Like in the case of Maine lobster, we may sometimes be better off managing commons as a community. Do unto others as you wish they do unto you. That may even work internationally, when it comes to solving some global problems. It's the basis for many of our international agreements and points the way to how climate negotiations could proceed. Don't try to find unanimous agreement among 192 countries. Pull up chairs for the 5 or 15 that matter.

But flying around the world signing international agreements and diplomatic communiqués will be worthless unless we have laws at home that guide market forces in line with these global pronouncements. Capping total catch and handing out individual catch shares did wonders for the Alaska halibut. Time to move from fish to carbon and from overfishing to a climate out of whack.

5

CURIOUS COMPANY KEPT

You may have noticed what I have—that there seem to be two types of people on airplanes: those who enjoy having conversations with perfect strangers . . . and the rest of us.

I am very much in the second category. I stow my bag in the overhead bin, get comfortable in my seat, open my briefcase, book, or newspaper within a few seconds of sitting down, sometimes even put on headphones just in case, and generally do my best not to notice anyone around me.

The other day I was on a flight out of Boston. I got on the plane, took out my book, and began to read. Then it came.

"Hi, how are you?"

"Fine, thanks." I struggled to look busy and kept reading, but I felt him itch for more.

"What do you do? What kind of business are you in?"

At that moment, I did something foolish. I told the truth. "I'm an environmental economist."

I turned back to my reading, expecting and dreading a follow-up comment, an additional question.

Nothing.

He just sat there in stunned silence.

Now it was me who was looking up. That was it? No hour-long conversation that ends with swapping pictures of the kids?

Did I somehow offend him?

But then it dawned on me: he had concluded that he's just met a living, breathing oxymoron. My seat companion simply didn't know what to say in response.

"Environmental economist?" Surely, it must be one or the other: it's either the environment or the economy, either an environmentalist or an economist. Pick your side. Not both, not in one person.

That is how Robert Stavins begins the first lecture of his introductory environmental economics course every year. I first heard it when taking the class as a freshman in college in 1999. I heard it again a few years later in the very same room when I was a Ph.D. student and a teaching fellow for the course.

Back then, it was just a story, sometimes with various embellishments. (I distinctly remember a purple velour jumpsuit mentioned in the 1999 version. Stavins vehemently disputes the charge.) By now, he has gone high-tech—complete with a PowerPoint slide showing a picture of two nicely dressed gentlemen talking in the back of a plane. The litmus test of how closely his former students who have gone out to teach their own environmental economics classes stick to the master's script is whether they, too, tell the same story.

Stavins's point, of course, is that "environmental economics" is not an oxymoron. The causes of environmental problems are economic. The same goes for their solutions. Economics is critical to our understanding environmental problems—and in our solving them.

Stavins is as methodical as they come. His day is split into fifteen-minute intervals. Undergraduates get one such slot, if they are lucky.

Graduate students get up to two, depending on the topic. Every class handout has a continuous number. Every lecture has an introduction detailing the main points to be conveyed that day, a summary at the end to put everything in perspective, and an outline to which Stavins sticks religiously. There is time for plenty of stories, but those, too, are well rehearsed and impeccably timed, and all fit within the larger theme of how to design "scientifically sound, economically rational, and politically pragmatic" policy solutions, which is also one of Stavins's favorite phrases.

One of these solutions, and another of Stavins's favorites, is cap and trade. It takes the logic from combating overfishing and applies it to pollution. With fish, who owns them matters. If no one does, catching fish turns into a global free-for-all with disastrous consequences. The most sensible solution—the only one, really—is to cap the total catch and hand out shares in that catch to fishermen. That can happen informally, as in the case of the Maine lobster gangs divvying up among themselves shares in a particular harbor's total sustainable catch. Or it can be done formally, through fishermen's associations, state regulators, and the federal government. More often than not, regulation is the only game in town. It's exceedingly difficult to form traditional, informal structures from scratch or re-create them once broken.

For pollution, the logic is similarly compelling: cap total pollution and hand out shares in the total to polluters. In the process, the government creates a market where there was none before and makes pollution costly.

Enviros get their limit on pollution. Capitalists get their market. It's not pro-left; it's not pro-right. It's the perfect marriage of common sense and environmental sensibility. And it's not the least bit oxymoronic. It focuses minds, refocuses market forces, and guides them toward a more desirable outcome for all. The lower the cap, the higher the price on pollution. The easier it is to combat pollution, the more the price decreases. The eventual goal is a zero cap and a zero price: no one pollutes, and no one wants to anymore.

Sounds like policy dreamland, but it isn't. We've heard this tune before. Countries and regions around the world from Europe to New Zealand are capping carbon pollution, and many more—including China—are looking into programs on their own, at least in pilot stages. State governments led by California and ten states in the Northeast are doing the same in America. And, if and when it gets around to embracing the solution, it will not be the first time for Washington either.

LEAD NO MORE

Gasoline has the annoying feature of igniting unintentionally when put under too much pressure, causing some of the earlier engines to self-destruct under constant knocking. Thomas Midgley found a solution to the dilemma in the early 1920s: mix in tetraethyl lead, a concoction of four parts alcohol and one part lead. Midgley could not know at that time that leaded gasoline would later be linked to self-destructing brain cells. (Midgley was a particularly unfortunate and prolific environmental antihero. He also developed dichlorodifluoromethane—Freon, for short. Midgley knew it as a nontoxic, safe refrigerant. We now know it as a substance that helped punch the hole in the ozone layer and has since been largely phased out.)

Some workers producing the gasoline-lead cocktail became psychotic and died. That should have been a tip-off, but it took three decades to conclude that even the much lower concentrations found in engine exhausts decreased children's IQs and increased blood pressure in adults. Lead also clogged newly mandated catalytic converters. When faced with the trade-off between old engines on the one side and brain cells *and* new engines on the other, the U.S. Congress reached the only sensible conclusion: lawmakers directed the Environmental Protection Agency to start decreasing the amount of lead in gasoline.

Between 1974 and 1982, the EPA phased down lead the only way it knew how: by setting lower and lower standards. Environmentalists and all kinds of brain cell conservationists loved it. Oil refineries and automakers resisted. Battle lines were drawn. It was the typical full-frontal collision of environment versus business.

During the ensuing debate, the EPA started to experiment with a new way of doing business. It created a business. It put in place a new market that would phase down lead.[1] The burden shifted from lawyers charged with fighting the EPA to engineers charged with reducing pollution. The successful engineers and the refineries that employed them freed up valuable "allowances," a company's share under the total cap, which could then be sold to competitors who couldn't meet their limits.

Lawsuits didn't disappear overnight, but reducing lead moved from being a legal nightmare to becoming a competitive sport among rival teams of chemists and engineers. The market was hugely successful. It saved the industry hundreds of millions of dollars in phasedown costs.

Time for another novel idea—novel, at least, for environmental legislation. The grand innovation was "banking," saving allowances for the future. Initially, many refiners found the targets easy to meet. They already owned the necessary technology, but they also knew that these standards—the cap—would become increasingly tighter. Banking enabled refiners to save allowances when meeting the standard was easy, so that they could use them over the next couple of years, when the tightening standard made it increasingly tough to comply.

That innovation alone saved around $200 million out of a total cost estimated on the order of $1 billion. It did so by shifting pollution into the future, or, in other words, by pulling pollution reductions forward. Say you expect to emit a hundred tons of pollution this year, and next year you know you will face a cap of eighty. Given the cap you know is coming, you may well decide that it's wise to reduce this year's emissions even if you don't have to. Instead of emitting a hundred this year and eighty the next, you emit ninety in both years. There's no particular magic to this logic. The results are striking nonetheless: companies save a fifth of their compliance costs; total pollution across time doesn't change, but it goes down earlier. Everybody wins.

Soon enough the business model flipped completely. Unleaded gasoline turned into the new business as usual. Consumers preferred the unleaded variety; producing it became increasingly cheaper. By 1988, the standard was at 0.1 grams of lead per gallon of gasoline, down 95 percent from over 2 grams in 1970, and the downtrend continued. The phasedown had run its course. Trading was no longer needed for compliance. By the time the EPA banned lead in gasoline in 1996, it had for all intents and purposes already been phased out. The ban was a logical confirmation of the successful market-based phasedown.

ACID REDUX

Sulfur dioxide spares brain cells but attacks airways and lungs instead. It also causes acid rain, which pollutes water, kills plants and trees, and is so caustic that it pockmarks stone figures on centuries-old cathedrals. We were supposed to take care of the problem in the 1970s through various Clean Air Act extensions and amendments. Alas, they missed a crucial point: power plants built before the regulation took effect, a large source of acid rain, were exempt.

That exemption managed to increase pollution by prompting utilities to keep their old inefficient, dirtier plants around as a way to avoid the new regulation. That was most certainly not in the spirit of the framers. Congress may have wanted to protect businesses, but I have a hard time believing they intentionally wanted to increase pollution. It's a cliché, but market forces do flow much like water. When a displeasing regulation stands in their way, they find every nook and crevice through which to pry themselves.

This time politics fortuitously came to the rescue. President George H. W. Bush wanted to prove his environmental bona fides and make good on a campaign promise to become an environmental president. He couldn't do a complete 180 from Ronald Reagan, who famously curtailed the EPA throughout the 1980s. Bush was looking to be pro-environment and pro-business at the same time, so he turned to Stavins and a few other academics as well as to the Environmental Defense Fund to help write a new sulfur dioxide market law.[2] It wasn't all happy-go-lucky, but it was clearly bipartisan. The final measure passed the Senate by a vote of 89–10 and the House by 401–25. The bill had something for everyone. The left got tougher pollution regulation; the right got the most business-friendly way of achieving those targets. Even companies with loads of coal plants, like Duke Energy, supported the bill.

The basics are much the same as with the lead phasedown, just here more explicit and on a larger scale, with over thirty-five hundred power plants covered. The idea comes in two simple parts: a cap on pollution, and the flexibility to meet it. Government—backed by science—sets the limit on overall pollution. Large polluters get allowances, each representing the right to emit one ton of sulfur dioxide, the total number adding up to the size of the cap. Businesses are free to trade the allowances among themselves. That flexibility is the ingredient that creates markets and empowers all players to act in their own self-interest while protecting the environment.

Anyone waking up now after lapsing into a coma during the environmental legal battles of the 1970s might feel he's still dreaming. The law passed over the objection of much of industry, but once in place the sulfur dioxide trading program saw near-perfect compliance. In fact, there was overcompliance during the first phase. Lawyers begone. Businesses were too busy doing what businesses are supposed to do: finding ways to make money by producing more at lower costs.

The flexibility of the law produced savings to the tune of $1 billion over the alternative of top-down, the-government-is-watching-you, command-and-control legislation, which would have required installing scrubbers on all power plants and would have cost $3 billion nationwide. Overall, benefits of the 1990 Clean Air Act Amendments outweighed costs thirty to one. Costs were so cheap compared with benefits that President George W. Bush's EPA—that's "W.," not "H. W."—tightened the sulfur dioxide emissions standard by another 70(!) percent in 2005. The tool of choice: cap and trade.

(There's a side story that isn't quite as rosy but harbors its own important lesson. Despite *The Economist* declaring the acid rain trading program "probably the greatest green success story of the past decade," in 2008 an appeals court invalidated the latest emissions-trading rules for reasons unrelated to cap and trade, and unrelated to much economic logic. Barack Obama's EPA has since tried to rewrite the rules to once again pass muster with the courts. While that's happening, the national sulfur dioxide market has all but disappeared. Ideal would be for Congress to step in and provide clarity. That may come eventually. In the meantime, the most likely outcome as of this writing would be an eventual system of state-by-state markets. That's not as good as a U.S.-wide market, but much better than none at all. The all-important lesson: markets don't work if rules are being changed in the middle of the game.)

None of this is how regulation is supposed to work. Government is the beast to be tamed, not the one creating business opportunities. It's the belief in the limits of government that makes cap and trade and its enormous cost savings possible. We don't need to trust bureaucrats to develop or even fund cleaner ways of generating electricity—even though government-led research funding in some areas would clearly be a good thing. We are entrusting entrepreneurs and innovators with that task. That's precisely what they are good at: getting better results, faster and cheaper. Cost savings don't just benefit businesses (and, ultimately, consumers through lower rates); they also benefit the environment (and, ultimately, each of us through cleaner air).

The entire system has the somewhat unfortunate name "cap and trade." It should really be called "rewards for innovation." Cap and trade is an enormous, publicly structured program to take money from the inefficient and unimaginative and pay it to the efficient and innovative, without deciding beforehand who is in which group. It's the definition of "doing well by doing good."

This all warrants a quick aside to anyone reading this while sitting in business class, and anyone else trying to make a difference showing companies how to do well by doing good. Andrew Winston, Michael Porter, and anyone who wants to be just like them, this one is for you: please keep doing what you are doing. All of us ought to do more of that. Much more.

AT&T is turning off the lights in its data centers; Google and Yahoo are opening windows rather than using air conditioners to cool their servers; Xerox is asking its own customers to use fewer printers more wisely; FedEx is using hybrid trucks; UPS is redesigning delivery routes to avoid taking left turns to save on time and fuel; Maersk is slowing down its ships. All great examples.

Let me repeat: we need more of that. Much, much more. But these are examples for a reason.

Andrew Winston talks about how we live in a "commodity world" and how "green can bring you out of the pack." That's great. Be greener than thy neighbor. Outcompete your competition by being leaner, smarter, and greener than the next guy. Let's give every company a chief sustainability officer and give every CSO enough resources to make a difference. Let's get to a point where green is the new normal.

But despite all of this enthusiasm for private enterprise and working with businesses to do good, let's not delude ourselves into thinking that we don't need the EPA or government to set the rules of the game.

Andrew Winston says as much. Every other green guru ought to agree. What goes for individuals also goes for corporate volunteerism. Sure, Walmart making a quick fix to its supply chain has a much bigger impact than you changing the way you source your raw materials for your next family dinner, but an overheating climate or overfishing is too big even for a company like Walmart to tackle on its own. The problem can't be solved by corporate volunteerism and do-goodism alone. Lead in gasoline wasn't. Acid rain wasn't. Smart government regulation guiding market forces in the right direction did the trick.

EUROPE TAKES THE LEAD

Acid rain has been as big a problem in Germany as it has been in the United States. Germans have a word for the response: *Großfeuerungs-anlagenverordnung.*

Laws don't come much more heavy-handed than that: emissions standards for each large electricity plant in the country. It has all the environmental components of the U.S. response to acid rain but none of the flexibility. German emissions have gone down significantly. Trees are no longer dying. Centuries-old cathedrals are no longer melting away under the acidity of the rainwater. But the cost has been much higher than it needed to be.

The *Großfeuerungsanlagenverordnung* fits neatly into all the stereotypes you could string together. Americans opt for flexible, market-friendly laws. Europeans take the centrally planned, top-down, command-and-control approach.[3] And Germans invent a word that promises to choke anyone who tries to pronounce it, as efficiently as the law chokes any semblance of a vibrant economy. Except that this stereotype doesn't fit for the most important pollutant of them all: carbon dioxide.

As crucial as combating acid rain has been in its own right, the U.S. cap-and-trade system used to address it to great success should be viewed as a test case for an even bigger challenge: capping greenhouse gas pollutants and stabilizing the world's climate.

The first big stage for that idea was Kyoto in December 1997. The U.S. delegation arrived with a proposal to institute a global cap-and-trade system of sorts: allow countries to meet their obligations by trading allowances with each other. Europe resisted at first. So did most developing countries. Through an odd diplomatic twist, the final agreement included some flexible elements—and Europe. It did not include the United States. President Bill Clinton never sent the treaty to the Senate for ratification, the outcome of any Senate debate being a foregone conclusion.

Months before Kyoto, the Senate passed by a whopping 95–0 the so-called Byrd-Hagel Resolution, declaring it would not ratify any treaty that didn't also include obligations for China and India. Kyoto didn't—it only included emissions-reductions targets for industrialized countries—so it never found its way onto the Senate floor.[4] The United States came away with no international obligations to start reducing its own emissions. Not so in Europe.

The European Union had an overall target: reduce average emissions between 2008 and 2012 by 8 percent below 1990 levels. To get there, it designed the European Union Emissions Trading Scheme, the first large-scale emissions-trading system for carbon pollution: thirty countries, ten thousand smokestacks, two billion tons of carbon dioxide emissions covered, tens of billions of euros at stake.[5]

The naming gods weren't kind. The Republican pollster Frank Luntz jokes about how whoever came up with "cap and trade" needs his or her knees capped. Now we have a "scheme" to boot. How's that for a conspiracy theory? "Brussels scheming to change American way of life." What's wrong with calling it an emissions trading system?

Trademarks aside, Europe's inexperience with cap and trade and the scale of the undertaking were enough to warrant a trial phase. That trial itself was already high stakes. Starting in 2005, it covered as many companies and emissions as the first compliance phase starting in 2008. One difference was that it hadn't yet been designed to produce serious emissions reductions. It was designed as a dry run, but reduce emissions it did.

System-wide—*pardon, monsieur*—scheme-wide carbon dioxide dumped into the atmospheric sewer declined by around 2 to 5 percent during the three years of the trial phase relative to where it would have been otherwise. The planet was breathing a bit more easily. That's an amazing achievement, and one that's even more surprising given a significant built-in handicap. The trial phase was set up to fail.

Let's take a quick look at the inner workings of cap and trade to see how all of this fits together.

Take the eminent B&A Steel Trading and Research Development corporation, BASTARD Inc. It just happens to be a heavy polluter and has traditionally been making lots of money, which helped dirty BASTARD overcome its highly unfortunate acronym and morph into a formidable force in Brussels lobbying circles. The annual BASTARD holiday party is the place to see and be seen.

On the other side is Agricultural 'n' Garden Engineering Limited. ANGEL Corp. is not just very successful in its own right; its most important characteristic is that it has particularly clean production facilities and an innovative engineering staff with lots of ideas about how to make things even cleaner.

The two companies have comparable revenues and, thus, lobbying prowess. In the EU's trial phase both ended up getting a similar number of free allowances. Environmentalists held their noses in the case of dirty BASTARD and cheered when clean ANGEL got its allocation, but in the end it didn't make much of a difference to the outcome. The planet doesn't care who gets the allowances as long as the total is set.

Dirty BASTARD didn't get enough allowances to cover all of its

emissions. Clean ANGEL, in the meantime, has more allowances than it needs, and its innovative engineering team has found a few cheap tweaks to its existing production line. It has more than enough to cover its annual emissions and is now able to sell unused allowances to dirty BASTARD at the going rate. Once the market was under way, that rate hovered between €20 and €30 for most of 2005. (You would get virtually the same final outcome even if all allowances had gone to one firm, only more money would have changed hands in order to get to the happy equilibrium.)[6]

So why was the trial phase set up to fail? Europe did things backward. Instead of first setting the total cap and then handing out allowances to each company, the EU essentially let each company set its own cap. Surprise, companies claimed they needed more allowances than they actually did. Dirty BASTARD and slightly sullied ANGEL lobbied their own national governments for as many allowances as possible, who then dutifully lobbied on their own companies' behalf in Brussels.

Once again, it jibes with logic. Just as you yourself can't save the planet, companies can't do it on their own. And we can go one step further: most countries by themselves, especially small ones like my native Austria, don't have much of an impact either. So forget the supposed European tendency toward environmentalism and self-sacrifice. When it came to asking for allowances, each nation's government had an incentive to ask for more than it actually needed. And so it happened for much of the EU.[7]

The moment of truth came in April 2006. EU regulators for the first time tallied up total reported emissions by all companies—not what each of them lobbied for initially to get their free allowances, but what their engineers determined was actually emitted during 2005. I think you see where this is going.

When emissions were tallied up for the first time, there were more allowances in the system than emissions for them to cover. Companies were essentially allowed to print their own money. Within a week, allowance prices tanked by half. That's a normal reaction in any kind of market with too many goods meeting not enough demand. In short order the price of an allowance to emit one ton of carbon dioxide crashed from €30 to €10. Carbon traders panicked. Enviros started pointing fingers. Most economists worth their profession's crest, in the meantime, looked on in amazement and with some satisfaction. The over-allocation of allowances was only one built-in flaw that had had economists scratching their heads for a while. Another was in the very way the system had been set up.

Dirty BASTARD and clean ANGEL could pretty much do whatever they pleased with their allowances, as long as they had enough at the end of the year to cover their emissions. They could buy, sell, or hide them under their CEOs' pillows for future use. But saving allowances had its limit: December 31, 2007, the end of the trial phase. Setting that limit seemed a natural thing to do—and EU regulators to this day insist it was the only way to organize a trial phase—but it had a devastating effect on the market.

Like a Christmas tree on December 26, a trial-phase allowance for a ton of carbon in 2007 should be worth exactly zero euro cents on January 1, 2008. Given the over-allocation in the system, that makes that same allowance worth zero plus a cent or two on December 31, about the same on December 30, and not much more on November 30 or even April 30, 2007, 2006, and 2005. Allowances, however, traded at above €30 at their peak before the crash at the end of April 2006. Supported by supply and demand it was not.

A much larger and decidedly more positive story was lurking in the background. While the trial phase was going on, Europe was already planning for its first compliance phase of the program—beginning with January 1, 2008. Companies started trading these compliance-phase allowances early to even out price fluctuations and allow them to plan ahead. In April 2006, while trial-period prices crashed, prices for allowances for the compliance period stayed around €20 and maintained their value throughout 2007. On December 31, 2007, while trial-period prices had long been zero, prices for compliance after the

New Year were well above €20. What a difference a day—and a well-designed market—makes.

Suddenly dirty and clean companies could be doing business once again. But in the end, of course, the point isn't to enrich the clean ANGELs and make them even cleaner, while the dirty BASTARDs of yore continue to spew out their gunk and buy up extra allowances. The point is to motivate all companies to clean up their acts—and to reduce total emissions enough for the planet to notice.

PRICE-FIXING

Putting a cap on emissions is the first and most important step, but how to actually get emissions to decrease? On the simplest level the answer is to set a cap that declines year after year. If the cap is properly enforced, emissions are bound to go down. The process of how emissions decline, however, merits a bit more exploration.

That process works via the price, the very first idea we encountered in chapter 1. Specifically, we need a higher price on the offending substance. That's another incredibly hard sell politically. The master pollster Frank Luntz doesn't like "cap and trade." I don't want to think about what he would do to whoever coined the four-letter word "t-a-x," the mother of all political insults. But that's, in the end, what it is. A price and cap on pollution are really two sides of the same coin, quite literally.

Zoom back to fish. Everyone knows there is a finite supply of fish in the sea. But left to its own devices, the market acts as if there were no limits. That might have been a good approximation for when you and your ancestral brothers were hunting the oceans with bow and arrow. Oceans didn't notice the handful of fish you took each week. But that's clearly no longer the case, with our satellite-guided industrial fishing fleets and billions of sushi and fried shrimp aficionados. The number of fish is finite, no matter that free markets left to themselves wish to treat it as infinite.

That's where the liberating hand of catch shares comes in. Governments set the overall cap of fish that can be caught in any particular fishery, and suddenly each share in that total catch has a real value attached to it.

Pollution is no different. We are spewing out greenhouse gases as if the atmosphere were a bottomless sewer. In that world—where we can have infinite pollution without any consequences—pollution is indeed free, at least to the polluter. Everyone else pays the cost. Once we limit fish or pollution, both have an implied price, what economists in a wayward attempt at decreasing the mysticism surrounding it call a "shadow price." That's the implied price of each fish or ton of pollution emerging from the shadows to achieve the same result as the cap.

Capping carbon emissions puts a price on each ton emitted. That opens up cap and trade to charges that it really is just a hidden tax, and a shadowy one at that. "Cap and tax" has become a rallying cry for opponents to a sensible step forward.

At one level, the answer to that charge is that cap and trade is much more than a hidden tax. It doesn't just punish polluters; it creates a market and, as with any market, opportunities as well as costs. When a CEO hears "market," she calls in her engineers to take advantage of the opportunity. When she hears "tax," she calls in her lawyers and accountants and switches into defense mode.

On another level, the answer is simply yes, it's a tax. Naming is important, but less so than its intended effect: making pollution costly. That's the point, at least at first. Rechanneling market forces doesn't just mean talking up low-carbon alternatives and making them viable compared with high-carbon fuels. It also means that fossil fuels ought to be more expensive. It's not a free lunch. No insurance is. You pay small premiums up front in order to get large sums back if disaster strikes and your home burns down. (And here, of course, it's more than that: there will be a steady payout in exchange for our investments now, even if ultimate disaster doesn't strike.)

Leave it to Google to put the relationship in the simplest possible terms. Google.org, the do-gooders funded by Google.com's advertisement dollars, put the goal into a simple equation:

$$RE < C$$

Making utility-scale renewable energy cheaper than coal.

Right now, the relationship is largely reversed. For electricity generation, coal is cheaper than most other sources of energy. Natural gas might be giving coal a run for its money, but it's still fossil energy. There's lots of it in the ground, and because we are treating the atmosphere as a free sewer, we don't account for the disposal costs of the resulting gunk and poison. For transport, the same holds true for oil. To get from A to B, the goal must be to flip that equation to Google's dictum in both cases: $RE < C$ for coal in electricity, and $RE < O$ for oil in transport. You can do that in one of two ways: by making renewables cheaper, or by making coal, natural gas, and oil more expensive. And seemingly the easiest way to do the latter is to tax pollution. Have polluters internalize the costs that are now socialized.

More than anyone else, Europeans have understood and—especially—acted on this understanding. Just drive up to any gas station between Scotland and Sicily, and you are reminded of the fact that cheap gas is no birthright there. Gas taxes are $2 and more a gallon across Europe. In Germany and the United Kingdom, they are above $3. U.S. gas taxes don't even add up to fifty cents. Largely as a result, Europeans consume about a third as much gasoline as do Americans.[8] Compact European cars and a low tolerance for long commutes may, in part, reflect ingrained cultural preferences, but they are not purely coincidental. The entire country of Luxembourg may be as wide as some Texas driveways are long, yet Luxembourgers are no homebodies. On average, they use as much gas as Americans. Luxembourg's prices at the pump? Consistently lower than elsewhere in Europe.

Gas taxes are an obvious first step to decrease pollution. Add ten cents to the price of a gallon of gas and watch carbon emissions decrease by around 1.5 percent, more over time as consumers take more radical steps like moving closer to work.[9]

Beyond gasoline, Europe has a much larger tolerance for green taxes in general. By 2000, overall environmental taxes accounted for 3 percent of Europe's GDP. In the United States, they were less than 1 percent. Yes, tax rates are higher in old Europe, but not three times as high. As an Austro-American dual citizen, I am proud to say that this does, in part, reflect a real belief among many Europeans that we ought to tax "bads" rather than goods.

Green tax reform—increase taxes on pollution, decrease taxes on labor—makes eminent sense. Tax what you want less of; don't tax what you want to encourage.[10] It was the Dutch who acted first and introduced a carbon tax in 1988. Scandinavian countries, which can usually be trusted to do the right thing even if it's not always in their self-interest, soon took the lead, with Norway and Sweden introducing carbon taxes in 1991. Denmark and Finland followed.

In the United States, in the meantime, a proposed energy tax—the so-called Btu tax—failed miserably. It passed the House of Representatives in 1993 but fizzled in the Senate. In 1994, twenty-eight of the House Democrats who had voted for the tax "got Btu'ed." They were voted out of office as Newt Gingrich swept in with his small-government revolution.

But not all is sunshine and roses in tax-happy Europe. Despite carbon taxes, emissions kept rising—over 15 percent since 1990 in Norway. That's not a bad outcome for an economy that grew 70 percent over the same period. It implies a massive decoupling and a real gulf between carbon emissions and economic growth. Get richer, and get (relatively) cleaner at the same time, but this wasn't all due to the tax. The largest effect was a general decrease in how much energy it takes to produce the same goods now as compared with in 1990. Some of that decrease was prompted by the tax; most wasn't.

A crucial factor was simply a change in the energy mix. Norway sits on the largest oil derrick in Europe, but it prefers to export the spoils. Its own economy uses comparatively clean energy and since 1990 has increasingly shifted toward services that require much less energy than heavy industry. All told, in Norway carbon taxes only accounted for an overall decline in emissions of around 2 percent in the decade after inception.[11]

A big reason for that low tax effect was that the taxes were anything but watertight. They harbored plenty of exceptions and loopholes for particular sectors. In fact, Norway effectively exempted all but offshore petroleum extraction. Onshore, the only sectors of Norway's economy with any carbon tax at all were the pulp and paper companies and the herring flour industry. (Apparently, ground-up herring meal is used as a fertilizer and to feed omnivorous cattle, which, I believe, have no choice in the matter.) The tax in the paper and herring flour sectors barely reached a quarter of what it was offshore.

Norway, sadly, is far from unique. Most nations have similarly leaky carbon tax systems, if they have them at all. The French president Nicolas Sarkozy's proposed carbon tax was struck down by France's highest court in 2009 for being too porous. It had exemptions for truckers, farmers, fishermen, and various industries, which violated constitutional requirements of not singling out individual companies. Instead of reintroducing a broader tax, Sarkozy followed Bill Clinton's lead from the early 1990s and simply scrapped plans for it altogether.

The U.S. federal tax code has seventeen thousand pages for good reason: politics. At least that's the reason, never mind whether it's a good one. (Indeed, these seventeen thousand pages are a good reason for fundamental tax reform.) Every time Congress tries to create a special incentive here or an exemption there, every time a politician tries to curry favor anywhere, every time anything gets tailored to anyone's wishes, it adds to the length of the tax code and makes things more complicated. Worse, it likely also leads to unintended exemptions somewhere that require more plugs. Much worse, every time there's an exemption for a carbon tax, emissions go up. If the French can't raise carbon taxes successfully, what hope is there for the rest of us?

THE INEVITABLE OUTCOME

Cap and trade is any political economist's dream creation. First debate the overall goal. But not endlessly. Arrive at a cap, and set it. Good. Proceed to step two.

Now focus on who gets what; distribute the allowances. Companies faced with the regulation will insist on getting allowances for free. That's akin to saying that they have the right to pollute. Enviros will insist that allowances are sold (typically auctioned off), akin to declaring companies have to pay for being allowed to pollute. Companies will fire back and say that, ultimately, it's the consumers who end up paying for the allowances in higher electricity and product costs. Enviros will respond that this is just as well, and if you, company, pass on too much of your costs to the consumers, they will end up buying their products from a different company—the beauty of the marketplace. Companies will retort that enviros aren't supposed to tout the advantages of well-functioning markets. And back and forth it goes. It's a philosophical debate and political fight worth having, but here's the gist: the atmosphere doesn't care who gets the spoils, only that it itself is less spoiled.

While all of that political funny business is going on, the cap remains intact. Unlike with a tax, the politics of who gets what doesn't jeopardize the environment. At least that's the theory, and how it mostly worked with U.S. acid rain regulation in the early 1990s and for carbon in the EU for the actual compliance system starting in 2008. The U.S. climate debate hasn't been quite as pretty.

Many businesses have realized how the game is played. Jim Rogers and Duke Energy, who had been among the first to play a constructive role in the acid rain debate, once again came to the table from the start. That's a significant step for the third-largest user of coal and, as a consequence, the third-largest polluter in the country. It's also a keen political calculation on the part of its CEO. In Rogers's words, it's better to "have a seat at the table" lest you "wind up on the menu." Having a seat at the table means being able to negotiate for free allowances. Duke wasn't alone.

Aluminum cans may be one of the most energy-intensive consumer products. That didn't stop companies up and down their supply chain—Rio Tinto, Alcoa, and Pepsi—from sitting down at the table. Across from them were Dow Chemical and DuPont. So were Shell, Siemens, all three U.S. carmakers, 300,000-employee-strong General Electric, and a couple dozen others. They all formed a coalition with a handful of environmental groups and called themselves USCAP, the United States Climate Action Partnership.

You would think that once enviros and some of the largest corporations in the country united in a call for climate action, it would be a done deal. Think again. USCAP did move things forward significantly. The discussions inside the umpteen CEO meetings, closed-door staff sessions, and mind-numbing, hours-long conference calls weren't always pretty, but the initial rounds of discussions yielded "A Blueprint for Legislative Action," which looks very close to the basic building blocks of the comprehensive, economy-wide cap-and-trade system that passed the U.S. House of Representatives on June 26, 2009. Then it was on to the Senate, and suddenly all the foolproof political economy logic went out the window.

Here's one indisputable fact: 25 percent of the House votes for cap and trade came from California and New York. In the Senate, these states have two votes each. Two out of a hundred, and the hurdle is no longer fifty. The hurdle when one senator can hold up debate forever in a filibuster is sixty votes.

I will spare you the sorry details. For an overview of what did or did not happen in the U.S. Senate in this process, turn to Ryan Lizza's terrific, terrifying, and terrifically sprawling New Yorker article on the very topic.[12] Or just read the title: "As the World Burns." Although an even more apt review might be an equally well-written, long, and appropriately titled New Yorker article by George Packer: "The Empty Chamber: Just How Broken Is the Senate?"[13] Very, it turns out.

The Senate was designed to choke change. It usually does the right thing in the end, but it first took several filibusters before we saw civil rights legislation. Woman suffrage took years. The problem is that we don't have another ten years to wait for sixty or more senators to join together in doing the wise thing.

Fortunately, there are other options. A 5–4 U.S. Supreme Court decision declared, in 2007, carbon dioxide a pollutant to be regulated under the Clean Air Act and mandated the Environmental Protection Agency to start regulating it. The EPA is indeed doing just that. Unfortunately, this regulation comes in the form of neither taxes nor cap and trade. Because the EPA lacks a clear, direct mandate, it needs to go back to some of the heavy-handed ways of the past, when pollutants were regulated through top-down, command-and-control measures. No one likes that, least of all the EPA. It requires many more staffers to implement the top-down approach than even the most comprehensive cap-and-trade system would have required. The threat of direct EPA regulation was supposed to spur the Senate into action; alas, no such luck. And anything that makes regulations more flexible begins to look like cap and trade.

In the meantime, while we are waiting for Congress to get back to its senses, we are left with the states. California has always been an environmental leader. It's the only state with an exemption in the Clean Air Act allowing it to set stricter standards, which other states are then free to join. And once again, California is out ahead. It has an ambitious cap-and-trade system on the books, slated to begin operation in 2013. New York together with nine other northeastern states has had a less ambitious system for a while. Some other states are moving in similar directions and may well set an example for Washington.

Comprehensive health-care reform eluded America for decades. It took a Republican governor in liberal Massachusetts to take the first step. Four years later, Mitt Romney's plan turned into federal law. Cap and trade continues to elude America, though notably a Republican governor in liberal California has taken the first step. Projecting out four years from the introduction of Arnold Schwarzenegger's ambitious cap-and-trade program would put us in 2016. Better late than never.

But all of that's idle speculation. We can't lose sight of the inevitable outcome. Eventually, whether in 2013, or in 2016, or, God forbid, later, we will have to move to a U.S.-wide system that joins the political left and the political right, takes market thinking seriously, and guides economic forces away from the planet-destroying ways of the past and toward that happy nirvana of using markets to help rather than hurt the planet. The goal is clear, and we have little time to lose. There's only one planet to go around.

6

MIND VERSUS MATTER

BUT ONE PLANET

Edward Gibbon's life's work details thirteen hundred years of the decline and fall of the Roman Empire and ranks as one of the great doom stories of all time. Methodically tracking blame for the slow descent of Rome and Roman supremacy, Gibbon's book is a magisterial work of finger-pointing, complete with insights and conclusions that have often been debunked by later scholars. It's only fitting that almost two hundred years later, in 1972, it was the newly formed think tank Club of Rome that ventured a prediction that the planet would be doomed and civilization on its way back to the Dark Ages. The club's *The Limits to Growth* employed the latest in punch-card-modeling technology to show that we are running out of clean air, water, land, and pretty much everything else that makes (modern) life possible. In contrast to Gibbon's opus, it contained no irony.

The Limits to Growth's argument wasn't exactly new. Gibbon's contemporary Thomas Malthus first wrote in 1798 that an infinitely increasing population doesn't mix well with a finite planet. No argument. If we multiplied like bacteria in a petri dish, we would soon spill into the seas. The same goes for accumulating stuff. Our planet can only support so many pairs of shoes. And even if everyone lived in Tokyo's cutting-edge, hyperefficient apartments (what California Realtors call "walk-in closets"), there will come a point at which we will have outgrown population growth. Infinite growth on a finite planet is not an option. By various credible measures, we have already exceeded the planet's carrying capacity—per some, many times over.[1]

What Malthus got wrong was the timing. He predicted imminent doom. Back in the late eighteenth century, there were a billion people on the planet, give or take. Today there are seven billion, and the average Londoner can expect to live almost twice as long and enjoy toys unheard of even at Buckingham Palace two hundred years ago.

In absolute terms, many of today's poor live better than kings not that long ago. Of course, the importance of keeping up with the Joneses and of racing to make more than your neighbor means that life as a king then was much more satisfying, blissfully ignorant of how antibiotics—let alone iPhones or an Airbus 380—could make things easier and mostly better. Malthus correctly showed that more money meant longer lives. If anything, he underestimated the power of modern medicine to extend lives by decades rather than years.

His logic broke down with the birthrate. Contrary to Malthus's expectations and some prominent counterexamples in our day, the great demographic transitions in the last centuries showed that richer parents had fewer children, not more. As a result, current consensus projections see global population growth slowing to reach around nine billion by 2050, and ten by 2100. If you ventured even further out, you would find perhaps ten billion by 2150. Not surprisingly, most of the additions will happen in still-poor countries.[2]

To arrive at his doomsday predictions, Malthus used pen and paper. Two centuries later, the Club of Rome relied on a set of equations by MIT modelers. No matter, they shared a similar, crucial flaw.

The Massachusetts Institute of Technology isn't ordinarily known for technological pessimism, and Jay Forrester, Dennis and Donella Meadows, and their colleagues manning the model didn't make many friends in Cambridge with their dour predictions, particularly among the economists down the hall. The MIT economist Robert Solow, who would go on to win a Nobel Prize for his work on economic growth, was one of the critics. He damned the model for using too little data for its bold predictions.[3]

That still misses the most transparent flaw: basic math. Linear growth implies equal jumps over time (1, 2, 3, 4, 5), which by its very nature gets dwarfed by anything that grows exponentially (1, 2, 4, 8, 16). That should be a fairly simple point. Alas, the Club of Rome models had population and pollution growing exponentially, while technology as well as checks on population and pollution grew, if at all, in small increments.

You could stop the entire exercise right there. The conclusions practically write themselves: the planetary petri dish starts filling up with ever more people consuming finite resources, unhinged by any kinds of checks and unimpeded by imagination to use limited space more intelligently.

Every model is only as good as its assumptions. If you assume doom and gloom, chances are you will get doom and gloom, no matter how many equations obscure that basic fact.

Sadly, there is rarely a clean solution to so fundamental a flaw. The argument that follows typically includes the doom-and-gloomer's countercharge that the optimist was wearing rose-tinted lenses from the start. And then the niggling of the arithmetic begins, each side conceding ground that builds into its modeling flexibility—usually resulting in pushing the date of destruction or salvation further out—but doesn't concede the basic point.

On the one side are ecologists (and many environmentalists). Most models they study see the world as overlapping waves of growth and decline. Bacteria in a petri dish run out of nutrients, collapse, and grow again. Hare populations run up against multiplying wolves that feast on them until the decimated hares take the wolves down with them, only for hares to thrive due to a lack of predators. Sometimes entire civilizations collapse in spectacular fashion: dinosaurs didn't adapt to meteors; they disappeared.[4]

Economists, on the other hand, study the world and see growth. Indeed, things are looking up, always. Every successful economic model for the last hundred-odd years shows unfettered growth, continuing forever. "Steady state" for economists doesn't imply no growth; it means a steady rate of growth.

The magical ingredient: technical progress.

There are limits to physical stuff, but human ingenuity knows no bounds.[5] It's easy to see the appeal of this way of looking at the world. While one set of MIT researchers was working with the Club of Rome to show how the world faces limits to growth, another was developing the board computer for the first moon landing. It weighed in at an impressive seventy pounds for a memory that held fewer than forty thousand words. Queue the jokes about how any toaster oven nowadays has more computing power than the lunar lander. No doubt. Things are getting better and better.

Yet even the tiniest microchip requires stuff. And the more powerful the chip, the more precious the stuff that goes into making it.

Economic growth models are as guilty as the models ecologists use in missing that crucial component. For economists, "stuff"—natural inputs into their equations, raw materials—is simply left out of the equation. We have labor, we have capital—the machines it takes to produce something—and we have technology or rather technological progress. Raw materials, for the most part, are missing. When they are included, they tend to be interchangeable, avoiding any kinds of real limits that can't be overcome by human ingenuity.[6]

That's the big folly of economics. Most economic models, instead of showing limits to growth, simply assume them away. Combine an absence of any physical limits with limitless human desire and ever-growing technical progress, and no wonder things look up all the time. It's clear, then, why neoclassical economists would occupy exactly the opposite corner from doom-predicting greens.

Few arguments are more consequential for the future of the planet and are more jarring to watch for any environmental economist who insists that environment and economy must go together. The debate between pessimists and optimists has a nasty tendency to pin the split nature of the environmental economist back into his respective environmental and economic corners. There really is no good solution.

As you may have noticed by now, this is a fairly uncomfortable chapter to write and—I'm sorry to say—also to read. There's no intellectual silver bullet. There isn't even a collection of silver bullets. I can't point to one economist superhero who has figured it all out, nor is there an environmentalist superhero who has ever demonstrated conclusively that economics has gotten it all wrong. There is no one in between either, no larger-than-life environmental economist who has straddled the two and come up with the golden middle path.

The closest we can come to a solution is to follow the lead of the Stanford historian Ian Morris, who in *Why the West Rules—for Now* does what every good historian does: he recounts the past in gory detail and then punts on the future. Or rather, in a somewhat surprising plot twist after hundreds of pages of historical prose, his conclusion as to whether East or West will dominate the future is both—or neither.

After pages upon pages on why the East led before it didn't and why the West led as long as it did, he doesn't come to the same conclusion that every armchair historian could draw by glancing at newspaper headlines: Asia is on the way up, and the era of U.S. dominance may be coming to a close. He does venture to say that 2100 will be the "*latest* point at which the Western age will end." Actually, in a comical twist of false future precision, he says the year will be 2103. But he immediately goes on to argue that this date does not matter.

Civilization faces a choice between the nirvana of "Singularity" on the one hand and total mayhem, dubbed "Nightfall," on the other. The difference is very much the split between mind and matter: between economist optimists and ecologist pessimists.

"Singularity" goes back to Ray Kurzweil, who defines it as "a future period during which the pace of technological change will be so rapid, its impact so deep, that human life will be irreversibly transformed . . . that technology appears to be expanding at infinite speed."[7]

That sounds almost like what an economist would say, and many do. It's tough not to see the world this way, when you have grown up virtually devoid of nature and all you know is the world of iPads, iHomes, iEverything that the billion or so rich inhabit. If the technological revolution continues at warp speed, eventually it will appear to be infinite and outpace any earthly constraints we could imagine.

On the other end is "Nightfall," so named because of the eerie similarity to total nuclear annihilation. Morris's words, not mine. He quotes Albert Einstein as saying back in 1949, "I do not know how the Third World War will be fought, but I can tell you what they will use in the Fourth—rocks." "After Nightfall," states Morris, "no one will rule." The forces that could bring about Nightfall, what he calls the "five horsemen of the apocalypse," are, in this order: "climate change, famine, state failure, migration, and disease"—with an increasingly unstable climate as the most fundamental of the bunch.

That sounds almost like what an environmentalist would say. Never mind, that's exactly what many environmentalists say—myself included. If an ever more unstable climate runs its course, eventually we will see more of the other four apocalyptic predictions play out in front of our eyes, and Nightfall may be nigh.

Morris doesn't exactly calm jittery nerves. Levels of innovation—"progress"—are so rapid, so unprecedented in human history that the question is not whether we will be making cross-country flights even faster or more convenient than they were only thirty years ago, or whether China or India will build faster planes than Boeing or Airbus. We don't know what the frontiers of travel itself will look like a hundred, fifty, or even twenty years from now. The question, says Morris, is how to avoid the entire system spinning out of control.

For Singularity, "everything has to go right." For Nightfall, "only one thing needs to go wrong," and that may well be the runaway greenhouse effect. The question is how far we have already spun out of control. We are clearly at the verge, but can we still right the past wrongs, or should we just keep on dancing all the way to Nightfall?

You know my answer: not doing anything would be illogical and insane. Morris's main theorem doesn't offer much solace: "Change is caused by lazy, greedy, frightened people looking for easier, more profitable, and safer ways to do things. And they rarely know what they're doing."

Except that last sentence is no longer the case. We know what we are doing by pumping billions of tons of greenhouse gases into the atmosphere, and we know what to do to avoid it. Ignorance about the global consequences is no longer an excuse. An atmosphere out of whack is the largest and most profound environmental problem facing society. But I will follow Morris's lead and punt on providing a real answer on the equally large question about the future of humankind running up against earthly resource constraints.

My ecologist self tells me that collapse is near. There's no way around it on a finite planet.

My economist self tells me that the future is bright. Look at how much better our lives are compared with those of royalty one or two hundred years ago.

But instead of waging a bet on the future, let's look to the past for some guidance.

BETTING THE PLANET

Even before the Club of Rome marched on the scene, the Stanford ecologist Paul Ehrlich took the downer-scepter from Thomas Malthus with his 1968 book *The Population Bomb*. He looked at the overcrowded, overheated streets of Delhi and saw imminent global catastrophe:

> The battle to feed all of humanity is over. In the 1970s and 1980s hundreds of millions of people will starve to death in spite of any crash

programs embarked upon now . . . Nothing could be more misleading to our children than our present affluent society. They will inherit a totally different world, a world in which the standards, politics, and economics of the past decade are dead.

Since the book's publication, people have indeed starved to death and fought wars over dwindling resources, and to this day Delhi is choked by traffic and horrific levels of pollution. It's a safe bet that there will be more wars and catastrophes to come.[8] But needless to say, Ehrlich's prediction of global demise was much too gloomy.

Unfazed, Ehrlich burrowed in and agreed to bet $1,000 with the economist Julian Simon over the future of the planet. Technically, it wasn't over the future of the planet, even though Simon would have liked to have claimed so. Simon offered Ehrlich to choose any natural resource: oil, coal, timber, metals. The bet was over rising prices: Would they, or wouldn't they?

Ehrlich bet that more and richer people would run up against resource limits and drive up resource prices for crucial raw materials. (Ehrlich and two colleagues—one, John Holdren, would later become Barack Obama's top science adviser—chose copper, chromium, nickel, tin, and tungsten, all of which are essential inputs in industrial production.) Simon bet that human ingenuity would win and prices for these materials would go down during the decade. Simon won.

What does this bet tell us about the future of humanity?

According to Simon, it gets to the heart of the matter: the earth didn't produce any more of these five metals during the 1980s, but humans found better and smarter ways of using them. Indeed, despite a growing number of wealthier, healthier, longer-living people, by 1990 we were actually using less of each.

Ehrlich drew the exact opposite conclusion and tried to explain away the results in language that made him Johnny Carson's favorite late-night scientist:

The bet doesn't mean anything. Julian Simon is like the guy who jumps off the Empire State Building and says how great things are going so far as he passes the 10th floor. I still think the price of those metals will go up eventually, but that's a minor point. The resource that worries me the most is the declining capacity of our planet to buffer itself against human impacts. Look at the new problems that have come up: the ozone hole, acid rain, global warming.[9]

It would be all too easy to dismiss Ehrlich once again. The ozone hole is getting smaller; acid rain is no longer the problem it was in the 1980s. In fact, technical progress helped us escape both crises. But the larger point is that none of that happened by itself. It took the right kind of innovation and technical progress to pull it off.

More fundamentally, it took government to redirect market forces to work for us instead of against us. Ultimately, it was government that put the necessary frameworks in place—the Montreal Protocol to fix the ozone hole and a cap-and-trade system for sulfur dioxide pollution to fight acid rain in the United States. The planetary-scale bet is whether we can once again get government(s) to put the right kinds of incentives in place to relegate worrying about global warming to an entry in the history books.

WHALE BLUBBER AND HORSE MANURE

We are running out of oil. That's a simple physical reality. The entire climate problem is a matter of simple arithmetic. Every day we extract carbon that took millions of years to put underground and pump it into the air. That makes oil one of the most inefficient energy sources.[10] It's easy to see why the age of fossil fuels will have to come to an end. We simply can't go on extracting oil at the rate we are doing now. The only question, really, is whether we will run out of oil, coal, and gas before we run out of atmosphere. Unfortunately, in a manner of modeling, the answer is no. If we ran out of fossil fuels tomorrow, the warming climate wouldn't be the problem it is without that hard stop. We'd naturally transition out of fossil fuels into a greener, cleaner alternative, or at least into one producing fewer heat-trapping gases.

We have seen that game play out before. If you listen to the technological optimists, they usually tell two stories with similar endings but rather unrelated protagonists: whale oil and horse manure.

I first heard about both listening to Martin Weitzman during his introductory economics class. In typical economist fashion, he looked to these stories as examples of how technological progress tends to save the day in the direst of moments. For once, Weitzman may not have gotten the full story right. Yes, technological progress is powerful beyond belief, and we ignore its power at our peril. Weitzman has made convincing, math-heavy arguments in support of this point.[11] But there's another twist here: technological progress doesn't happen all by itself. We sometimes trumpet it too loudly without looking at the deeper forces that lead us to start innovating in the first place. Once again we are back at setting the right goalposts, at putting the right incentives in place.

Throughout most of human history, the day started at dawn and ended at dusk. Reading at night was a fickle, smelly, and often eye-ruining experience, which was particularly unfortunate because ophthalmology wasn't all that advanced either.

The middle of the eighteenth century saw the invention of "a new kind of Candles very convenient to read by," as Benjamin Franklin wrote in a letter in the dark of winter in 1751: "They afford a clear white Light . . . their Drops do not make Grease Spots like those from common Candles."[12] He likely referred to candles made from spermaceti, a fat found in the heads of sperm whales. Those candles were a step up from wax derived from the blubber of the right whale, named that way for no other reason than that for a long time it was the right whale to harpoon at sea. And harpoon we did, to the point where whaling turned into a global hunt for every remaining right and sperm whale slow and unfortunate enough to be caught with the technologies available to nineteenth-century whaling fleets.

Sound familiar? It should. Just substitute bluefin tuna, cod, salmon, and sea bass, and bring the story forward a century. Repeating history, however, is usually the signal flare to study it all the more closely.

Whale oil production peaked sometime in the mid-nineteenth century. That coincides roughly with the discovery of "rock oil," the literal English translation of "petroleum." One conclusion: innovation saves the day yet again. "Greenpeace should have a picture of John D. Rockefeller on the wall of every office," says Matt Ridley, the Rational Optimist, citing Warren Meyer, an irrational climate denier. And indeed, it looks that way at first blush.

It takes a particular kind of obsessive-compulsive to set out to discover the true story. The Italian chemist Ugo Bardi did just that and sifted through a sea of whale oil production and pricing data. He came up with a surprising result. Whale oil production hit its peak before 1850 and began a steep decline in the subsequent decade, cresting and falling well before the first rock oil from Titusville, Pennsylvania, became available in 1859. Whale oil production was at less than half its pre-1850 peak when kerosene started to become commonly available. (Kerosene would soon be replaced by electricity as the light source of choice, although that took another few decades. Thomas Edison made his first announcements about the incandescent lightbulb in 1879.) Bardi concludes that "the peaking and the initial phase of decline of whale oil production were not caused by the availability of a better technology, but by the physical depletion of the resource."[13] Whale oil production went down because whales were increasingly harder to find.

A look at the size of the whaling fleet confirms the real story. Whale oil production declined about a decade before the size of the fleet peaked. In short, whalers weren't cutting back on their efforts. They were out in force with their harpoons, just not having much luck finding many suitable targets left.

Indeed, if there was a single event beyond resource depletion that saved the whales, it would have been the Civil War, which started in 1861 and prompted Union whalers to keep their ships in port lest they risk getting captured by Confederate raiders. By the time Union troops emerged as the victor in 1865, kerosene had made sufficient market inroads to make renewed whaling efforts not worth the investment. The boats that did venture out found fewer and fewer whales. The seas had been largely emptied of them save some treacherous and frigid Arctic territories. Steamboats offered renewed hope for whalers, but by then it was too late. Kerosene and later electricity had replaced whale oil as the luminescence of choice.

The parallel—or rather lack thereof—to our current situation is striking: it's as if we were transitioning away from oil, coal, and gas because they are increasingly harder to find. That may be true to some extent for some oil fields that are past their prime, but there is still plenty of oil underground that, when pumped into the atmosphere, would wreak tremendous havoc. And what goes for oil goes for coal and gas even more so. We have tremendous deposits of both still waiting to be tapped. The atmospheric sink turns out to be the limiting factor.

Oil provided the impetus for another revolution. While whales were declining, horses multiplied—not out in the wide-open plains, but right in the heart of major cities. Horses had been the most important mode of transportation for thousands of years. It wasn't until the late nineteenth century that they really took off. New Yorkers made over thirty million trips on horse-drawn carriages in 1860. By the end of the decade, that figure had topped a hundred million, and there was no end in sight. In the 1890s, 200,000 horses produced twenty-five hundred tons of manure a day. It took thousands of horses just to haul the manure away. Much of it was simply dumped into empty lots. One doomsday scribe infamously predicted that by 1930 horse manure would blanket Manhattan three stories deep. In 1898, the world's first urban-planning conference broke up in disarray after only three of ten scheduled days. Delegates could not see a way out of the gridlock and stink. Mobility was as essential and addictive back then as it is today. It was a transportation, environmental, and public health nightmare rolled into one. The model of cities looked wholly unsustainable.

We know what came next. John D. Rockefeller, Henry Ford, and others saved the day with oil-powered cars that pushed horse-drawn carriages out of New York.[14] In 1900, cars were still a luxury turning heads. That year 4,192 cars were sold in the entire United States. By 1912, sales topped 350,000, and cars for the first time outnumbered horse-drawn carriages in New York City. Five years later, the last horse-drawn streetcar was retired for good, and by the 1920s horses were all but gone from city streets save for horse carriages shuttling tourists through Central Park and the occasional mounted cops, who to this day roam through Times Square and Central Park and look considerably more stately than their unfortunate colleagues on Segways.

The advent of cars was an awesome transformation of society and arguably only paled in impact compared with the speed of the spread of the Internet. While we would like to think that free-market capitalists, when they weren't racing heartwarmingly undersized horses named Seabiscuit, presided over the rise of the car without any assistance, the fact is that anticompetitive and anticapitalist behavior played a decisive role.

A heavy dose of government policy helped the rise of the car all along the way: from the building of interstate highways to navy ships patrolling the Persian Gulf and even more direct subsidies for oil drilling. When General Motors bought up streetcars and converted them into buses through a wholly owned subsidiary, it effectively destroyed mass transit in over forty cities throughout the United States between the 1930s and the 1950s.[15]

As always, incentives played a key role, and they were manipulated by a host of actors to favor the car. Detroit, as well as Saudi Arabia, knew full well what it meant to get Americans hooked on affordable cars and cheap gas. Why let a functioning rail system get in the way if you can help it? If it means that trains running between Chicago and New York take longer now than they did a century ago, so be it.

• • •

We can't sit around and hope for the next grand technological break-through to rescue us all. We'll keep inventing better, faster, and cheaper stuff. No doubt about it. We could even have government-directed research that may lead to some of these breakthroughs. It worked for the Internet. Why wouldn't it here?

For starters, the Internet grew into a void. No one knew what to expect. We know exactly what we will have to achieve in the clean energy revolution. Governments and corporations have been nudging our grand-parents, parents, and us into cars. The overwhelming odds are someone is going to have to nudge us out of them. Which brings up another irritating truth about energy: it's so not cool.

People literally wait in line overnight to get the latest iPad. Some crazies show up at midnight to get their hands on the newest operating system. No one, however, waits for clean electrons, and far too few will choose to pay premiums for them. Apple's ingenious branding department would be at a complete loss if it came to selling a steady stream of clean electricity. That points to a big fallacy in the way we think about new energy technology in general. When we think "innovation," we think iPhone. We don't think boring old commodities that have turned into everyday staples.

Clean electrons deliver few additional benefits to me that I couldn't get from electrons piped in from a dirty old coal or natural gas plant. There's certainly no fun factor attached. Yes, there are some pluses to cleaner air, but the key benefit of lower carbon pollution from my own actions doesn't matter to me personally.

Repeat after me: my actions are less than a drop in the bucket, and my making a personal sacrifice won't make the atmosphere notice or be appreciative. Unless ubiquitous clean energy becomes very cheap very soon, dirty energy needs to become more expensive to enable the transition.

Sometimes price is not an issue. To this day, the Hubble Space Telescope and the *Voyager* space probe exploring the outer reaches of the solar system are lubricated by sperm whale oil, prized for its property of not freezing even in subzero conditions. NASA can afford to pay premium dollars to lubricate its space missions with the finest spermaceti and can write off the need for it as falling under scientific research rather than now-banned commercial whaling. For most everyone else, price is the deciding factor—as it should be. By 1850, the cheapest right whale oil cost $200 a barrel in today's dollars. The superior spermaceti cost a whopping $1,500, and the price was going up as the whales became more scarce.

Crude oil, by comparison, promised a bonanza. By the 1870s, it came in at under $100 a barrel in today's dollars, and the price went down from there. Throughout the twentieth century, oil mostly hovered around $20 a barrel before spiking during the Arab oil embargo in the 1970s and then again in the first decade of the twenty-first century.[16]

That latest rally has been particularly curious. If you wanted to know the price of oil in the early aughts, there was a simple rule of thumb: take the last digit of the year and add a zero. The year 2002 saw prices in the $20s; 2003 in the $30s; 2004 in the $40s. Prices climbed through 2007, when they reached the $70s. Then things overheated. Oil spiked above $140 in 2008 before crashing down to less than half that as the financial crisis hit. By this writing, they are back near $100, with many signs pointing up.

Some of this roller coaster was speculation, particularly at the height of the bubble in the summer of 2008. The general euphoria surrounding the housing and stock bubbles spilled over into commodities. The proof? Oil prices weren't the only ones spiking. Aluminum, barley, coffee, cocoa, copper, corn, cotton, gold, lead, oats, silver, tin, wheat, and plenty of others hit similar records. Commodities were flying high, largely fueled by a generally overheating economy.[17] But not all of it was folly.

Much of the run-up in the first decade of the new millennium was due to fundamentals, the underlying factors that are chiefly responsible for any longer-term price movements: demand went up; supply didn't keep pace or even went down. Anyone interested in the main reason only had to look east.

Chinese oil consumption shot up by over 500,000 barrels a day in only three years, between 2005 and 2007.[18] That's not speculation. That's physical barrels changing hands and being burned up to fuel hundreds of millions of people escaping poverty during the last throes of the fossil fuel age. By comparison, the United States, the most successful energy hawk in history, siphons off around 20 million barrels a day. China's demand crashed much like everyone else's during the global financial crisis, but it soon picked up steam again and by 2010 had surpassed the United States in total energy consumption. That by itself foreshadows a major geopolitical power shift. Yet another factor might have played an even bigger role.

Supply didn't keep pace with demand increases. Worse, world oil production actually fell slightly. That's not how things are supposed to pan out in a market. China wants more oil; prices rise; oil companies take the hint and supply more oil. Except they didn't.

Oil markets fail in two important ways to prevent that from happening.

One is due to Saudi Arabia.[19] Oil markets are anything but perfectly competitive. The Organization of Petroleum Exporting Countries often gets blamed for deciding the fate of global oil markets. In the end it's the Saudis, OPEC's single largest producer, who hold the strings. That doesn't make the problem any easier to solve. Saudi Arabia is fortunate to sit on both the cheapest and the sweetest crude, the kind that's easiest to process into useful forms without too much unusable residue. That, combined with the magic elixir of excess production capacity, is the true source of Saudi dominance. It allows them to open the spigot up when people want more and clamp it down when prices seem to go too low. It's why oil prices were relatively stable at around $20 a barrel for most of the twentieth century—except when the Saudis wanted to make a point, like showing their displeasure with U.S. and European support of Israel during the Yom Kippur War of 1973. The Saudis, however, soon realized that keeping oil too high had its drawbacks. It motivated consumers to try to break their addiction and search for alternatives. When solar panels went up on the roof of the White House during the Carter administration, Saudis were the first to get the message. They reopened the spigot. Oil prices dropped, the solar panels came down once Ronald Reagan moved in, and with them the drive to tackle the problem seriously—four decades of presidential rhetoric from Richard Nixon through Barack Obama notwithstanding.[20]

The price rally of the first decade of the twenty-first century may have felt like a repeat of the 1970s, but it was something else entirely. Instead of showing Saudi dominance, it showed the limits of Saudi Arabia's powers. The Saudis no longer had the excess capacity necessary to open up the spigot to satisfy increases in Chinese demand. No one knows what the price of oil is going to be next year, but no one thinks we are going back down to $20 a barrel. There's still plenty of crude, but it's increasingly difficult to get to. What the price gyrations in the early twenty-first century point to is the simple fact that the Saudis and the world are running out of the cheapest, easiest-to-find oil.[21]

Economists have long struggled to merge the reality of $20 oil with predictions from some of their standard models. The most basic of them goes back to Harold Hotelling, who showed why the price of resources like oil that don't replenish themselves ought to rise at the rate of interest.

The logic goes like this: You have $100—or perhaps $100 million—and are deciding whether to put it in the bank or invest it in an oil field. As a savvy investor, you would only put it in the oil field if you knew that the value of the oil in the ground increased at least as quickly as the same money in the bank. Otherwise you would simply put it in the bank.

The rule itself isn't all that interesting. It's more like a straw man than a real description of reality. What's more important is trying to see why, in reality, the rule more often than not doesn't work.

• • •

Prices of most minerals didn't rise at the rate of interest throughout much of the twentieth century. Not even close. Many prices stayed nearly constant or, if anything, seemed to decline at times, as the Ehrlich-Simon bet made clear.

Hotelling's basic formula is missing at least two major factors: first, the more oil you take out of the ground, the harder it is to find the next barrel; second, technical progress counteracts that first effect. By now we are digging for oil miles under the seabed, which proves both of these factors to be true.

Balancing the two effects can explain near-constant prices. But it only works up to a point. I can speak from painful personal experience here—painful as far as grad school research stories go. I teamed up with Cynthia Lin to work out the theoretical quirks that would allow us to add these two effects to the Hotelling formula, and all seemed to go just fine.[22] Except that as soon as we pulled our heads out of the equations, we realized that in the real world prices for most resources had just gone up significantly after around 2005. Technical progress had successfully kept prices down since the 1970s, but it seemed to be losing the race against natural resource limits. Our figures ended in 2004, just missing that rise. The paper might have elided the implication, but the findings didn't: there is a point at which the two effects no longer balance and resource limits trump all else.

Being trapped with ever-increasing prices brings back the drama of the whale oil story. The world was running out of whales by 1850, but John D. Rockefeller had yet to strike his first liquid gold. For about a decade, without real alternatives, investors underwrote more whaling ships, which dutifully set out to kill ever fewer whales. How do we avoid that trap? How can we jump-start technical progress in our search for new, alternative, cleaner sources of energy and avoid having our addiction to oil drain not just the last cheap wells but our wallets to boot?

Put differently, how do we jigger incentives to direct market forces to produce the desired result?

One way is by jump-starting innovation through a price on carbon or a market for emissions reductions. Cap carbon in line with our finite atmosphere, in turn making investments in carbon reductions pay, and investments in carbon reductions will come. In time. The logic is compelling, yet there must be a more effective way. Why not regulate technologies directly? Flat out declare that everyone shall use compact fluorescent lights instead of nineteenth-century incandescent technology.

That's what's happening. Between 2012 and 2014, the United States will phase in such high performance standards that they will bar all but the most efficient incandescent bulbs from even reaching store shelves. The EU started implementing its bulb standards in 2009 and will complete the phase-in by 2012. We'll encounter that ban again in chapter 8. For now, let's stick to barnacles.

PRESCRIBE NEW TECHNOLOGY, IN TWO SIMPLE STEPS

Pity the whaler. I know, few environmentalists would ever utter these words. It's the economist in me. It's the half of me that sees not only the decimated natural resource on which the whaler's life depended, not just the Civil War that docked most of his fleet, but also his dirty bottom. Barnacles and algae like to attach themselves to the hulls of ships, putting a drag on the boat, not only compromising its speed, its captain's pride, but also exerting a negative environmental effect. Boats afflicted with barnacles use more fuel than those with smooth hulls.

Yet barnacles and other organisms aren't the nuisance they once were when entire whaling fleets succumbed to their draw while waiting harbor-bound during the Civil War. The solution: copper-based antifouling paint. Sadly, copper is toxic and slowly seeps out into the water. That's actually the point, or at least part of it. Barnacles don't like to cling to toxic substances.

For each individual boat, that logic makes some sense. Problems emerge when copper-leaching boats converge near recreational piers,

turning entire harbors into copper cesspits. It may not be quite on par
with the consequences of a warming planet or worldwide overfishing,
but for some fish and other marine wildlife, as well as anyone attempting to swim in these harbors, the immediate consequences are real
nonetheless.

Any economist would have the perfect solution: make polluters pay
in a way that limits copper pollution. Create a market for copper reductions by capping total copper in any one harbor. Suddenly it becomes
valuable to reduce the use of copper-based antifouling paint—and
paint manufacturers, hull painters, and shipowners will switch soon
enough to alternative methods of keeping boats barnacle-free. If alternative paints are already available, newly incentivized markets will
ensure that they get used. If they have yet to be invented, markets will
allocate sufficient innovative willpower to generate the right patents. If
the cheapest and most effective solution is something else entirely—
using different hull materials or perhaps keeping boats on dry land
when not in use—markets will find ways to make that happen as well.

All of this is surely the case. Flexibility pays and often creates the
kinds of win-win situations that bridge the business-environment gap
or at least the one between recreational boat owners and recreational,
harbor-bound fishermen and others worried about harbor ecology.
Sometimes, though, a more direct, heavy-handed approach can be just
as effective, just as cheap, and easier to pursue.

Technology standards have long been a favorite tool of politicians and
regulators. They spell direct action: mandate and thou shalt receive.

Creating environmental markets instead is often a humbling experience. The entire point of enabling innovation and creative new ways
of adopting existing technologies to achieve particular environmental
goals is to give up control. Markets, by their very nature, are decentral-
ized and don't easily lend themselves to micromanagement from the
top. Dictating technology standards is at the opposite end of the spectrum. That's why economists have an almost allergic reaction whenever
they hear the words, but there are ways to both design smart technology
standards and alleviate spring allergies.

The most important way is not to design a technology standard and instead focus on performance. The right paint "performs" by not leaking copper into the water, and there are more ways than one to ensure that happens. Boat owners can opt for paints with silicone, epoxy, water, or polymer bases. Rather than prescribing any particular alternative, a smart standard focuses on the copper content. That avoids picking winners from afar, hardly ever a good idea, and instead calls out the loser: copper.

Next in our quest for the perfect standard is to decide on how fast to move. Demanding zero tolerance overnight would be extremely costly for everyone involved. It would also be impossible. Boatyards can only hoist, scrape, and repaint so many hulls at a time. The sweet spot seems to be a two-part copper ban: first require all *new* boats to use greener paints from day one, then set a future date when all boats must comply.

It's the kind of solution that has a certain "duh" effect attached to it. The Clean Air Act faced considerable problems when it forgot the second part. It simply exempted existing plants, which resulted in power companies extending the lifetime of the polluting plants for years and sometimes decades. The other extreme is forcing all existing power plants to comply on day one, which would come with immense conversion costs and stiff industry headwinds. Setting a future date when all existing plants must meet the new standard seems like the logical middle path.

As a graduate student at the University of California, San Diego, Maria Damon and some of her colleagues ran the numbers to show that this kind of two-part copper ban can be as cheap as the most flexible market-based solutions and ten times cheaper than the next best technology standard.[23] By now, Damon has joined New York University's faculty, and she has moved on from studying copper pollution in San Diego Bay to look at applying two-part bans to some of the larger environmental problems.

One example is lead in gasoline. We have already seen how cap and trade made the switch away from leaded gasoline much less costly to refiners in the 1980s. What about consumers? They faced a two-part ban:

In the United States, many European countries, and elsewhere, regulators required new cars to burn unleaded gasoline. This alone would still allow old cars to spew out lead and may even have prompted particularly lead-friendly car owners to keep their clunkers around for longer, but regulators were one step ahead. They also announced a later date when there would be no more leaded gasoline available, so everyone had to convert. Other economists—and by now, I hope, you, too—may cringe, but Damon has even identified conditions where two-part standards can be better than markets.

If the goal is to get boat owners to move away from copper, what matters is to find the optimal moment to get them to switch to environmentally friendly paint. Copper paint has to be reapplied every couple of years. That adds layers and layers of paint, so every few years the boat's painted bottom has to be stripped entirely, which is the exact moment for its owner to switch to more environmentally sound paint—and also the exact moment when the regulation ought to bite. Say each boat gets stripped every nine years. Then set the phaseout date by which no copper-painted boat can be in the water ten years into the future, and you have your desired outcome. It also keeps things simple. People don't need to think about the new law except for when their boats get stripped.

Contrast that with a market-based solution. Cap and trade for copper would mean that boat owners get allowances to use a certain amount of copper year after year. Now suddenly they need to think about it and pay the price every year, not just the one year when it matters. That makes life more cumbersome without any inherent benefits. Economists could cook up plenty of redistribution schemes to make each boat owner whole and have the dollars come out even in the end. But that all seems to be more trouble than it would be worth if a simple two-part standard can do the trick just as well.

What's the catch?

With dictated standards, there's no more (or, to be fair, little additional) innovation. It's tough to put a standard in place calling for a technology that hasn't been invented yet. As a result, standards are most often less ambitious. Alternatives to copper-based paint had already been invented. Most major boating paint companies saw the water pollution problems their toxics caused and figured that stiffer regulation must lie in their future. Some also wanted to appeal to the enviros among their customers who would opt for the greener alternative regardless. In a sense, all the regulator had to do was get everyone, not just the greens, to buy the new, at first slightly more expensive, slightly less convenient paint. The emphasis was on deploying existing technologies, not inventing new ones.

Whenever the Clean Air Act opts for mandates, it prescribes something akin to "best available control technology." The emphasis here is on "available." If it doesn't yet exist, the EPA would have a hard time mandating it. Banning incandescent lightbulbs works only because alternatives are already available.

Directly mandating innovation is out. It doesn't work in theory, let alone in practice. You could imagine increasingly tighter standards announced in advance that would spur further innovation, but it would be difficult to see that play out in reality for environmental problems that go much beyond copper leaching into harbors.

Markets, by contrast, are marvels of innovative power. Put the right incentives in place, and entrepreneurs have a way of finding the appropriate solutions. And we already know the best solution to make it all happen: cap pollution. Still, there's a good reason why we would want to pick some winners and outright subsidize them, although it's most certainly not to replace a cap.

CAP AND SUBSIDIZE

It doesn't happen every day that a group of academics looks at a government program and says: "Yep, nailed it." Since they are academics, that's not exactly what they said. Their conclusion was just a tad more nuanced and couched in academic parlance: "Under central-case parameter estimates, including nonappropriable [learning by doing], we find that maximizing net social benefits implies a solar subsidy schedule similar in magnitude to the recently implemented California Solar Initiative."[24] In other words, California's approach to subsidizing solar panels appears to be close to optimal. What makes a group of Stanford economists and engineers think that meddling in markets via subsidies would be a good idea?

Lord Nicholas Stern is wont to say that "climate change is a result of the greatest market failure the world has seen." We know the solution well: limit pollution. Make polluters pay for the full cost of their actions, and soon enough they will pollute less. Without a cap on pollution, there's too much of a bad thing—the definition of socialized costs.

The world also faces the exact opposite: socialized benefits. Now instead of getting too much of a bad thing, we don't get enough of a good thing. We don't get enough crucial research, development, and deployment of new, cleaner technologies, because today's scientists and tinkerers don't enjoy the full value of their positive contributions to society.

The patent system is supposed to help inventors cash in on their new and improved toys, but it doesn't go far enough to capture all positive effects of innovation. For starters, patents expire. They aren't universal, and sometimes serve as "inspiration" for others. All of which puts a damper on new inventions. If you know that your neighbor will steal your invention right out of your garage, you won't invest quite as much in your own research. But that's not all patents fail to do. They also don't capture the full benefits of learning by doing, or rather of learning by watching someone else having done it. We may all be standing on the shoulders of giants, but when making our own decisions, we don't incorporate the fact that whichever small contribution (or screwup) we make provides others with shoulders to stand on (or alerts them to pitfalls so they do not repeat the same mistake).

The solution: subsidize research, development, and deployment of new technologies. Smart environmental policy comes in a combo package: cap the offending substance to limit pollution and increase its price while at the same time subsidizing new technologies to move away from it altogether.

California is doing just that. State legislators have capped greenhouse gas pollution through its statewide cap-and-trade system. As governor, Arnold Schwarzenegger also launched the California Solar Initiative—at first dubbed the "million solar roofs initiative"—and put up money for direct subsidies to make it happen. Solar energy costs are rapidly declining, but by 2006, when the California Solar Initiative was inaugurated, solar energy cost more than fossil-based alternatives.

Some of that cost was due to the fact that solar panels themselves were still expensive. Another was because local electricians, roofers, and home owners weren't yet familiar with installing and maintaining them. That, it turns out, was the more important factor of the two and the one that warranted large initial subsidies.

The California Solar Initiative provided exactly these kinds of subsidies: a decade-long subsidy that started high and decreased by 10 percent each year. That's close to what the ideal policy would suggest. The Stanford engineers and economists calculated the optimum to be $3.23 per installed solar watt in 2006; the California bureaucrats came up with $3.10. On average, the academics say the subsidy should be $2.04; in reality, it's $2.09. Overall, the initiative deserved a $1.1 billion budget; California was prepared to spend $1.2 billion. That's a policy slam dunk if there ever was one.[25]

What goes for California goes for the optimal global climate policy as well: step one is to limit overall greenhouse gas pollution and combat the negative spillover; step two is to subsidize new energy technologies and internalize the positive, learning-by-doing spillover.

More important, there's no need for permanent government handouts of any kind. The ideal subsidy is high, starts immediately, and gets phased out almost as quickly. The faster and stronger the action, the better it will be for the planet, the economy, and government budgets. Done right, "environmental goals can be achieved without permanent intervention and without sacrificing (much or any) long-run growth." That's the hopeful conclusion provided by another set of economists who looked at the global picture.[26]

The magic ingredient to make everything work in their model is "substitutability." As long as the world can get from clean technologies what it now gets from the dirty kinds, things look rosy indeed. That may seem like a heroic assumption at first, but it's probably a pretty accurate description of the world—at least for the most important cause of pollution: energy.

For the most part, electricity now gets produced from dirty fuels: coal and natural gas. The clean kind still produces the exact same electrons. Your fridge wouldn't notice whether its electrons came directly from the sun instead of indirectly via dug-up fossils.[27] Even dirty gasoline has a direct cleaner substitute: "next-generation" biofuels generated through efficient plant matter that don't lead to unnecessary pollution during their production (in contrast with corn ethanol, which receives plenty of undue attention and subsidies—coal might be king, but Iowa corn decides the next U.S. president). And the wider the definition of energy, the easier it is to substitute cleaner alternatives. Who says cars have to be powered via gasoline or other liquid fuels? Hybrids and fully electric cars increasingly provide a viable alternative.

If you go one step further and look at transport overall, you can even substitute trains, buses, and other ways of getting around for individual, fossil-powered cars. Substitutability is all around us, and the greater the potential for it, the greater the possibility of sustainability. Yet we can't take substitutability for granted. We can switch from Hummers to hybrids and make ever more qualitative improvements to have GDP grow without bound. Consumption of "thoughts" has no limits, but clean water and air do. We live on a finite planet after all, and we are right back at square one—at the beginning of this chapter.

7

CARS (AND PLANES)

TRAVEL CHOICES

I stand in the rain outside the European Commission in Brussels asking for the best way to get back to my hotel during evening rush hour: the Métro, no question. To Berlin the next morning? A six-hour journey by train, which sounds rather painful before you consider the conveniently timed lunch break in historic Cologne and glimpse my seat. It feels closer to a mobile office—including high-speed Internet access to guarantee all the online distractions found at home—and has a window with views changing at 150 miles per hour.

The Berlin train station looks like any three-year-old's paradise: trains, trams, buses, and undergrounds on three different levels with over a thousand departures a day. I ask at an information booth about the best way to get around Berlin for the next three days only to be met with a blank stare: trains, trams, buses, and undergrounds. How else? And all that for under $30, which comes to much less than one cab fare from the airport to the city. The next tram to my hotel? "Upstairs, every five minutes."

Three days of conferencing and tram hopping later, I'm back at Berlin Central Station, this time to catch a night train to Vienna to see my family. You need to like the slight rocking motion to fall asleep comfortably, but it's tough to beat the built-in vanity and shaving mirrors and especially the schedule: to bed at 10:30 p.m., wake up at 7:30 a.m. at your destination—and all that for less than one night in a hotel room.

None of this comes as news to anyone who has ever traipsed through Europe on a whim. Road trips on the old continent usually don't involve all that much road. It might be a bit unusual for your typical business trip, often more cab and airport lounge than overnight train and grandparents, but, hey, I work for a green group after all. My boss's boss spent twenty hours slumped next to me in economy class on our way to a meeting in Hanoi to save money and carbon. (Check the index for: "Business Meeting, flying halfway around the world for a.")

It's easy to dismiss these Eurotrain stories when discussing transportation choices elsewhere, especially in the United States, where travel by train is an exercise in nostalgia laced with frustration rather than convenience. Europe, the argument goes, developed differently out of necessity and predetermination. Swiss trains must run on time and in fifteen-minute intervals through the dead of winter. How else would the Swiss get from one valley to the next without skis? And the French were just historically lucky, at least as far as train travel is concerned. France's cities are just far enough apart to make TGV high-speed trains worth the investment.

Except Europe is far from perfect. Look at most trains in the United Kingdom and weep. Italian trains making it into Switzerland must be embarrassed. When the Zurich train dispatcher announces a delay past half an hour, chances are the holdup has happened across the border. And Europe has many more important problems. As long as there are flights offered between Vienna and Linz, less than a two-hour train ride away, something is rotten in the country of Austria.

Europe, too, has a deep-seated car culture. Too many towns are off the grid, and not just quaint honeymoon spots à la Cinque Terre along the Italian coast, only accessible by foot and boat. I'm lucky that my small hometown made it on the main Austrian east–west train corridor between Vienna and Salzburg. Visiting my cousins five miles north means arriving soaked in sweat after the hilly bike ride, being at the mercy of an erratic bus schedule, or just taking the car.

Cars seem to be the default answer to most transportation questions. Leaving out New York, Boston, Washington, and a couple of other Euro-style enclaves, the only way to get around much of the United States is to drive. Most of Houston presumes a five-minute drive to get a quart of milk. No one even bothered adding sidewalks.

Full disclosure is in order here: There are plenty of cities, Houston among them, that would question my street cred. I live in New York, where more than half of the inhabitants don't own a car. More specifically, I live in Manhattan, where almost four-fifths make do without one. And even for around here I'm an oddball. I never got my driver's license. My reason back when I had the chance and refused was that if a billion Chinese all start to drive, the planet will be toast, so why should I?

The problem with my logic was precisely that a billion Chinese are going to start to drive sooner rather than later. Chances are they won't take their cues from my behavior. My making the sacrifice and not driving contributes nothing to the solution: $1,000,000,000 - 1 = 1$ billion.

One billion isn't far off. As of 2010 around a billion cars, trucks, and buses roam the world's roads, and things are picking up quickly. We will likely add another billion by 2030. If you count in motorcycles and scooters, we will pass two billion by 2020.[1] So, rather than grandstand about my sacrifice, I'll say what most New Yorkers say: I don't own a car, because it's too damn hard (and expensive) to find a parking space.

Now we're onto something.

IN THE EYES OF THE BEHOLDER

Fortunately, these two billion cars won't all be competing for the same already-crowded roads and parking spots. In the United States and Europe everyone who wants a car already seems to have one, and populations aren't growing all that fast. The biggest growth in car ownership will happen in China, India, and other still-poor countries where most roads have yet to be built.

Unfortunately, all two billion tailpipes, no matter where their attached cars are parked, are spewing carbon into the same already-overflowing atmospheric sewer. A fifth of global carbon dioxide emissions come from cars.

Once we talk policy, though, the fortunes flip. A limit on parking spots or roads would serve as a rather neat cap on car ownership that could also help meet climate policy goals.

Yet, *unfortunately*, the next billion cars won't be competing for existing lanes and parking spots, which would act as a rather neat cap on car ownership. Alas, even after a century of road building, there remains plenty of ground left to cover with asphalt, especially in countries where the largest growth in ridership will occur. And, of course, we simply can't and wouldn't want to cap cars, roads, or global parking spaces at current levels, at least not immediately. The real constraint is not mobility or even cars; it's the atmosphere.

So, *fortunately*, the billion new cars are competing for the same, overflowing atmospheric sewer. That puts real environmental constraints on how many more century-old internal combustion engines we can add, and the answer is simple: none. Most of the existing ones on the road now ought to be replaced soon, too. The trick is to translate these constraints into policy to avoid having uninhibited and misguided market forces lead us right over the edge.

Sadly, the atmospheric constraint isn't nearly visible enough, and it doesn't help that it's diluted across all seven billion of us. When you sputter along the road looking for a parking spot, the atmosphere doesn't register. Going once more around the block might add another few grams of carbon into the global sewer, but no one notices that extra pollution. Not the planet, not your wallet. Not yet.

TOO CHEAP

Gasoline is too cheap. Deliberately so. Too often it's being subsidized. Kuwaitis pay eighty cents a gallon, Saudis forty-five cents, Nigerians thirty-eight cents, Turkmen thirty cents, and Venezuelans pay nineteen cents a gallon at the pump.[2] Don't hold me accountable if on your next drive through Venezuela you end up paying double the nineteen cents advertised here, but these numbers do indeed stay pretty stable, even though market prices fluctuate widely. It turns out to be rather easy to come up with the difference when you are sitting on your own oil derrick. As oil prices go up, you need to scrape together higher and higher subsidies, but your income from oil exports goes up in tandem. The same logic holds when oil prices fall. Why not share some of the spoils with your own populace? It keeps everyone happy and you in perpetual power.

Similar scenarios play out in nominal free-market democracies. The question these governments confront is whether to increase gas prices to account for the carbon and soot now dumped for free into the air. In some countries—America most blatantly—the answer is no. The U.S. federal gas tax was last changed in 1993 to exactly 18.4 cents a gallon. Why 18.4? Because the Senate didn't have the votes for 18.5. Politics, not policy. Pure and simple. There was no grand analysis supporting the 18.4 cents.

So, yes, gas is too cheap. Another word for it is "socialized." But cheap gas is only half the story.

Driving is too cheap for reasons other than subsidized gas. It's too cheap because of subsidized driving. Free roads, free parking, and a free infrastructure geared toward the car all contribute to America's car culture. Of course, it's only free for the one doing the driving. We all pay for the consequences with our tax dollars, lungs, and lives.

Once you consider all the socialized costs, from traffic congestion, pollution, noise, accidents, and just the space it takes to accommodate cars, the numbers quickly add up to anywhere from $500 billion to the trillion-dollar range for U.S. drivers alone.[3] Europe has its subsidized train culture. America has its subsidized car culture.

HIGH ACCIDENTAL COSTS

Economists have a funny relationship with cars. When you see an intersection with stop signs on each corner, the logical thing to do would be to stop, right? Wrong. Economic game theory tells you to duck your head and speed right through it. Each driver expects everyone else to stop, so the rational response is not to. (Things change if there is a chance that you live in a neighborhood with another game theorist on wheels, but that's a level of realism beyond the basic model.)

There are decidedly better ways to apply economics to the art and practice of avoiding traffic fatalities. Leave pollution aside for a moment, which tends to kill people silently and over time, and instead focus on the kinds of traffic deaths that make it into the local news. If you sit behind the wheel, you increase your chance of getting into an accident. That's a personal decision and should be no one else's business. People do all sorts of crazy things that are inherently dangerous. If jumping out of a plane with a flimsy parachute or reading while driving only endangers you, go for it. The trouble is that 70 percent of all car accidents involve more than one car.[4] In that case, one driver's accident is at least one other driver's problem, and this doesn't even count innocent pedestrians who might be harmed in the making of this thought experiment. Brought to its logical conclusion, it implies that driving entails an enormous socialized cost of accidents.

That cost depends heavily on how many others are on the road. In California, where driving is required to get practically anywhere, as I discovered painfully while living there for a year sans license, the cost each additional driver afflicts on others solely taking possible accidents into account adds up to between $1,000 and $3,000 each year. These are staggering figures. Add it up, and the annual cost per year is over $40 billion, a bit less than all California state taxes combined. For the United States, the socialized cost of accidents adds up to more than $100 billion a year, and this is a significant underestimate: it only includes costs covered by private insurance. Figure in all uninsured costs, and the total comes in a bit under $400 billion, and we are still only focused on direct socialized costs from accidents. No word on the costs of traffic delays due to accidents, or increased pollution because of idling cars—or any other socialized costs of driving, like pollution itself.

The numbers don't look much smaller when you bring them back to earth and see what they mean for each of us individually. It's no longer billions. Now we have between $2 and $3 in additional socialized costs per gallon of gas, and that's only for accidents.[5] Contrast that with the actual 18.4-cent-per-gallon federal tax. Even if you add up all state and local taxes, the U.S.-wide average does not get above 50 cents.

But let's leave politics aside for a moment. There is another economic phenomenon at play here. With a $2 to $3 additional gasoline tax, the number of drivers and miles driven would go down dramatically. And, as Aaron Edlin and Pinar Karaca-Mandic, the authors of the accident cost study, conclude a bit nonchalantly: "That would be the point." The less people drive, the fewer accidents.

MORE PAIN AT THE PUMP, LESS PAIN ON THE ROAD

When the price of something goes up, people buy less of it. Few other economic ideas have more staying power. Price goes up, demand goes down—a relationship so ubiquitous it has been elevated to a status usually reserved for real sciences like physics: the law of demand.[6]

The law's existence doesn't yet mean we actually know the full effects. An age-old question is how high gas prices have to go to have a measurable effect on driving. Generations of economists trying to provide the definitive answer have uncovered some surprising twists.[7]

Higher gas prices prompt people to leave their cars at home once in a while and walk the half mile to the nearest mailbox. Good. They also prompt car buyers to forgo Hummers in favor of Priuses.[8] Better. But owning a Prius makes you feel good about driving and also makes driving cheaper exactly because you use less fuel, so you may actually drive more. One effect—buying the more fuel-efficient car—may, in part, cancel out the other: driving less. That's true, but fortunately only in part.

An entire cottage industry of economists has crunched the numbers and has come up with some basic rules of thumb: Increase gas prices by 10 percent, and drivers use around 1 to 3 percent less gas immediately. Keep gas prices up, and eventually they use between 5 and 8 percent less gas.[9] As gas prices rise, you space out your visits to Grandma and skip other nonessential trips. As prices stay high, soon enough you opt to replace your old clunker with a newer, more fuel-efficient car. By now you have already gotten used to visiting Grandma only every other month, and—averaged over millions of drivers and grandmas—that tends to stay this way or go down even further. All in all, the law of demand prevails and grows stronger over time—a crucial conclusion when we set our sights on nudging the billions.

Fewer drivers driving fewer miles means less of all these other unaccounted side effects: fewer accidents, less pollution, shorter traffic jams. Down the road, it also means fewer roads built, fewer parking lots, and less dependency on oil with all that entails, like fewer troops stationed in the Middle East. Not a bad place to be.

Getting there means increasing gas prices, or so would be the common answer among economists: make people pay for the costs they now shove off onto others. And, indeed, few economists would argue against higher gas taxes, though they usually preface their arguments with statements like "Let's leave politics aside."

But are gas taxes enough? Say we add up all socialized costs and try to privatize them so that drivers see the full cost of every gallon purchased and every mile driven and are able to react accordingly, would we enter the nirvana of maximum good for the maximum number of people?

WHY DON'T WE ALL DRIVE HYBRIDS?

Here's the classic economic view of your car-purchasing behavior: You walk into a dealership, choose a car based on brand, color, cylinders, looks, and general feel, and then start comparing prices among different options. And you don't just look at how much you pay to drive home with the car; you also include all likely future expenses. You look at maintenance costs and might decide that paying a bit extra for a Mercedes is worth the up-front expense because it tends to break down less often than the Yugo next door. You also look at gas mileage, today's price per gallon, form an opinion about future gas price trends, attach probabilities to them, calculate expected total gas costs over the lifetime of the car, balance all of that information against expectations over future inflation rates and interest earned were you to just leave your money in the bank, take into account how your preferences for driving will evolve over time, make a few assumptions about how future buyers will perceive your choice when you are ready to sell the car, and you do all that and probably a few things I'm missing, while the car salesman at the dealership explains to you the awesome industry-leading warranty and zero-down loan program offered through the end of the month. In the mind of economists, you are this hyperrational super-calculator and more.

To be fair, no sensible economist really thinks this is how you buy a car. Individuals make mistakes, focus on the wrong things, and manage to remember only some of the points that they should as they are lulled by the dealer's promise of the free child seat with any car bought with the DVD player and nine-inch screen built in for the little one. It's just that on average they behave *as if* this model holds.

That's a subtle but crucial point. It wouldn't even be rational to stand in the dealership with your calculator trying to solve ridiculously complicated optimization problems. That's a waste of everyone's time. But most economists do believe that when you look at a million car-purchasing decisions, this is what comes out in the end—taking into account and averaging across all the individual mistakes people make.

Indeed, given all the assumptions holding up the rational edifice, it's surprising how well this model works in reality—until it doesn't. Hyperrational house buyers, on average, would have foreseen the financial shenanigans others tried to play with their mortgages and would not have fallen into the subprime-mortgage trap, just as hyperrational car buyers would not be falling for sales gimmicks that cause people to make rash decisions at the dealership. Any good economic model would take these limits to rationality and other quirks in human behavior into account. An entire branch of the profession is attempting to do precisely that, with some limited success so far. While we await the behavioral economists to come up with all the answers, we can test whether the hyperrational model holds—and if not, how far off it is.

Hunt Allcott and Nathan Wozny set out to test just that for gas prices and car buyers.[10] Allcott got his training at Stanford and Harvard before moving down the road to MIT and taking a faculty job at NYU. Wozny moved from Caltech to Princeton. They combined their brains and brawns to assemble what they call "perhaps the largest collection of data ever used in the economics literature on the automobile industry": over fifty million individual purchasing decisions, combined with survey data of twenty-five thousand households. The result: consumers aren't quite the hyperrational math geeks standard economic models assume. They only make it 60 percent on the way to super-geekdom.

In theory, car buyers ought to be "willing to pay one extra dollar in vehicle purchase price to decrease the expected present value of future gasoline costs by one dollar." You'd expect drivers to think every dollar is worth a hundred cents no matter where they find that dollar. They don't. Car buyers only pay sixty cents for every dollar of gas saved. They apparently don't include the full cost of gas over the lifetime of the car when they make a decision at the dealership.

Forget socialized costs ignored by drivers that lead us, as a country, to make the wrong decisions. Drivers apparently don't even include their own personal costs that would lead them as individuals to make the right call.

One response to this paradox would be to just let it go. Stupid is as stupid does. Perhaps try a bit of education to inform buyers willing to learn about their optimal choices, but no more. Everyone is free to make his or her own mistakes. That's true insofar as these mistakes only affect the individual. If you make a mistake on the road, chances are you also affect someone else—hence, the large socialized cost of accidents. If you make a mistake in the dealership and buy a less fuel-efficient car than would be good for you, and everyone else follows the same logic and falls into the same trap, you are also affecting people around you, and many more. The global nature of global greenhouse gas pollution makes sure of that.

MEDDLING WITH CAFE

Politicians hate taxes. Hate them. Raising them requires an up-or-down vote forever attached to their public voting record, there for constituent and rival to see. Gas taxes are particularly onerous to justify when predictably every Memorial Day weekend prices rise all by themselves just as people are filling up their tanks ahead of the summer driving season. Wouldn't it be nice if there was a way to get the same effects of higher gas prices without actually voting for a gas tax?

The magic system that emerged from the political sausage-making process of the 1970s in response to this question was CAFE: Corporate Average Fuel Economy. Back then, Allcott and Wozny hadn't yet been born, and neither had behavioral economics that shows how consumers have lives besides thinking about prices all day long. Still, CAFE hit a sweet spot of sorts. Instead of taxing gas to nudge drivers to drive less in more fuel-efficient cars, it forced car manufacturers to produce, on average, more fuel-efficient cars. So if General Motors sells a lot of Cadillac Escalades, which drink gas like a marathoner guzzling sports drinks, it needs to make up for it by selling more diminutive Chevy Cruzes or—even better—electric Volts.

This is the kind of direct meddling in markets that economists love to hate, and for good reason. Either it's toothless, or companies race to fulfill the standard, but no more. Innovation stops. Why go above and beyond a standard that forces consumers to buy what they don't want? One strike against CAFE.

The much smarter, less paternalistic approach would be to raise the gas price and then let markets figure out the optimal result all by themselves. With more expensive gas, more consumers actually *want* to buy more fuel-efficient cars *and* drive less in them.

Which would point to strike two against CAFE. Forcing consumers to buy the smaller, lighter, more fuel-efficient cars while keeping an artificially low gas price doesn't address the issue of driving less. Quite the opposite. Now drivers have fuel-efficient cars *and* cheap gas. Suddenly visiting Grandma once a month got a whole lot cheaper. But that's only a theoretical strike.

Grandma turns out not to be all that important after all. Give drivers more fuel-efficient cars *and* cheap gas, and they start visiting Grandma a bit more often than with their old clunker, but not that much more. The grandma effect only accounts for around a tenth of the total. Ten percent of the savings go toward driving more. Drivers pocket the other 90 percent of fuel savings themselves.[11] That's bad for Grandma, good for CAFE—and the planet.

There's another important factor at play. Car emissions aren't just caused by consumers driving too much. Oil companies, car makers, and urban planners all play a role in the interlinked system that defines our driving choices.[12] Gas guzzlers come out on top because of the proverbial systemic failures of what has grown into our current misguided transport policy. CAFE standards tackle car companies' contribution to the problem directly. That would be a clear plus, even if we already had the perfect gas tax in place.

CAFE guides drivers in the right direction without them knowing. Another word for it is "paternalism," but it also does what taxes don't. If car buyers regularly choose to spend only sixty cents to save a dollar in fuel costs, perhaps there's a case to be made for some more direct nudging. CAFE is the most direct nudging imaginable. It's closer to a shove, an actual mandate.

We should be pretty darn sure that the shove is indeed warranted. That's far from settled. The best economic studies answer this question with a resounding "maybe."[13] It's not one of the areas of economics where the question has been answered sometime in the last century, and where some of the luminaries have already picked up their Nobels. It's an active battlefield for the young-and-coming environmental economists. Only time will tell who emerges on top at the end.

In the meantime, we can be clear about one thing: if you can't increase the price at the pump because "t-a-x" is a four-letter word, CAFE might have to be part of your political tool kit. Anyone who opposes CAFE because it screams "paternalism" ought to take a long hard look at the best way to accomplish the same goal. CAFE may indeed be a four-letter word. A gas tax or an actual cap on emissions are just ways of fighting planetary socialism.

THE HIGH PRICE OF FREE

Environmental economists look at the world and see market imperfections all around us. The guy in front of you in the checkout lane yapping into his cell phone? He's only doing that because the cost of excess noise is being socialized. The obnoxious speaker doesn't pay for the inconvenience he bestows on others. The same goes for too much traffic noise, too many traffic accidents, too much time spent in traffic jams, too much waiting for free parking spots, too many parking garages obscuring pristine views, too many highways encroaching on pristine wilderness areas, too much wildlife killed on roads, and—not to forget—too much pollution. Let's focus on one aspect of this equation for now: free road use.

Free roads inadvertently subsidize driving and our car culture. Insofar as that leads to vital services being provided—the expectant mom making it to the hospital on time for her delivery, firefighters rushing to an emergency—that's clearly good. Most driving does not quite entail these noble pursuits.

Charging for road use isn't exactly a new idea. The mythic knight on the bridge or the troll under it echo the fact that the powers that be made sure travelers in the Middle Ages paid their dues. Modern-day planners realized early that drivers ought to foot the bill for using roads. Someone, after all, has to pay for them being built in the first place.

The knight and the troll were onto something. Ideally, drivers would pay for the number of miles driven. That would be the fairest, most obvious way to charge for road use. But putting up tollbooths is a costly proposition. The booths have to be staffed at all hours of the day. They slow down traffic quite considerably, with the inconvenient side effect of increasing pollution from idling cars.[14] Up to a third of tolls collected go to paying for and staffing the booths themselves.

Road planners opted for the next best alternative. Transportation officials in the state of Oregon were the first in the country to introduce gas taxes. They did so not to deal with pollution, nor to get people to buy more fuel-efficient cars. These gas taxes were squarely aimed at paying for roads. If gas mileage stayed constant and the price of oil kept pace with increases in the cost of living, Oregon might have gotten away with it. Alas, gas taxes did encourage drivers to opt for more fuel-efficient cars and drive less—just as you would like to have happen if your goal was to deal with pollution. If your goal is to pay for roads, you are out of luck: right policy, wrong use.

What goes for Oregon also goes for the entire country. Ever since 1993, the revenues from the 18.4-cent gas tax have gone into a federal trust fund to cover road maintenance. That fund has seen costs soar and revenues stall precisely because gas mileage has improved, albeit ever so slightly. As a consequence, in 2010, Congress had to appropriate almost $20 billion to bail out the national highway fund.[15] Instead of bailing out the funds year after year, we could, of course, increase the gas tax, and we should—to tackle socialized costs of pollution. To pay for road use, there is a much more direct way: pay-as-you-go.

Most new cars come with GPS built in, and it may not be necessary to beam your travel habits into space. Replacing tollbooths with automatic sensors that recognize when a particular car passes by may be enough. That's exactly the kind of system already in use across tunnels and bridges in New York and many other metropolitan areas. It ought to be used everywhere.[16]

Cities, meanwhile, have come up with their own models to charge for road use. London was among the first to implement a "congestion charge." Everyone driving into the city center during business hours pays a fee for the privilege. Beginning in 2005, the amount was eight pounds, much higher than a trip on the tube or on a city bus, and significantly lower than the fine for scofflaws who attempt to evade payment. One easy, legitimate way to dodge the fee is to drive a hybrid or electric vehicle, but few Londoners have made that transition. The result: car trips are down, public transport use is up.

London's system is far from perfect. It exempts everyone who lives in the city, which includes the loathed Chelsea "tractors"—SUVs owned by the glitterati in one of the poshest districts in town. Still, London's congestion pricing is a good model for others to emulate.[17] Sadly, efforts in New York City have so far been nixed by state legislators in Albany. Tolls for bridges and tunnels are scant replacement for comprehensive congestion pricing.

Most cities, New York included, have a wholly different issue to deal with: too many drivers chasing too few free parking spots. Few things in life are truly free. The same goes for supposedly free parking.[18] Parking spots may seem free to anyone who manages to secure one, but the costs are extremely high and get higher the scarcer the spots become. One issue is time wasted looking for them in the first place. If you have to drive five times around the block and then walk ten minutes, the spot you found isn't exactly free. You just paid for it with twenty minutes of your life and the gas, wear and tear, and risk of accidents it took to repeatedly circumnavigate the block. And that's only the cost to you personally.

The cost to the city is much higher. It has to set aside prime real estate for use as free parking spots. Buildings in some of these same areas rent for thousands of dollars per square foot. Why shouldn't parking spots cost the same or else be put to better use?

Free parking doesn't do anyone any favors. It makes finding a spot a competitive sport. It also encourages people to drive into the city center. That comes with significant costs by itself. I'm sitting in my living room overlooking Broadway as I write this. The only noise I hear is that of cars, trucks, and buses going by underneath, but noise pollution is the least of my worries. Actual pollution is much more significant, and it affects everyone in the city and beyond.

One approach is to banish most cars from city streets altogether and generally make getting around by foot easier. Bike paths, sidewalks, and designated bus lanes for all—complete with ribbon-cutting ceremonies for politicians. That might be good politics. It also raises the cost of driving and should make the city much more livable for everyone involved. A more livable city also means it will attract more visitors, some of whom will be drivers. You simply can't win, unless you tackle driving costs directly: road pricing for road use, gas taxes to combat pollution, pay-as-you-go for insurance, all of the above to address the costs of accidents, and the list continues.

Conspicuously missing from this policy wish list is an actual cap on cars or car pollution. There's a simple reason: America, Europe, and China have thousands or tens of thousands of major polluters each. They have millions or tens of millions of drivers.

A carbon cap-and-trade system for large factories and power plants works well. A direct carbon cap for millions of cars would complicate matters by orders of magnitude. Moreover, a comprehensive carbon cap for large polluters would, in fact, manifest itself in something akin to a gas tax. Big Oil and oil refiners face the cap. Consumers down the line only see the price. That results in small price increases—pennies rather than dollars—but it's a start, for cars as well as for planes.

Going from one to two billion cars in the next two decades will have major implications for the climate. It would be even worse if every Chinese and Indian suddenly flew as much as Americans—or, still worse, as much as New Yorkers. The typical New Yorker might not own a car and might live in a crammed apartment, but flights often make up for the difference. That times a billion would easily push the planet over the edge. A flight from Delhi to New York emits more carbon per passenger than the average Indian uses in a year.

So far, I have been rather quiet about plane travel. The subject makes me cringe. My parents live in Austria, my in-laws in Thailand. My job led me to four continents in the last twelve months. And I'm supposed to be on the do-gooder side of the global laptop-and-carry-on crowd. I flew much more still when I was working as a management consultant, where not boarding a plane on a Monday morning means you aren't working.

Should marriages (and jobs) like mine be illegal? People got married and lived happy and fulfilling professional lives before plane travel. Why is it necessary to fly halfway around the world to meet your mate or to have a three-hour business meeting, and all that in a world that has supposedly gotten a lot flatter? Can't get as much done in an hour-long phone call as in an hour-long face-to-face meeting? Make it a five-hour call. It probably still saves at least one of the two parties significant time.

And just think of the waste that is the modern vacation travel market. You spend twelve hours on a plane to lie ten days on a beach or hike up a distant mountain, only to arrive home after another twelve-hour flight as exhausted and jet-lagged as you were when you started.

I fondly remember vacations with my parents in Seeboden in southern Austria. Every one of them involved a four-hour car trip—the longest all year—and two or three weeks at the very same campsite, fifteen years in a row. It was the most relaxing way to spend the summer, swimming, hiking, and eating ice cream paid for with twenty-schilling coins we had saved all year. Since moving to the United States, my wife and I spent one more summer vacation with my parents and brothers (after an eight-hour flight, no less). It was divine. Shortly after, the campsite went the way of the Austrian schilling—in a nod to more modern vacation behavior, which apparently must include at least one flight, and which makes having the more universal euro that much more convenient.

But nostalgia is no solution. Once again, it's a question of the law of demand, which is even reaching down and touching how we relax. Vacationers aren't paying for the full costs of vacations. If prices go up or flights are capped outright, people—I included—will surely fly less.

The Conservative-led U.K. government scrapped plans for an expansion of Heathrow when it came into office in 2010, declaring it incompatible with climate policy goals. That's a start. Why should the U.K. government be subsidizing its citizens buying weekend homes in Spain? But banning air travel or just making it as inconvenient as possible can't be the answer. The solution must go via a tax or cap on pollution.

As with everything else, flights, too, ought to include the full price of all socialized costs: carbon and other air pollution, noise pollution, and the slew of other costs now rolled over onto everyone else. Instead, we actually subsidize new airports and runways under the guise of economic development while socializing the costs.

Travel is fun. I'm the first one to admit this. (Commuting sucks, especially the kind done by plane. Sadly, I can attest to that, too.) Travel, of course, also has plenty of positive side effects—from increased cultural understanding to helping otherwise marginalized regions get a piece of the global vacationer's or business traveler's pie. And right now, there often simply is no good alternative to having the full travel experience other than to board a plane. (An overly committed, nonflying Dutchman friend of mine tried for months to plan a trip from Amsterdam to Boston without a plane—without success.)

Going to Costa Rica on an "eco"-vacation will be nothing but a cruel sham if getting there allows me to shove off my costs in pollution, noise, and space onto everyone else. And no, having the chance to voluntarily offset my carbon emissions by paying a few dollars extra to save a couple of trees doesn't cut it. Volunteerism will not rise to a sufficient scale, not in time to make a difference. Everyone landing in your fair nation, and sooner rather than later at every other one of the fifty-thousand-odd airports around the world—especially the dozens of major hubs—ought to be paying the appropriate charge.

Part of the solution is also a shift in the way we look at plane travel. Entire cities, and even countries, have been able to largely get rid of one-way plastic bags with tiny PlasTaxes. Plane travel requires a similarly fundamental shift in attitudes. Flying from New York to London for a three-hour meeting is absurd, to put it mildly. Unless it's the prime minister waiting to have a heart-to-heart conversation, few clients should warrant the costs for everyone involved. That one round-trip flight pays for new videoconferencing systems on both ends.

Once again, volunteerism won't do. If I'm not willing to board a plane for that meeting, someone else will be waiting to cross the Atlantic to make the sale. As long as showing up in person is expected practice, a handful of dissenters taking the hit won't make a difference other than to their own pocketbooks.

Many people, myself included, will keep flying as long as it's much too cheap—and the accepted practice to get the job done. That won't change unless we start with the PlasTax equivalent for plane travel. Tax the full now-socialized cost of flying. Tax runway use. Tax take-offs. Tax landings. Tax every mile flown. Tax the land used to build runways. Tax business class more than economy class—not because of class warfare, but because a business-class seat causes at least twice as much in socialized costs as the seat in row forty-five. Tax up to the point where a plane ticket costs me what it now costs the planet and everyone around me.

That's a cringe-worthy statement to make, and sadly it's a slight understatement to say that taxing isn't the most politically viable solution. That may well be a cap on pollution (in addition to appropriate fees and other limits to account for the other socialized costs).

Europe has made some first laudable moves in the right direction, proposing to cover flights within as well as to and from the European Union in its carbon-emissions-trading system. It's still only a start—airlines at first get 85 percent of their allowances for free instead of paying for their fair share—and it won't happen before 2013. But it's a start.

The goal, of course, must be worldwide coverage. Any global industry requires global regulation. Right now, newly developing hubs like Abu Dhabi or Doha are already planning for increased business from travelers wanting to avoid the surcharge incurred on a Chicago–Frankfurt–Delhi flight. This year I took my first flight from New York to Bangkok via Doha, avoiding the usual European hubs. It's by far the cheapest itinerary. Qatar Airways goes to great lengths to become a global player, and Qatar is not going to stand in the way by taxing flights in and out of its major hub.

Brussels, fortunately, has realized the global dimension of it all: flights to and from the EU are covered no matter who the carrier is. And every country is encouraged to pursue its own policies. Instead of Air India sending money to Brussels, New Delhi could collect the money itself through appropriate policies. That creates important dynamics. It wouldn't take long for New Delhi to decide that it should not treat flights to Frankfurt differently from those to Doha. It's a roundabout way of covering the world's flights under a uniform system, but short of a world government or airtight global agreement applying a universal cap, a cascading bottom-up, one-by-one approach may well be what we'll have to take.

One big hope is that all of this prompts a real rethinking of what it means to travel. Just as there is no birthright for cheap gas, there's none for $300 flights from San Francisco to New York or for £50 ones from London to Barcelona. It'll be painful to realize that flights will be pricier, but who's to say that we would not appreciate more spaced-out yet longer and relaxed visits? I would think little wrong with spending summers—instead of weekends—in Austria with my parents, and winters—instead of a few days—with my in-laws in Bangkok. It certainly beats outlawing our marriage, as much as it beats polluting the planet beyond recognition.

Merchandise is already moving slower across the oceans as shipping companies realize that the fuel-cost savings more than make up for the extra time at sea.[19] I would love to take a boat across the Atlantic (at least for the experience, if not my personal environmental "sacrifice") if tickets sold for a price comparable with plane travel. Sadly, the comparison isn't even close, and it won't be as long as all seven billion of us are paying the price for a small and growing number of privileged jet- and pollution-setters.

ALL OF THE ABOVE, AND A FEW SILVER BULLETS

Transport is a hard nut to crack. There is no one-size-fits-all solution. As good a start as carbon caps and gas taxes would be, it's still not enough. Every socialized cost has its own ideal policy response. And the best solution for holding everyone accountable for their socialized pollution cost of driving, a gas tax, is usually dead on arrival in Washington. Frying the planet is much easier than getting burned at the polls.

What else is in our tool kit? Adjust insurance premiums to charge for miles driven? Absolutely. Free bikes for everyone? More bike lanes to use them on? More buses and bus lanes for those who can't or wouldn't want to bike? Better train service for moving more people longer distances? A fundamental shift in how traffic, transport, and travel are approached? Yes, yes, yes, yes, and yes.

As long as each driver and flier is subsidized to the tune of thousands of dollars a year, there will be many more miles driven and flown, and many fewer walkers, bikers, and riders than is optimal for your health and the planet's.

Smart urban planning is another piece of the puzzle. The magic phrase there is "high-density, mixed-use development." An alternative term for it is "a city." Lots of people living with a relatively small footprint doing things close by.

The running joke on New York's Upper West Side is that you need a passport to head over to the East Side. It's not necessarily that the East Side is so different or that far away. It's that on either side you have everything you could possibly need within a five-minute walk of your home. When we run out of milk for our cereals in the morning, it's quicker to head across the street and buy a new jug than it is to fire up the stove and make an omelet instead. Granted, that's an extreme situation, and it clearly spoils you. It also happens to be fairly popular, which implies ridiculously high real estate prices—and ridiculously small apartments for those not willing or able to shell out millions for their dwellings.

A common refrain, then, is that suburban living is just a lot cheaper. It is, on the surface. The same real estate dollar buys a lot more land in the 'burbs than on Fifth Avenue. But once you carefully account for the true cost of commutes to yourself—both in time and in money—living in the suburbs comes to the same as living in a comparable house in the city. Figure in the socialized costs of driving, and the city comes out ahead by a long shot.[20]

Would removing socialized costs mean we'd suddenly all be living in cities? Some will always prefer suburban life (and will pay a premium for the privilege), but it's highly unclear that we should be subsidizing it.[21] Urban sprawl is not a free-market outcome. It's caused by having developers and home buyers not being held accountable for the socialized costs they shove onto others beyond their suburban subdivisions.

A final big piece of the transportation puzzle is technology. I won't go into the pros and cons of electric vehicles versus biofuels, or the technologies down the line that might revolutionize plane travel. Oil companies are well on their way to developing biofuels ripe for jet engines, and change won't stop there. The first experimental flight powered by solar energy has already landed successfully after twenty-four hours in the air. Who's to say that flying—or otherwise zooming across the landscape—won't be an entirely different experience a couple of decades hence?

Few of these technologies are as simple as just getting the prices right. Widespread use of electric vehicles requires more than just capping or pricing carbon. It requires a whole new infrastructure for plugging in cars at night and during the day wherever they are parked, although none of that's too revolutionary. Electric vehicles, after all, do everything cars do, just cleaner. No need for anyone to move closer to anything. Switch from Escalades to Electrolades, and keep on driving.

That's also part of the problem. Electric vehicles are much better cars—but they are still cars. Larger-scale shifts will require even greater leaps of technology, faith, and transport policy.

We can't sit idly and hope for new technologies to save the day. Getting the prices right won't be everything, but it's the most fundamental step. Look at the now-socialized costs and make sure people are paying their full share. Traditional car and plane manufacturers, airlines, and many others will want to keep the status quo in place as long as possible. We don't need to give them extra help by subsidizing their—and our—collective exploits.

8

BRIGHT IDEA

LIGHT INVENTIONS

The very first thing I remember learning about lightbulbs was not the magical transformation of night into day, of being able to wake up and bother my parents at every possible hour and have them transform midnight into midday, food and reading time included. The first thing I remember learning was "Don't touch." Lightbulbs are hot. "You'll burn yourself," my parents would warn.

The bulb in question, of course, was what everyone of my, my parents', and my grandparents' generations, and a few further back, would recognize as the illuminator of choice: the incandescent lightbulb, which produced its first faint glow in Menlo Park, New Jersey, at 1:30 a.m. on October 22, 1879.[1] At first people came to the light: wealthy New Yorkers in their horse-drawn carriages trekked by the thousands to marvel at Thomas Edison's invention. It wasn't long before the light came to people, as incandescent bulbs took the rich world by storm.

Sales of gas and even kerosene lamps were still on their way up at the time, but only because vested interests and established infrastructure had locked in their ascendancy. Electric light was here to stay. It had overtaken all other forms of light by the first quarter of the twentieth century, and there has been no looking back.[2] A great leap forward, no doubt.

Incandescent lightbulbs, though, are much closer to the most elemental form of earthbound light—fire—than most would like to admit: 90 percent of the energy they use radiates into space in the form of heat. Which is why it's still not possible to leave an infant in close proximity to a lit lamp and why many a children's book and warning label extol the virtues of "Don't touch."

The threat posed to little hands, however, isn't the reason incandescents are finally on their way out. They are beautiful, convenient, and cheap to purchase, but largely in a backward-looking, nostalgic, and present-focused, myopic kind of way.

Better lighting technology is brighter, gives out more natural-looking light, and, lasting far longer than incandescents, is cheaper. CFLs, compact fluorescent lamps, cost more at the register—a few dollars rather than a dollar or less—but only use a quarter of the energy. And prices are coming down quickly as the technology gets better and better. Indeed, CFL is no longer the acronym that gets technophiles excited. The latest is LED, short for light-emitting diodes, also known as solid-state lamps. These lamps are modeled after the steady glow emitted by alarm clock displays and tiny lights on standby buttons.

So why wouldn't everyone just buy these newer, more modern lights? After all, we didn't mind when film cameras gave way to digital ones, prop planes disappeared in favor of jets, and polio was stamped out by vaccinations.

One reason is resistance to change and a preference for the incandescent glow of yesteryear—no doubt, back in the day, there were folks still swearing by kerosene while their neighbors installed electric lamps. As we ponder the persistence of incandescent lighting, we might well ask why the most modern of homes, stocked with plasma screens, iPad docks, and continuous floor heating, also tend to boast of fireplaces that have lost all practical function other than to serve as reminders of simpler times.

Perhaps a more compelling reason is price and the purchaser's failure to account for future energy savings. It's akin to car buyers systematically miscalculating future fuel savings and not wanting to spend a little more now to save a lot in fuel costs later. CFLs pay for themselves after a year or two. By that calculus, everyone ought to buy them—for their own pocketbooks, not for the planet. But not everyone does, and there's a simple reason for it.

Car buyers could be accused of displaying some irrationality by not making the proper calculation on an investment worth thousands of dollars. Bulb buyers, by any definition of "rational," should not be spending any brainpower on calculating future energy savings on a purchase worth less than the cost of getting to the store. Purchasing bulbs is simply not worth the brainpower it would take to make any such calculations.

I have tried hard to retrace my own thought process for buying the spare bulbs now sitting in our hall closet and came up with nothing, which is probably pretty accurate for what went through my head in the store that day one or two years ago: need bulb, get bulb. We needed one. I apparently bought three, to avoid having to go to the store in the future. Never mind that our next move would likely come before we would need another bulb and that the packing material to ensure safe passage of said bulb would cost more and possibly waste more resources than just tossing it and buying a new one at the other end. This situation all but calls for guidance from above.

Every time you buy McDonald's fries or your morning cereal, you entrust your food decisions to someone in a lab coat who creates just the right formula to maximize taste, minimize cost, and have you come back for more. The U.S. Department of Energy employs scientists who spend their entire careers trying to find out which bulbs are best. It would only be logical from an individual perspective—and certainly from that of society and the planet as a whole—to entrust your bulb-purchasing decision to that scientist.

That's especially true because the Ph.D. at McDonald's gets paid by how successful he is in making fries taste as good as possible so that you ask for the supersized option and return for your next meal. There's a good reason why restaurant meals are generally worse for you than Mom's home-cooked dinner. Few restaurant chefs hesitate when it comes to adding another stick of butter to their stew. Mom—or especially Grandma—may be known for stuffing you whenever she can, but that's just because she thinks it best for you. Her intention is clearly not to clog your arteries. She may simply not know or worry about the larger consequences, which leads right back to the scientists whose job it is to do just that—and save you from yourself, and from your mom and grandma.

The Ph.D. at the Department of Energy doesn't get a year-end bonus if his research points to a new way to make you buy more bulbs. Plenty of research documents that large government bureaucracies do not always operate in the best interest of the general public and are sometimes also in it to further their own gain—grow their own departments, make themselves look busy in light of waning demand for their services, or work to further their private financial interests. But there's a reason why there's precious little research showing the same conflicts for corporate staff scientists. That's the expected outcome. They wouldn't be doing their jobs if they were working in the interest of the general public or of the planet and not that of their corporate bottom line.

This is anything but a diatribe against capitalism, corporatism, or the big bad companies trying to trick us into buying things we don't want. It's their job to act in their own interests. It's our job to make informed decisions and spend our money wisely. Individual actions, of course, only go so far, which points to the government's role in helping to protect us and the planet and have everyone take full responsibility for their own decisions.

One difference is that you aren't obligated to head to McDonald's for your fries. Wendy's, Burger King, and plenty of others are working hard to get your business. If you don't like the Department of Energy's recommendations, you are free to move across the border, but that's about it. Then again, when Coke decides on the formula for its signature drink, Walmart stocks only concentrated detergent, or an airline strikes your route, there is often little you can do. Companies—especially the corporate behemoths any five-year-old can name—make decisions every day that inescapably affect our daily lives.

I certainly don't want government, corporations, or anyone else to decide what I can or can't do in many situations, but I draw my line when it comes to deciding how much of a particular toxin I would want to ingest or, for that matter, to buying lightbulbs. Someone is going to make that decision for you regardless, and I would much rather have that be the Department of Energy than General Electric. When the American Cancer Society establishes guidelines for colorectal cancer screenings, the Environmental Protection Agency sets toxicity standards, and the Department of Energy determines which lightbulbs produce the brightest light most cleanly, these recommendations are made for the benefit of all. What's good for General Electric may sometimes be good for America, but it's not (nor should we expect it to be) in its job description.

Life is complicated. I am thankful others put considerable thought into helping me maneuver it. Regulating the size, type, and energy efficiency for most bulbs is but one of these tiny ignorable aspects where I trust a bunch of Ph.D.'s working in the public interest to give me a helping hand. They are there to guide my purchasing decisions in a more desirable direction, solving well-known behavioral economics problems in the meantime. That's not a nanny state. It's behavioral science at its best.

SIDE EFFECTS MAY INCLUDE ...

No good deed goes unpunished. One complicating factor is mercury. Incandescents consist of many components best not ingested, and the electricity used to light them causes significant additional pollution. But the bulbs themselves have one thing going for them: they are free from mercury. CFLs are not.

The amounts are tiny—so tiny, in fact, that they are less than the mercury released into the air by burning the coal necessary to produce the same amount of light with a traditional incandescent bulb.[3] So, on average, CFLs come out ahead of incandescents even on the mercury score, but even these tiny amounts are infinitely more than the safe amount for anyone to ingest: zero. Moreover, the difference is that these tiny amounts of mercury in CFLs are concentrated in a precarious position above your nightstand. Most days, that's not a problem. The mercury is securely sealed inside the bulb—until it's not.

When a CFL breaks, mercury escapes. The amounts are far from hazmat territory, but the EPA still recommends a set of precautions: air out the room for at least fifteen minutes; pick up the pieces and put them in a sealed glass jar or plastic bag; don't vacuum or, if you do, change your vacuum bag when you are done; if the bulb breaks directly over your bed, throw out the bedding or definitely wash it; wash your hands after you are done with the cleanup.[4]

Some of these steps are common sense. If any glass breaks over your bed, you are well advised not to put your head down before first washing everything thoroughly. Most others are not: you wouldn't leave your room for fifteen minutes before starting the cleanup. Mercury in your bedroom clearly poses a problem. Installing CFLs is good for society and even for your pocketbook. Good for your kid's cognitive development it is not.

To be clear, none of the bans on incandescents prescribe the use of CFLs. Technically, they don't even ban incandescents. They simply prescribe a certain level of energy efficiency, the most sensible kind of performance standard possible. CFLs happen to be the ones that come out on top for the time being as the cheapest lights that meet the standard. It's certainly conceivable that somebody somewhere will come up with a way to build brighter and better incandescents that achieve similar energy savings. And soon enough, other alternatives will overtake CFLs as the energy source of choice. LEDs are quickly becoming cheaper. The cost of an equivalent level of illumination already beats incandescents.[5] LED technologies, however, have yet to hit store shelves the way CFLs already have.

So far, so good: set ambitious performance standards; take care not to breathe in any of the CFL mercury. But could that logic be entirely backward?

CONQUERING THE NIGHT

To catalog wealth around the world, look no further than a map of Earth from space at night. Rich, densely populated areas show up as bright spots. Vast barren swaths of Siberia, poor areas of China and India, the region around the Amazon, and almost the entire continent of Africa appear completely dark. The richer we get, the more light we use.

No wonder, then, that cheaper light begets more light, and light is getting cheaper all the time. The true price of artificial lighting has decreased over a thousandfold in the past two centuries alone, while its use has increased by even more—from a few candles in the eighteenth century to panels of light switches in your typical living room, with a spotlight for the mantelpiece, and a heat lamp for the tropical plant in the corner.[6] That trend is here to stay. At least, few signs point to it letting up. Rich households may hit a plateau at some point in the foreseeable future, but many more are playing catch-up to this moving target.

To be sure, that's the global view, taken over decades, centuries, and millennia. Over days, weeks, months, and years, the perspective is decidedly different. There, the results mirror something akin to the "rebound" effect for driving—buy a Prius, visit Grandma more often.

We have already seen that the effect is but a small fraction of the overall fuel savings. A Prius gets twice as many miles per gallon as a typical sedan, but Prius owners don't suddenly visit their grandmas twice as much. The rebound effect nixes less than 10 percent of the savings at the pump.

The same goes for lights. Just because CFLs use a quarter of the electricity doesn't mean you would turn on your lights four times as long, nor would you suddenly buy four times as many light fixtures for your living room. You are not going to change the number of light sockets overnight.

Over decades, centuries, and longer, the number of lights is anything but fixed. Over that time frame, what we consider the very idea of light to be—much like the idea of travel—changes dramatically. The step from candles to kerosene lamps didn't just decrease the use of relatively inefficient candles; it also brightened rooms and increased energy consumption. Kerosene to gas lamps was another such jump, and we didn't just try to mimic the illumination of gas lamps when incandescent lightbulbs came along. Suddenly rooms became much brighter, and energy use for lighting increased even further. Jeff Tsao and his colleagues at Sandia National Labs ran the numbers on these transitions. They fully expect this trend of increased energy use to continue with the switch from incandescents to CFLs and onward to LEDs. Times Square notwithstanding, much of the night, even in a city like New York, has yet to be conquered.

None of this implies that CFLs or LEDs are bad. They produce light at lower cost and higher quality than incandescents. Energy efficiency is good. Period. The opposite of it is energy *in*efficiency—waste. That's never a good goal, but we need to be clear about what we get in return. Banning incandescents and promoting CFLs and LEDs instead does not reduce overall energy consumption all by itself.

Politicians love bans. They make them seem decisive. They give them control, much more so than the cap-and-get-out-of-the-way approach would promise. Incandescent bulbs are not the only scourges that have seen bans of late. Styrofoam food containers, bottled water, plastic bags, outdoor wood furnaces, phthalates in children's toys, and deepwater drilling have been banned in various ways, shapes, and states. Many of these bans come for very good scientific reasons; others mainly come for reasons of the political sort. Banning incandescents is a step toward a brighter future; a step toward guaranteed lower overall energy consumption and pollution it is not.

We can't solve socialized costs through waste reduction alone. "Reduce, reuse, recycle" will decrease these costs, but the underlying forces still point in the exact same, misguided direction—and the less waste there is, the cheaper it will be to increase overall consumption. Planes are more efficient for traveling longer distances than cars or horses, and longer distances we go. Over time, lights have the same effect.

A much smarter way to tackle emissions from travel as well as from lights is exactly that: tackle emissions. That is, in the end, what we are interested in. We don't want to shackle light; we want to put pollution in an ever-shrinking box.

Once again it's the boring, hands-off, market-based approach that ought to form the basis here: tally up the now-socialized costs, and increase the price of electricity by the corresponding amount. Given the nastiness of the word "tax" and the difficulty of tallying up costs to begin with, an even better approach would often be to limit emissions directly. Cap total emissions, hand out allowances, and let companies trade them to achieve the cheapest, most effective way of decreasing overall pollution: cap and trade.

Of course, putting a ceiling on emissions by itself isn't a complete fix. Let's say we do have the perfect carbon market in place. Emissions are limited and become more so over time. Companies are outcompeting each other on their way toward a new, cleaner energy future. But neither companies nor consumers would do everything that is in their own best interest.

Markets clearly aren't perfectly efficient all the time. Companies hire management consultants for a reason, and McKinsey has identified plenty of energy-saving opportunities that aren't currently being pursued to the fullest, even though they'd be in the selfish, economic interest of everyone involved. I don't spend a lot of time studying which lightbulb to buy when I walk into the store, and that's a perfectly rational thing to do. I shouldn't be thinking about that, because the energy savings for each more energy-efficient bulb are literally pennies, worth less than the cost of having to worry about it. So yes, by all means, ban those offending bulbs, but ban them in addition to capping emissions and making sure I pay for the $20 per ton of carbon dioxide I release into the atmospheric sewer. Not either/or, but both.

JUST BAN IT

In a cruel twist of fate—cruel, at least, for whoever dreamed up the incandescent ban—it's mercury that ought to be banned. If the optimal amount of a chemical that you come in contact with over your lifetime is zero and any trace amount puts your child's brain at risk, market solutions are out.[7]

A cap set at zero is no longer a cap in any meaningful cap-and-trade sense of the word. That's a ban, and that's the appropriate step. This goes for mercury as much as for many of the other tens of thousands of chemicals we release into the wild every year that come back to haunt us later. It may well be appropriate to allow for a temporary reprieve, while zero-mercury technologies like LEDs are catching up with CFLs or while car companies are looking for alternatives to lead in batteries, but no ban would be effective immediately anyway. The key is to get the hazardous materials out of the environment sooner rather than later and to signal now where companies ought to focus their innovative prowess.

When the President's Cancer Panel comes back with a two-hundred-page report that lists three hundred chemicals found in umbilical cord blood, I frankly don't care how much it will impact profits in the petrochemical industry or whether any of these chemicals help make plastic bags crackle less.[8] Call me a radical, or a hysterical first-time dad, but I don't want my newborn to come prepolluted.

9

A BILLION POLLUTERS

TOP OF THE BARREL

It's easy being an environmentalist when you are among the privileged billion of global high emitters. You can show your allegiances by remembering to bring a cloth bag to the grocery store, refusing bottled water, or—the classic—using your frequent-flier miles to plant trees and offset emissions for your next flight.

Getting your personal carbon dioxide emissions from twenty down to eighteen tons a year is noble. For anyone confronted with going from two to zero, the task isn't just a lot harder. Today's dirty technologies and misguided markets with socialized costs all around us render it impossible. Not to mention that it's also obnoxious to ask anyone living on two tons a year to decrease emissions, giving up even the bare necessities for life.

Add to that the fact that the global poor are the ones who feel the worst and most immediate effects of a warming and increasingly un-predictable planet. For the poor, starving or dying en masse because of environmental catastrophes is not a distant, future event flickering across TV and computer screens every once in a while. It's already happening—some of it due to global warming, some of it not. Just as the American poor were the ones worst affected by Hurricane Katrina dev-astating the Gulf Coast and drowning New Orleans, the global poor are the ones worst hit by a changing climate. The rich adapt; the poor suffer.

The surest way to protect yourself against the impacts of ever rising temperatures is to get rich and hide behind your air condi-tioner. Chances are that air-conditioned supermarkets frequented by the global rich will be the last places on Earth affected by the loom-ing food squeeze.

It's clearly those emitting twenty tons and more per year who are to blame for the planetary crisis we are in, not those emitting two. Our world and our climate are being shaped by the now-industrialized coun-tries. Still, all of us need to be part of the solution.

China has been engaged in a massive get-rich-quick scheme for de-cades, and I am using "scheme" here in the best possible sense of the word. China's awesome growth, doubling total incomes at least once a decade, pulled hundreds of millions out of abject poverty. This very process has ensured massive additional pollution—both the local kind, manifesting itself in the form of asthma attacks and neurotoxins in drinking water, and the global kind, in the form of an increasingly unstable climate.

But is it really the Chinese who are pushing the planet over the edge? We know that one out of seven billion is less than a drop in the bucket. One billion out of seven matters. But it's probably not the bil-lion you are thinking of.

One way to look at the world is by country: 300 million Americans spew around twenty tons each of carbon dioxide a year into the atmo-sphere; 500 million Europeans emit ten tons each; a billion-plus Chi-nese emit three tons each; and a billion Indians emit around one ton each, on average.[1] That's a convenient way to pit nations against each other. It also provides a poor view of the world as a whole.

We need to add a bit more nuance to the bucket analogy from chapter 2 to see how that pans out. Not all drops are created equal. Let me see whether I can explain the slightly more complicated version as well.

Instead of slicing the world by countries, how about we look at people?[2] Beijing's and Delhi's nouveau riche are as profligate in their use of fossil fuels as the best of them in New York, London, and wherever the rich congregate. If we slice the world that way, we are left with a billion global high emitters without regard to national borders. That's one billion out of seven, each consuming twenty times more than each of the bottom four billion. Those on top—me and, most likely, you included—collectively account for over half of global carbon emissions. The four billion on the very bottom barely register with 10 percent of the total.

That picture won't change for quite a while. By 2030, the billion at the top of the carbon-wasting scale will likely have grown, from a bit under 1 to perhaps 1.2 billion. Their—our—contribution will still account for over half of global emissions. The bottom 4 billion will have grown more rapidly, from 3.6 to around 4.3 billion. Their average pollution will still be less than one ton, and they will still barely tip the global scale with less than 10 percent of overall emissions.

Emissions from the poor don't matter—not now, and not anytime soon. What matters are emissions from the global rich and from those who are rapidly joining them. China tops that list as the one country with by far the largest number of people growing into profligate carbon users.

These numbers say a lot of things: one, teach your kid Mandarin; two, China is at least two countries, the urban, coastal rich and the rural, inland poor. By 2030, China will have 350 million of its citizens in the high-emitter category, easily eclipsing the United States, and many more will be in the middle-income and middle-polluter league. Yet plenty of people will remain poor. Many may be on their way up,

2010

2030

but not nearly as fast as the top earners and top polluters. In the end it's those top polluters who tip the balance and on whom we ought to focus.

So now we have a better handle on the numbers. We have also just made our lives considerably more complicated. It's not as easy as laying blame on a handful of countries, but there are some clear avenues to tackle the problem with a bit of systematic thinking.

LESS INTENSE

One key ingredient in this puzzle is "emissions intensity": how much carbon per dollar of economic output.[3] Ironically, once we look at intensities, we are back to dividing the world into countries as the most convenient point of comparison. France, with its nuclear power plants, has a low intensity. The French could be promiscuous users of electricity, yet their emissions would be low compared with almost anyone else in the industrialized world. Many other western European countries are close to France. The United States and especially Australia have large intensities. They use lots of dirty energy relative to what they produce. China, with its large number of old, inefficient factories and its large and growing coal fleet, is a bit higher still—though not by much. It's roughly on par with Australia, and China's energy goals in its five-year plans all but ensure that intensities are coming down relatively quickly. Watch out, Down Under.

This is one possible approach: do everything to decrease energy and, therefore, carbon intensities as rapidly as possible. There's lots of room for improvement, especially in formerly or currently Communist countries. Eastern Europe is more carbon intensive than its western neighbors. North Korea's economy is over three times as carbon intensive as the South's. China's is a fifth higher than America's, and three times that of France.

None of these improvements in carbon intensities depend on new breakthrough technologies. They simply require replacing old with new (something China has become good at) and shifting to other, cleaner existing technologies (something China's only starting to do, but it's already in the lead).

DEVELOPMENT VERSUS ENVIRONMENT

Tackling emissions intensity is one answer, although it's not yet the solution to decreasing global emissions. If the economy grew 10 percent a year, total energy use could still *increase* 5 percent each year for China to meet the goal of decreasing its energy intensity by 20 percent over a five-year period, something enshrined in its current five-year plan. That's better than no intensity improvement at all, but it still pits development against environment in the starkest terms.

China weathered the global economic downturn in 2008–2009 better than most. The slump still meant that it could shut some of the most inefficient Mao-era factories. But the natural order of things wasn't enough to meet the 20 percent energy intensity goal, so Beijing tried a more ironclad fist. It flat out ordered over two thousand steel, cement, and other inefficient factories to shut down before the last quarter of 2010 to help meet the goals of the tenth five-year plan.[4] That still didn't cut it. Frustrated local officials, who had to meet Beijing's targets or face personal consequences, resorted to turning off street and traffic lights and instituting rolling blackouts affecting factories, homes, and hospitals. It got their provinces closer to the energy-efficiency target, but it did so in a decidedly heavy-handed, nonmarket way. Beijing didn't like those measures and started reminding and reprimanding local officials that environmental goals ought not to come at the cost of economic development. That's easier said than done.

Environment versus development is *the* trade-off, and *the* struggle, that will define the world's climate for centuries to come. The question is how to strike a sufficient balance that will avoid too many significant trade-offs.

I remember buying our first set of canvas shopping bags at Whole Foods in Cambridge over ten years ago. I mainly remember it because they were expensive—$15 each. Now any store that wants to strut its environmental bona fides—and its logo—hands them out for free. We knew it was the right thing to do, but it still took a jolt to decide that it was worth it. That jolt came when one of our paper bags slung over a bike handle broke, ruining a dozen eggs and half the groceries around them. Equally important, Whole Foods had just started giving a ten-cent credit for each bag you brought to the store. A hundred and fifty shopping trips later and we would be printing money. Thirty whole cents each trip.

I'm not telling this story simply to get public credit for my good deeds (although, in truth, the psychological value of the approving glances of the people around me in the checkout lane probably far exceeds the dime I get every time I schlep a bag to the store). I'm telling this because it's a larger metaphor for going green: the start-up costs are often high, but the payoff comes soon enough; and once you get ahead, you stay ahead. That goes for cloth bags as much as for energy-saving lightbulbs, clean-burning cookstoves for the poorest of the poor, and large-scale power plants and electricity grid investments for the well connected.

Shift from $15 canvas bags to billion-dollar investments in power generation. Coal and natural gas are dirty and expensive. Yet barring major technological breakthroughs, fossil fuel plants are still cheaper to build than most renewable-energy plants, just as plastic bags are cheaper than ones made out of sustainable cotton.

Fortunes flip once the plant is turned on. To operate a renewable-energy plant means paying for regular maintenance, the kinds of expenditures every factory incurs regardless of what raw materials it needs for its products. The raw materials themselves—sun, wind, waves, and waste—however, are free. Year after year, renewable-energy plants are cheaper to keep running than those powered by coal and natural gas.

This same conclusion repeats itself over and over: putting up leaky buildings is cheaper than properly insulating them, never mind that whoever lives and works in them will be stuck with the higher energy bill; clear-cutting forests is cheaper than managing them well, never mind that the next generation will be left with deserted soils; building roads to yet another suburb is easier than rethinking urban plans, never mind that in the long term a well-built city will prove more livable than quickie subdivisions next to unsightly strip malls.

It's one thing to have a bunch of greens shouting these truths from their solar-paneled rooftops and extolling the virtues of sustainable living. It's quite another to have a group of hard-nosed management consultants take a close look at the actual numbers and show the exact same thing in a sleek PowerPoint presentation.

McKinsey is hardly the place you think about when you think long-term sustainability. (And I'm not saying that because I worked for the Boston Consulting Group, a rival haven for twentysomethings in suits, armed with spreadsheets, frequent-flier miles, and rings under their eyes.) McKinsey has created a cottage industry around tallying up the costs and savings of decreasing greenhouse gas pollution. The results are a slew of "cost curves" that show the costs and impacts of particular actions. They should really be called "saving curves."

McKinsey put on paper what many suspected but were shy to admit lest they get laughed out of the room or stamped as environmental fundamentalists: many of these actions pay for themselves over time. Some have significant start-up costs, and many have plenty of other obstacles from simple ignorance to real market barriers, but the savings dwarf them sooner rather than later, sometimes significantly.

Economists tend to be skeptical of these pronouncements. There's no such thing as a free lunch after all. Stereotypical University of Chicago economists, known to be the most conservative of the bunch and also known to subscribe to this mantra to a fault, have a joke about two economists finding a $20 bill lying on the ground. Says one to the other: "It can't be. If it were real, someone would have picked it up already." It turns out McKinsey discovered plenty of these bills.

No surprise there. If markets were as efficient as Chicago economists proclaimed, there would be no need for consultants in the first place—nor, for that matter, for business schools, including the one at the University of Chicago. Why hire McKinsey, or any M.B.A.'s, if you already operate at maximum efficiency and for the maximum benefit of your shareholders?

Alan Greenspan, the long-serving Federal Reserve "maestro" and high priest of free-market ideology, had to admit that he watched in a state of "shocked disbelief" when market self-regulation didn't prevent banks from doing things that threatened their very survival, throwing billions of $20 bills out the window all at once. Milton Friedman, an even higher priest of free marketeers, hailed the "effective transmission of accurate information" in markets.[5] He worried about everyone getting the right information "without clogging the 'in' baskets of those who have no use for it." Here, McKinsey is lending a helping hand.

It's not as easy as pointing the searchlight in the right direction. There may be plenty of real obstacles that explain why companies (not to mention all of us individually) don't take advantage of each of these money-saving opportunities. One is that these savings aren't really $20 bills lying on the ground. They come in the form of dimes, nickels, and pennies. There might be lots of them, but it's still a pain to bend down and pick them up. Some are stuck to the pavement, some are hidden from plain view, some require a bit of creativity to get them out of a pond.

Developing new technologies (like finding new ways to insulate buildings) and deploying them at scale (plastering every building with the new insulation material) have plenty of obstacles themselves. Once again, that's only natural. Innovation means figuring out how to get around these hurdles. If it were effortless, we'd already have done it all.[6]

There is no such thing as a free breakfast. Lunch, however, may well be free. And those free lunches can add up quickly.

In the United States, energy-efficiency measures alone add up to over one billion tons of reduced greenhouse gas emissions annually by 2020, and all of them, in theory, pay for themselves: their operational cost savings over time exceed the initial investment.[7] To put the one billion tons in perspective, these reductions are on par with the most ambitious climate bills ever seriously considered in Congress.

Globally, McKinsey finds emissions reductions of fifteen billion tons by 2030, all with net savings. Once you add in available technical abatement measures at reasonable costs, you get to over thirty billion tons by 2030.[8] That's thirty out of a bit over sixty. These potentials are a big reason why the most credible economic studies insist that stabilizing the climate is eminently affordable, if we only put the right incentives in place.

That's the big if. We know that the only eventual solution is for market forces to point in the right direction, and governments ought to be the ones putting the right incentives in place to make that happen. But the transition won't come for free. Switching from incandescents to CFLs, retrofitting buildings with better insulation, replacing clinker with fly ash in cement production, rolling out hybrid and electric vehicles, improving management of cropland nutrients, putting in place better waste-recycling systems, and dozens of other seemingly small, low-hanging fruits on the McKinsey saving curves might all pay for themselves or come in at low costs, but someone has to invest the money up front. Breakfast isn't free after all.

The added up-front investments for a transition to a green economy are in the billions—somewhere on the order of $500 billion annually through 2015, rising to the dreaded trillion by 2030. That's no longer chump change; it's closer to financial-crisis bank-bailout territory. It's also a global figure. For China, the number is around $50 to $100 billion now, and less than $300 billion by 2030. More important, we ought to put these numbers in perspective. The private sector globally invests some $20 trillion a year. The world currently spends around $5 trillion on energy each year and up to $500 billion alone on fossil fuel subsidies.[9] The money is clearly there. The task is to redirect it from planet-destroying behavior to actions that would actually help.[10]

BORROWING FROM THE ATMOSPHERE FOR A GOOD CAUSE

We know that eventually we need to rely on market forces. The task is to overhaul a $5-trillion-a-year global fossil-fuel-based energy sector—something that can't be done through public funds or charity. In the meantime, though, it may well be possible—and necessary—to unleash public funds and other large investment opportunities in that direction.

One way to come up with the cash up front is to borrow money from the atmosphere. That's a strange statement from an environmentalist, less strange from an environmental economist. Actually, it should be downright familiar to all of us. Borrowing from the atmosphere is what we've been doing all along by treating it as a free sewer. Except that we have done exactly the wrong kind of borrowing. We've been borrowing and using the money to burn even more coal, oil, and gas, year after year. The atmosphere rather wishes we'd just stop with borrowing altogether. Overnight. No doubt, this would be best for the planet, but then we are right back to the epic battle of development versus environment. And the question still remains: How do we come up with billions of dollars?

So why not take some of the money—and breathing room—we now borrow from the atmosphere to build dirty tech and shift it over to building clean tech? We can't do that forever—we've been borrowing for too long—but we could do it perhaps for a few years or even a decade, if that's what it takes to turn things around and reorient market forces. Of course, the atmosphere isn't exactly printing actual cash, so who would give us the money? Once again, the answer lies in the carbon markets: cap and trade.

In 2009, Chinese companies made somewhere around $2 billion a year from selling Clean Development Mechanism credits for reducing emissions, by building renewable-energy plants where coal would have been cheaper, destroying industrial greenhouse gases much more potent than carbon, or pursuing simple energy-efficiency measures. The main buyers of these credits were European companies, the only ones already obligated to either reduce their own emissions or, within limits, pay others to reduce theirs. That implies emissions are being reduced where it's cheapest to do so, and China was by far the largest source of these credits globally. These project-by-project transactions are rather cumbersome, and there's little hope that they can be scaled up sufficiently fast and far. The $2 billion is nothing compared with the money that could and should change hands if China and others were to put caps on emissions instead of dabbling with individual projects.

That same absolute cap in Europe led to emissions reductions even before its full inception in 2008. It also generated the demand for the $2 billion in Chinese credits in the first place. For China and other developing countries, though, the cap wouldn't have to be immediately binding. They could set their caps slightly above current emission levels, thus enabling emissions to grow for a few years. That enables a bit of space to grow emissions for a few years. All that comes in exchange for binding commitments to significantly reduce emissions later, and a commitment to use the extra money generated in the meantime and put it toward the kind of clean-tech projects McKinsey identifies as being free lunches after the breakfast has been paid off.[11]

The gut reaction of many climate campaigners who remember their history tends to be to cry foul when they hear this proposal. They point to "Russian hot air," the extra emissions allowances Russia negotiated for itself as a condition of its signature to the 1997 Kyoto Protocol. Russia insisted on linking its carbon reduction goals to 1990 levels, just like everyone else. This belied the fact that Russia's economy crashed shortly after 1990, its emissions crashing with it. It was a foregone conclusion that Russia would meet its Kyoto emissions targets without doing anything at all.

Things are very different here. The point for China, of course, is not to crash its economy in hopes of cutting emissions. It's the exact opposite. China is supposed to grow, but do so smartly and cleanly, without repeating the mistakes the now-rich world (including Russia) has made all along its development path.

Another twist to ease the transition to a cleaner development path is that China's carbon cap could at first be focused on particular sectors. Power generation is by far the most significant contributor to greenhouse gases and the one that penetrates most everything else. It also links into many other concerns related to energy and national security. Beijing's leadership is no different from Washington's. Talking about climate instability might get some attention, but what really riles up politicians is talk of dependency on imported oil, coal, you name it. McKinsey lays out how pursuing a green development path would drop oil imports and coal use by 40 percent each by 2030.[12] That would make coal imports for China superfluous. Now suddenly we have generals at the table talking climate policy.

THE LONG ARC

China so far has been a convenient stand-in for developing countries in general. It's certainly the one that matters the most for the climate. India comes in at a close second. Its growth hasn't lifted off as early and as quickly as China's, which also means it has a lot less environmental baggage to deal with. There are plenty of problems, to be sure. Delhi is a mess, and the government in New Delhi often doesn't have the power to change things quickly enough. But one thing India doesn't have is quite as much old, dirty infrastructure. The technical term is "path dependency," or here, the lack thereof. India is still largely able to chart its own course into a low-carbon, high-efficiency future without having locked much of its country into the old pathway.

Simon Kuznets was one of the all-time economic greats and one of the first Nobel laureates. He won for his work on economic growth and was particularly worried about the actual process of development: how to get from A to B. For inequality, more often than not, that path seems to lead via an upside-down U, later dubbed a Kuznets curve. Inequality first rises as countries get richer before the income distribution becomes more and more equal once again.[13] When no one has anything, incomes aren't far apart. When incomes increase, everyone looks out for No. 1, and inequality goes up. When a country is so rich its citizens can afford to worry about things other than making money, societal fortunes once again equalize. It turns out this holds for some countries (think Sweden) but clearly not for others (think the United States, where inequality has continuously increased of late as the richest of the rich have taken home an increasing share of earnings).[14]

Starting in the early 1990s, environmental economists became curious about the same relationship for pollution. The first studies struck gold—at least when it came to finding nice little curves that purported to show how pollution first rises and then falls with economic riches.[15] These upside-down-U relationships—"environmental Kuznets curves"—struck a chord.

Development and environment can and must go hand in hand, but the marriage is not automatic. When you look at the entire arc of development—from the extremely poor to the too-rich-for-their-own-good—you find a curious phenomenon. The very poor don't pollute; the very rich don't seem to, either, at least when it comes to local pollutants that impact air and water. It's the ones in the middle who do.

That's a beautiful result—almost too beautiful, especially for anyone prone to oversimplification. Ardent anti-environmentalists tend to shout, "See, environmental regulations aren't needed after all. Just let countries get richer and they will get cleaner, too." If only it were that easy. It's the classic fallacy of mistaking correlation for causation. Just because two things go hand in hand does not mean one causes the other. Pollution does not decline in rich countries simply because countries are getting richer. Localized pollutants decline because richer citizens start demanding cleaner air and water, and governments step in with laws to make it happen. We had to witness the Cuyahoga River burn in

1969 before the United States passed its first set of major environmental laws. China is now approaching this point.

Rivers may no longer burn in the United States, but there is one pollutant still shooting straight up without a global turning point in sight: carbon. Thousands of graduate students ran millions of regression analyses in every which way, trying to relate pollution to economic growth. Xavier Sala-i-Martin published a serious academic paper called "I Just Ran Two Million Regressions" about his search for anything and everything that goes hand in hand with economic growth. (He later upped the ante with "I Just Ran Four Million Regressions.") He didn't focus on pollution specifically, but many others did. To no avail. However hard you try, carbon simply doesn't want to follow the convenient pattern of turning around and declining. Few researchers ever claimed to have found environmental Kuznets curves for carbon emissions, and those who did had largely been wrong—at least in the interpretations.

Say you do find that the very rich (let's call them "Americans") don't dump quite as much carbon into the atmosphere each as the slightly poorer (let's call them "Americans ten years ago"). What does that tell you? One of two things: either that Americans have really gotten their act together and are decarbonizing their economy, or that they've somehow managed to wiggle themselves out of being account-

able for their pollution. There are a few reasons why you might think the latter to be true, but here's one solid economic argument.

When we look at emissions, we generally focus on one aspect of them: the gunk associated with *producing* a particular aluminum can, for example. That's how things had typically been tallied and still are to this day: the aluminum smelter pollutes; the resulting emissions get added to the country's balance sheet. But then it turns out we don't always consume what we produce. We trade. I don't make my own aluminum cans but instead buy them at the store, and sometimes an entire country doesn't make its own but imports them from somewhere else. So while pollution from production might come down a bit after all—the beginnings of another one of these upside-down Us—pollution linked to consumption could still shoot straight up. The richer we are, the more carbon we spew into the atmosphere. We just no longer make it ourselves. Pollution goes the way of U.S. manufacturing jobs: to China.

China can't be let off the hook quite this easily. It gets the benefits of jobs, tax revenues, and everything else those jobs entail, but ultimately, American and European consumers are the ones buying the steel, laptops, and toys. A fair accounting of carbon pollution ought to include trade and look at total pollution consumed rather than produced. The buck stops with the consumer.

Everything I have said so far in connection with the environmental Kuznets curve should be fairly uncontroversial. Not every economist may give the exact same answer as to why we'd expect upside-down-U relationships between income and pollution or why we wouldn't, but the reasoning is fairly well established. That won't be the case with what I'm about to say.

Let me try to cushion the blow a bit with economists, and instead miff a few fervent environmentalists, by emphasizing that *trade is good*. Most of it is, anyway, but not so fast. First I need to boost some of my free-trade credentials: no trade, no gain. That goes for "trade" among individuals as much as for trade across national borders. It's how prosperity evolves, how we evolve as a species, and why I'm able to eat what I eat, wear what I wear, and do what I do. Every voluntary trade means both sides are better off, because otherwise they wouldn't bother making the deal.

Matt Ridley, the Rational Optimist, has made a name for himself arguing how trade helps ideas have sex, and how no single individual knows how to make even the most basic items. Forget laptops, no one knows how to make a pencil—and that's largely a good thing. If we all needed to know how to make everything we use, we'd be finding ourselves back in trees or in caves, and even there a division of labor existed. I doubt every hunter was also a gifted toolmaker or cave painter. Hunter-gatherer societies didn't get this designation by accident. Some hunted; some gathered; then they traded their spoils. So to be clear, I'm pro-trade. Repeat after me: trade is good.

We can up the ante even further: trade is (often) good for the environment.[16]

Several factors are at work here, but two dominate the equation: free trade makes everyone richer and leads to more output; even more important, free trade spreads ideas of how to produce things better and cleaner. Across a broad swath of pollutants, that second part dominates all else and makes free trade a friend rather than a foe of the environment.

Okay, so with that out of the way, here goes. Companies move across borders to where production is cheap. Always have, always will. They move in droves from the United States to Mexico, or from everywhere to China. It's only natural, and it's a tried-and-true practice. Many factories in New England got their start because costs were cheaper in the colonies than at home in England. Aluminum smelters locate in cities with unpronounceable Icelandic names for a reason: geothermal power makes electricity cheap and plentiful.

The same goes—to a much lesser extent—for climate policy. Say Europe has a price on carbon through its cap-and-trade system. That means some European factories may decide to move across the Bosporus or the Strait of Gibraltar and produce their products there to avoid the additional costs of environmental policy at home. That threat is often overblown, but it's not nil. Shifting from production-based to consumption-based emissions numbers makes this particularly apparent.[17]

Anytime we talk about carbon pollution associated with consumption—which is fundamentally the right way to look at things—we immediately get to something akin to border tariffs. Some call it "border carbon adjustment" to avoid the treaded "tariff" term. But let's not mince words here. We are talking about tariffs on anyone who doesn't have a similarly strong climate policy. That's not a tariff for the sake of throwing a wrench into world trade. It's a tariff that would help throw a wrench into our unbridled desire to use the atmosphere as a free sewer.

Here, I said it. Yes, I'm an economist arguing for tariffs. It goes against a basic tenet of my religion.

But there's a rub: I don't want any of these carbon tariffs to come into force—ever. Ideally, they would simply be nudges to get other countries to adopt equivalent measures. The best policy, then, is to announce tariffs to come into effect in, say, five or ten years. That won't have any direct harmful effects on trade now, and it would still accomplish the goal of getting others to see the policy light.

Ardent free traders often cite the World Trade Organization as a potential obstacle to such a policy. There are surely ways to design border

tariffs that would run afoul of WTO rules (as if that were the only criterion); there would also be plenty of ways to design tariffs that would
pass WTO's muster, most likely under another name. In the end, they
aren't tariffs at all but closer to "antidumping penalties" for high-carbon
products. These penalties ought not to create undue competitive advantages for domestic firms. That much is clear. As long as they only level
the playing field, these antidumping penalties should be yet another
area where environmentalists, economists, and even international trade
lawyers may come to a happy medium.[18]

RACE TO THE TOP

By now, we're about as far removed from individual action as we can
get. The energy-saving lightbulbs you and I use in our homes don't
matter, but to get the United States to act and put the right policies in
place, we could at least put our elected representatives on speed dial
and start berating them (or send them each a copy of this book).

How do you get the whole world to act? Global problems require a
global government. Sadly, there is none. The United Nations and the
UN-sponsored climate talks are poor stand-ins, and other forms of
cooperation—like governments mimicking lobstermen gangs—only
go so far. National governments are all we have to make a difference.

Fortunately, we don't need all 190-odd countries to make that difference. Washington, Brussels, Beijing, and Brasília control over half of
global greenhouse gas emissions. Add in Tokyo, Moscow, New Delhi,
and Jakarta (Indonesia's emissions from deforestation put it almost on
par with Brazil's), and we're at over two-thirds of the global total. Now
suddenly everyone fits around a single table, even if the Europeans send
a handful of their own to represent their views. One oft-heard analogy
in the climate world is trade. The World Trade Organization, the comparison goes, is a club of joiners. It started out as a small group of willing nations rather than an attempt to forge an agreement among all
countries. Joining—or rather, being allowed to join—excites trade

ministers and national parliaments, if not the masses. WTO membership comes with a commitment to free(er) trade and with subjecting oneself to certain rules, but in the end, it is still a voluntary club.

That certainly has appeal for climate policy as well: organize climate talks around the nations who want to join (which, ideally, matches the ones who actually matter) rather than let global talks be hijacked by the likes of Saudi Arabia and others who have the most to lose. Of course, the stalled Doha round of trade negotiations makes this analogy imperfect at best and points to the dangers of even letting a club of joiners get too big for its own good.

Another link to trade provides an even less hopeful picture. The "race to the bottom" is almost synonymous with free trade: cheaper production, lower standards, more pollution. No one, it seems, other than some high-minded Europeans, the ever-green Costa Ricans, and the doomed-by-rising-sea-levels Maldivians, can afford not to play the game. When the true environmental costs of our daily actions are socialized and exploiting the planet fattens your wallet, that's not too surprising.

Why, then, can some significant players afford to be cleaner and greener than others? (And by "significant," I mean the likes of Germany and Spain.) One response goes that none of them really are greener than need be. A handful of Europeans might do a bit more because government meddling in private business is part of their DNA, but that's about it (and they certainly can't seem to be able to afford it, either). It's not nearly the full story, though. Plenty of countries go far beyond the lackluster U.S. climate policies—not always, of course, for climate reasons.

For one, there's the local environment. Coal doesn't just spew carbon into the atmosphere when you burn it; it throws up a lot of other gunk and toxins that end up in drinking water and lungs, and digging it up in the first place isn't clean either. Decreasing greenhouse gas pollution often goes hand in hand with decreasing other pollutants. As a result, Germany moving away from coal means that both Germans and the planet breathe more easily. That's why democracies tend to be cleaner and greener than autocratically run states. It's tough drawing attention to polluted rivers when every attempted protest ends in jail.

So what explains China's move to go green? Ultimately, a much bigger reason than any environmental argument is the competitive advantage gained from getting a head start in the race to thrive in the new-energy future. In other words: "industrial policy." The type of direct meddling to nurture infant industries that free traders hate to love. It's become a cliché to say that whoever owns the technology and supplies the world with cheap, clean electrons owns the twenty-first century, but that's indeed the key ingredient and the real reason why the trade game is increasingly turning itself into a virtuous cycle of countries outcompeting each other to be greener and leaner than their neighbors. The real question is whether that transition is happening fast enough and whether politicians have the audacity to put the right guideposts in place to unleash market forces and innovation in the right direction.

In the end, it all still comes down to national policies. Spurring innovation might be a global race, but it's a national game. Nations decide on the right combination of sticks (carbon caps and prices) and carrots (a modicum of subsidies).

10

MARKET MORALS

STARFISHING

Once upon a time, there was a wise man who used to go to the ocean to do his writing. He had a habit of walking on the beach before he began his work.

One day, as he was walking along the shore, he looked down the beach and saw a human figure moving like a dancer. He smiled to himself at the thought of someone who would dance to the day, and so he walked faster to catch up.

As he got closer, he noticed that the figure was that of a young man and that what he was doing was not dancing at all. The young man was reaching down to the shore, picking up small objects, and throwing them into the ocean.

He came closer still and called out, "Good morning! May I ask what it is that you are doing?"

The young man paused, looked up, and replied, "Throwing starfish into the ocean."

"I must ask, then, why are you throwing starfish into the ocean?" asked the somewhat startled wise man.

To this, the young man replied, "The sun is up and the tide is going out. If I don't throw them in, they'll die."

Upon hearing this, the wise man commented, "But, young man, do you not realize that there are miles and miles of beach and there are starfish all along every mile? You can't possibly make a difference!"

At this, the young man bent down, picked up yet another starfish, and threw it into the ocean. As it met the water, he said, "I made a difference to that one!"

Type the first sentence of this parable into Google, and you will get twenty-six thousand search results. There are Starfish Societies, Starfish Clubs, Starkids, and at least one Starfish Story Appreciation Society. Humane societies use it to justify being good to dogs; doctors use it to show their humanity toward patients; foster-parenting organizations use it to shore up interest in their services; motivational speakers use it to strut their credentials.

I first heard it from my wife, who heard it from someone counseling her on whether to go to medical school. "You'll be touching starfish every day on the job and making a huge difference in every one of their lives." The story has clearly done a lot of good. It's the classic tale of pay-it-forward. At least a half dozen charities have used it directly to raise more money: "You, too, can be a member of our Starfish Society for the low, low price of a tax-deductible gift of $1,000."

More often than not, this story is attributed to either some wise mentor, former boss, or an "anonymous" scribe. In fact, the author of the original is the late Loren Eiseley, invariably called a latter-day Thoreau.[1] Eiseley's version is a much longer meditation on science and humanism, replete with cameos by Charles Darwin, Francis Bacon, Einstein, Freud, and Goethe.

Although he would have never put it this way, the "wise man" in the Internet sensation is Eiseley himself, meditating about the meaning of life in a world where Bacon and Darwin have shown that "individuals do not matter." Eiseley points to the star thrower as someone who demonstrates that individuals can matter after all. "There is a hurler of stars, and he walks, because he chooses, always in desolation, but not in defeat." That's already a slightly more gloomy perspective than the children's book version.

But the story need not end with the young man crying out that he made a difference to that one starfish. The other protagonist is a wise man after all. Let's give him the microphone once more:

The wise man replied: "Young man, have you ever considered why these starfish are washing up on the shore?"

He led the young man up the shoreline, up a hill, and onto a rocky cliff overlooking the ocean. Pointing toward the horizon, the wise man said: "You see that fisherman? He's using dynamite to kill the fish, so he can just skim them off the surface. Starfish get washed onto the shore as innocent bystanders. If you want to save the starfish, go stop the fisherman."

Talk about economist killjoys. But wait; there's more.

The young man is tired and hungry from picking up starfish and throwing them back into the water day after day. There's no food stall in sight as far as the eye can see.

Spying the fisherman pulling up onshore, his boat full of fish, he says, "Oh, please, can I buy some?"[2]

PEOPLE ARE MOTIVATED BY MOTIVES

Economics jades you. Not in the "There's no God but money" kind of way. Plenty of economists—too many—subscribe blindly to the "Greed is good" mantra, and that surely casts a spell on the entire profession, but that's not what I mean here.

Economics jades you because it teaches you a set of inalienable principles that you then feel compelled to apply to anything and everything in sight. That's also what distinguishes economics from many other social sciences (and ensures that economists tend to come across as imperialists with one-track minds and opinions about everything).

Petroleum engineers spend years studying ways to push off the date of "peak oil." Conservation biologists study intricate human-animal interactions, listening carefully to community needs to help formulate sustainable management plans. Transportation specialists and urban planners look at our car culture and infrastructure and come up with itemized plans to transform both to realize a lower-carbon world. Economists often just shout "gas tax," or "limit total fish catch," or "cap emissions."

That's largely due to the fact that economics is different from other social sciences. Economists often see themselves more like physicists, with their laws of thermodynamics and gravity. There are differences, of course. Humans aren't emotionless atoms moving around in a frictionless vacuum, but we can't just throw our hands in the air and pretend it's impossible to say anything about how humans, on average, behave. Indeed, there are some fairly well-established rules that most of us follow most of the time.

N. Gregory Mankiw lists ten such principles on the first pages of his introductory economics textbook. The first is an easy one to swallow: *people face trade-offs.*

Life is full of them, whether it's between going on that morning run or sleeping in, between buying a red or a blue sweater, or between funding a war or improving primary school education. Mick Jagger put it best: "You can't always get what you want."

Simple enough. Except, once you start looking at the world through these trade-off goggles, it's amazing how often this principle gets violated. The Endangered Species Act is a marvelous example. It has done enormous good, but it has done so without any regard to trade-offs. Once a species makes it on the endangered list, the law states that everything must be done to save it. We'd all like to save as many ivory-billed woodpeckers, bald eagles, and polar bears as possible, but the act doesn't even include the "as possible." It just says, save them all no matter the cost.

If not, you pay to the tune of $100,000 per dead animal or with a year in jail. Despite all this, the Endangered Species Act hasn't saved the ivorybill (which was very likely extinct before it was listed as endangered), it didn't save the bald eagle (that was thanks to the ban on DDT), and it won't save the polar bears (that will require serious efforts to stabilize the global climate). What makes me so certain about the latter prediction is the fact that an all-or-nothing conservation approach simply won't do. We can't stop global warming by edict.

I'm not arguing against conservation. Far from it. Not conserving comes with enormous costs, but it's equally true that the problems we and the planet face will not be solved by saying we'd like to protect all species, all land, all water. We can't declare the atmosphere a national park untouchable by humans. We have to face trade-offs, and we have to face them head-on.

That's especially true because of Mankiw's second principle: since people face trade-offs, *the cost of something is what you give up to get it.*

It's not just money; time matters as well, and so do all those other forgone pleasures that you miss out on when you hunker down and write a book or read one, run or sleep, work or shop, and so on. Sometimes a wind turbine is an eyesore and kills the occasional bird. The relevant question is what we are prepared to give up for the clean energy it produces. Coal plants kill more birds and do far more damage to the planet—just silently, out of our sight line, and over years and decades. That's often not well understood, but once you get it, it makes forehead-slapping sense. Welcome to the club of jaded economists.

The principle, though, that really makes economists look like greed-obsessed simpletons and jades the outlook of everyone who has gone through an economics boot camp makes it to number four on Mankiw's list: *people respond to incentives.*

It seems so obvious as to be almost comedic. Yoram Bauman, the self-declared world's first and only stand-up economist—who is quick to remind people that, yes, he does have a Ph.D. in economics, and also happens to be an environmental economist—agrees. After looking up the definition of "incentives" in the dictionary, he has translated Mankiw's fourth principle to: "People are motivated by motives." For him that's a bit like saying tautologies are tautological: "People would have to be pretty stupid to be unmotivated by motives."

And indeed, people are smart in this regard. Mankiw is one of them. He hit it big in December 1992 with an up-front $1.4 million paycheck to write his introductory economics text. Mankiw had been a rising star in Harvard's economics department, earning tenure before he turned thirty—at which point it was seemingly time to cash in. He played publishing houses against each other to set the new record for textbooks, which still stands today. His motive was clear: money.

None of this is to say that being motivated by money is either good or bad. It just is.[3] It's convenient shorthand for how authors, economists, most dedicated environmentalists, and everyone in between—on average—behave. Bill Gates may not wake up every morning worrying about his next billion. You can also ignore a few yoga-obsessed yuppies and nature-obsessed hippies, but the other seven billion of us at least behave *as if* money mattered. Never mind what people say, or want to believe, it's how they behave that's important. And there money—more often than not—plays a central role.

Generations of cultural anthropologists, cognitive neurobiologists, economic sociologists, social psychologists, organizational behaviorists, behavioral economists, and all sorts of other decision scientists have made productive careers poking holes into the basic principles governing economics. Daniel Kahneman and Vernon Smith have shared the Nobel Prize in Economics for developing psychological insights and laboratory experiments, which they and others have used to show why people eat too much, donate too few organs, and save too little for retirement.[4] We can use these insights to show why people get plastic bags at the checkout counter and don't buy more fuel-efficient bulbs, cars, and appliances even if it's in all our economic self-interest to do so.

These same disciplines have also developed important and often strikingly simple solutions. Reposition veggies in the cafeteria, and more people will eat them. Make organ donations and retirement savings the default option, and people will donate and save more, even though they are perfectly free to opt out. Charge pennies for plastic bags at the register, and shoppers will bring their own canvas bags. We ignore potentials for these nudges at our peril.

Yet, nudges have their limits. Strategically positioning vegetables in the cafeteria does wonders for your rear end, but it does not explain the obesity epidemic. That's where the bottom line comes in. Americans are obese not because they can't find their veggies. A whole host of factors contribute to entire generations eating themselves into diabetics, but the single most significant factor for why Americans have ballooned over decades is cheap, processed food.[5] One of the best economic studies on the U.S. obesity epidemic shows just that. Lower prices mean people consume more. That's not necessarily bad. In theory, cheaper food could also mean that we have more money left over for other things. Alas, people don't tend to think about their retirement savings when they see a cheap McDonald's burger. They just stuff themselves with more burgers.

Overeating is no different from overfishing or overpolluting. We catch too many fish because their price in the ocean is essentially zero. We pollute too much because the atmosphere serves as a free Dumpster.

It's boring. It's obvious. It's old news. No one will win a Nobel Prize for that discovery. The one economist credited with coming up with the idea, Arthur Pigou, died a decade before the prize was first given out.

Yet after all these years, we still have not implemented his ideas. It's not just boring and old news. It's also difficult. Much more difficult than fiddling with nudges and other psychological tricks to get us to do things we should have been doing all along. These nudges will be crucial to make the system work, but first we ought to have a system or at least a goal. That system revolves around setting up a market that makes people pay for pollution and makes pollution reduction pay for people. The price we pay for our private actions needs to reflect the now largely socialized costs of those actions. Even myopic car buyers seemingly unaware of the full energy savings a more efficient vehicle would provide seem to stick to this basic mantra over 60 percent of the time. They spend sixty cents on more fuel-efficient cars for every dollar in fuel savings later. Psychologists and sociologists can help get us to 80 or perhaps even close to 100, but that's all based on having the right incentives in place to first get from 0 to 60.

Moreover, psychologists, sociologists, and a stable of other decision scientists can help explain "What's the matter with Kansas?"—why politics has yet to get us to 60 in the first place. And they can help us try to get there by finding ways to convince the heretofore unconvincible. We need all the tools imaginable as well as those social scientists who can better understand the minds and behaviors unseen to economists. But once again, the goal itself is no secret: it's getting from 0 to 60; it's putting the necessary guideposts in place that help us rechannel market forces—to internalize those externalities.

Greg Mankiw is arguing for exactly that. He clearly understands the basic economics, and he clearly believes in well-functioning markets. Markets can't function well when the largest costs are socialized. Mankiw calls for a carbon tax—a "Pigovian tax" in honor of Arthur Pigou—to privatize these costs and no longer shove them onto everyone else, because he says it will be simpler.

Simple is good, and green tax reform—decrease labor taxes and increase environmental taxes—would be terrific. But of course, the U.S. tax code has seventeen thousand pages for a reason. A tax in reality wouldn't be quite as simple as one drawn up on paper, and in the end what really matters is the limit on pollution. That's where cap and trade comes in.

LIMITING POLLUTION TO FREE MARKETS

Libertarians put individual freedom above all else. If you sell a kidney, hire a surrogate mother, or enjoy consensual cannibalism, it will be no one else's business. If I choose not to wear a helmet when riding a bicycle, feel free to call me suicidal. That's your right. But don't tell me to wear one. That would infringe on my personal freedoms.

Taken to its extreme, libertarianism equates taxes—any taxes—with slavery. Giving up a third of my income to pay for roads and national defense is akin to spending a third of my working hours fixing roads and fighting in wars. That's slavery. Mailing in my tax payment on April 15 might not be as dangerous as actually serving in the military, but the principle still stands. And there's little wrong with the principle. My body, my life, my decision.

Utilitarianism sits on the opposite end of the spectrum: the greatest good for the greatest number of people. At the height of his decade-long reign as the richest man on the planet, Bill Gates owned more than $50 billion. Forcing him to give up $1 million to spread the wealth around would make thousands of people happier, and Gates would not even have noticed the missing million. He has 50,000 millions more where that came from. And he may even be happier himself, knowing that he made others happy without noticing the difference in his own pocketbook. That, in fact, seems to be how Gates himself sees it. He supports higher taxes for the rich and is giving away much of his own wealth voluntarily.

Economists are of two minds when looking at these extreme positions. Philosophically, libertarianism appeals to many, me included. What's not to like about wanting everyone to have full dominion over his or her body? Free markets are largely based on the philosophy. Yet much of economics is also grounded in utilitarianism: grow the overall pie; get to a place where we can't make anyone better off without cutting into the pie for everyone else; maximize well-being.

Well-being, however, means different things to different people. Environmentalists tend to be more holistic in their thinking. Birds have feelings, too, they'd argue. Most economists have a much narrower definition. First, their focus is on humans. More important, well-being often gets equated with economic output, GDP. That's where we are back in chapter 1 and the debates around green accounting, putting dollar values on the environment to make nature count. You can't see what you can't measure. Or, in this case, you can't maximize what you don't quantify. Even Simon Kuznets, the father of GDP, has warned that it's inadequate as a measure of overall well-being. Yet that's exactly what we are using it for.

Environmentalists as a group are much closer to the utilitarian school of thought. Free markets, after all, are destroying our environment. When avowed libertarian Rand Paul captured a Senate seat from Kentucky in November 2010 running on the Republican ticket, the faux pundit Stephen Colbert declared that Kentucky's state bird would now be a can of lead paint—once Paul manages to dismantle all existing environmental regulations.

Rand Paul's logic around free markets and no government regulation of any kind quickly leads to real absurdities. Holding personal freedom as a good to be treasured above all others is well and good, but few would be prepared to live with the consequences. Having the freedom not to wear a helmet or seat belt is one thing. Be my guest, kill yourself. But what if your not buckling up means your ejected body endangers others? Or when your not wearing a helmet makes the job of rescue personnel that much harder? There's a cost to everyone around you when you drive past without a seat belt.

The same goes for pollution. Socializing costs of private actions is the exact opposite of what libertarians would want to do, but that's what the market does, when left entirely on its own. So yes, by all means, make your own decisions about how much you would like to drive, fly, and pollute, but be prepared to pay every last dime of the consequences. That's all I'm asking for. It doesn't get much more libertarian than that.

A LICENSE TO SAVE THE PLANET

The other end of the spectrum counters all of this free-market talk by saying that cap and trade provides a license to pollute. It does. You get a piece of paper that says you are allowed to emit one ton of carbon dioxide. Call it what you want. In the end, it gives you a permission slip to pollute.

The political philosopher Michael Sandel makes this argument forcefully: "Turning pollution into a commodity to be bought and sold removes the moral stigma that is properly associated with it."[6] He argues that fines for pollution are okay; fees are a different matter altogether.

From a moral perspective that's all well and good. Too bad it doesn't get us anywhere. Sandel made this argument most prominently in a *New York Times* Op-Ed under the heading "It's Immoral to Buy the Right to Pollute." That was in December 1997, shortly after the Kyoto climate conference that brought us the Kyoto Protocol. The same crowd has since reconvened at least once a year: in Buenos Aires in 1998, Bonn in 1999, The Hague in 2000, Bonn and Marrakech in 2001, New Delhi in 2002, Milan in 2003, Buenos Aires in 2004, Montreal in 2005, Nairobi in 2006, Bali in 2007, Poznan in 2008, Copenhagen in 2009, Cancún in 2010 . . . The moral case for action has been getting stronger every year. At the same time, the climate has been getting more and more out of whack. And the prospects of strong, global action based on moral persuasion have been fading all along.

So, by all means, make the moral case. Teach it in philosophy classes and preach it from the pulpits, but let's not wait for it to have an impact while the planet burns. A loud and clear "told you so" won't do anyone any good.

Eventually, in fifty years perhaps, hopefully much sooner, carbon pollution will go the way of child labor or slavery. It would be possible to make purely economic arguments that child labor ought to be allowed, yet not even the bête noire of left-wing activists, the World Trade Organization, would touch these arguments. There has not been a single challenge in front of the WTO on whether barring child labor constitutes uncompetitive behavior.[7] Nations debate where the cutoff should be, and there are plenty of violations of both anti–child labor and anti-slavery laws all around the world. Economics—"keep kids in school so they can be more productive later in life"—has nothing to do with this. In the end, it's a moral issue. Child labor and slavery are things not to be done.

We need to work hard to achieve such a shift. Carbon pollution, overfishing, and all these other exploitative behaviors that are bringing the planet to the brink ought to go the way of child labor laws and slavery. Some European countries are much further along than the United States toward realizing this end. Pollution is immoral. Recycling is good.

But Europe hasn't managed to limit its carbon emissions from the power sector by preaching alone. Moralizing may have caused it to take the appropriate steps, but it was not until Brussels put the right incentives in place that emissions started to decline. Europe's cap-and-trade system limits carbon emissions by law. It's the power of incentives at work: economics, not morals.

Your pollution is a tiny, ignorable portion of the global total. Everyone else is in the same but-one-in-seven-billion boat. Most of us reading these words are in the but-one-in-one-billion-high-emitters category, and still our personal actions won't tip the scale.

By all means, de-clutter your life. Move to the city and, once there, downsize your apartment. Carry around a canvas bag. Bike. You'll be that much better prepared when everyone else catches up to your good deeds. But everyone else won't catch up to your good deeds voluntarily— not in time, and not with sufficiently strong action.

That's where economics enters the room. There's simply no way to go about tackling this problem other than taking seriously the incentives all of us face. Getting several billion of us to behave differently—to behave morally—means guiding market forces in the right direction, making it in our interest to do the right thing. It's the only way to make the planet notice.

FINE PRINT

Welcome, scholar. Notes galore for anyone seriously interested in a particular topic discussed in the main text. As a general rule, if you can find a reference for something mentioned in the text simply by typing it into Google, you probably will not find it here. Similarly, if I first found a fact on *Wikipedia* and only later verified it by clicking through to the one source mentioned in the *Wiki* entry, I won't cite that either. That's just embarrassing. You will find the occasional technical explanation, additional nuance, or further references beyond what's in the text.

DOING GOOD

1. *The Validity of Food Miles as an Indicator of Sustainable Development*, a report produced for the U.K.'s Department for Environment, Food, and Rural Affairs (Defra), provides a comprehensive analysis and questions the use of food miles as a valid indicator. Sarah Murray's *Moveable Feasts* (St. Martin's Press, 2007) is a terrific guide to where our food comes from. For the specific flower example, see Patrick Foster, "Why Roses from Kenya Are Greener Than the Flowers from Amsterdam," *Times* (London), February 10, 2007. For another striking comparison, see Ben Webster, "Tofu Can Harm Environment More Than Meat, Finds WWF Study," *Times* (London), February 12, 2010.

2. Calculate your own carbon footprint at http://www.terrapass.com/carbon-footprint -calculator or plenty of other tools like it.

3. The technical term for shipping pollution overseas is "pollution haven effect." We will encounter it and the associated "pollution haven hypothesis" in chapter 9 on the global dimension of the problem. Both are different from the simple accounting exercise that says that the United States is importing on the order of 10 million barrels of oil per day directly, and that it is also importing 2.5 million barrels of oil-equivalent energy per day embedded in imported manufacturing goods. This accounts for the energy required for producing the goods; it does not yet include energy used for transport. (I crunched these numbers in "Energy Content of World Trade," *Energy Policy* 38, no. 12 [2010].)

4. The Yale economist Matthew Kotchen provides a wealth of examples in "The Good, the Bad, and the Reality of Voluntary Environmental Offsets" (paper presented at the Environmental Defense Fund Climate Economics Seminar, May 6, 2010).

5. Karen Ehrhardt-Martinez and John A. "Skip" Laitner survey the latest studies to arrive at the 10–30 percent rebound figure for consumers ("Rebound, Technology and People: Mitigating the Rebound Effect with Energy-Resource Management and People-Centered Initiatives," ACEEE Summer Study on Energy Efficiency in Buildings [2010]).

6. Columbia University's Center for Research on Environmental Decisions has a terrific guide related to the psychology of climate change communication and cautions about the single-action bias (http://www.cred.columbia.edu/guide/guide/ sec4.html). See also Nate Silver's hypothesis in "When Hope Is the Enemy of Change," *FiveThirtyEight*, April 22, 2009. Psychological effects may go even further, with green consumers possibly being less trustworthy due to a "moral license effect"; see "Are 'Green' Consumers Less Trustworthy?" *Green* (blog), *New York Times*, March 17, 2010.

7. According to an analysis of state data by Jason Deparle and Robert Gebeloff, "Living on Nothing but Food Stamps," *New York Times*, January 3, 2010, approximately six million Americans receiving food stamps report they have no other income or cash aid.

8. The CIA's *World Factbook* (2009) ranks the United States forty-ninth in the world for life expectancy at 78.1 years. Cubans' life expectancy in 2009 was 77.5 years, only six ranks behind the United States. Several studies cite rising levels of obesity as a reason for recent declines in U.S. life expectancy. See S. Jay Olshansky et al., "A Potential Decline in Life Expectancy in the United States in the 21st Century," *New England Journal of Medicine*, March 17, 2005; and Susan T. Steward et al., "Forecasting the Effects of Obesity and Smoking on U.S. Life Expectancy," *New England Journal of Medicine*, December 3, 2009. For a general

argument for why wealthier means healthier, see Lant Pritchett and Lawrence Summers, "Wealthier Is Healthier" (Policy Research Working Paper 1150, World Bank, 1993). For a more recent debate and some nuance, see "Healthier or Wealthier? Which Comes First in the New Global Era" (debate, Harvard Institute of Politics, February 25, 2002). Robert W. Fogel, Roderick Floud, Bernard Harris, and Sok Chul Hong provide one of the most comprehensive accounts in *The Changing Body: Health, Nutrition, and Human Development in the Western World Since 1700* (Cambridge University Press, 2011).

9. Between 250 million and 1 billion are predicted to be displaced by climate change by 2050. See Craig Johnstone, United Nations Deputy High Commissioner for Refugees: "Climate Change Future Is Now" (2008); and IPCC, *Climate Change 2007: The Physical Science Basis: Contribution of Working Group I to the Fourth Assessment Report of the Intergovernmental Panel on Climate Change* (Cambridge University Press, 2007).

10. If you read one book on the science of our changing climate, read Elizabeth Kolbert's *Field Notes from a Catastrophe* (Bloomsbury, 2006). It's the most beautifully written and most comprehensive account. If you are looking for a second, have your pick among several others. Heidi Cullen's *Weather of the Future* (HarperCollins, 2010) talks about future predictions and current realities. Tim Flannery's *Weather Makers* (Grove Press, 2006) combines well-researched science with beautiful prose to tell the history and future impact of a changing climate. Ross Gelbspan's *The Heat Is On* (Perseus Books, 1997) is one of the first; his *Boiling Point* (Basic Books, 2004) is one of the best. Mark Lynas's *Six Degrees* (National Geographic, 2008) lists degree by degree what impacts to expect and how they will affect us all. Bill McKibben's books are too numerous to list here. His 1989 book, *The End of Nature*, is a classic. Al Gore's *Earth in the Balance* (Houghton Mifflin, 1992) is similarly iconic, and *An Inconvenient Truth* (2006) earned him an Oscar and ultimately led to him sharing the Nobel Peace Prize with the Intergovernmental Panel on Climate Change (IPCC) in 2007. Mark Hertsgaard's *Hot* (2011) both raises the alarm and provides a clearheaded way forward. Carl Safina's *View from Lazy Point* (Henry Holt, 2011) provides another beautiful and disturbing account of our changing world. The late Steve Schneider was one of the scientists sharing the Nobel Prize as a member of the IPCC. His book *Science as a Contact Sport* (National Geographic, 2009), part scientific treatise, part autobiography, provides an enjoyable firsthand account from the climate science trenches. Similarly, I will not delve too deeply into the science of overfishing and other large-scale environmental issues. Plenty of writings exist on these problems. Again, start with Elizabeth Kolbert and her essays in *The New Yorker*. A notable book on overfishing is Paul Greenberg's *Four Fish: The Future of the Last Wild Food* (Penguin, 2010).

11. One of the latest reviews of climate science, conducted by the U.S. National Academy of Sciences, summarizes the scientific case as such: "From a philosophical perspective, science never proves anything—in the manner that mathematics or other formal logical systems prove things—because science is fundamentally based on observations. Any scientific theory is thus, in principle, subject to being refined or overturned by new observations. In practical terms, however, scientific uncertainties are not all the same. Some scientific conclusions or theories have been so thoroughly examined and tested, and supported by so many independent observations and results, that their likelihood of subsequently being found to be wrong is vanishingly small. Such conclusions and theories are then regarded as settled facts. This is the case for the conclusions that the Earth system is warming and that much of this warming is very likely due to human activities." See http://americasclimatechoices.org.

12. The Intergovernmental Panel on Climate Change's *Fourth Assessment Report* said that "summer sea-ice is projected to disappear almost completely towards the end of the 21st century." The latest observations point to a total loss of Arctic summer sea ice possibly before 2020; see the Public Interest Research Centre's 2008 report *Climate Safety*.

13. If you doubt my calling out Obama for dropping the f-bomb, see "Hackers and Spending Sprees," *Newsweek* web exclusive, November 5, 2008.

1: CUE THE ECONOMISTS

1. Daniel J. Weiss and Susan Lyon catalog oil industry profits, tax exemptions, and subsidies at http://www.americanprogress.org/issues/2010/04/without_a_gun.html and related articles.

2. The idea of a financial transaction tax dates back to John Maynard Keynes's *General Theory of Employment, Interest, and Money* (1936), where he proposes "a substantial government transfer tax on all transactions" because "it is usually agreed that casinos should, in the public interest, be inaccessible and expensive." James Tobin popularized a currency transaction tax in a lecture in 1978 ("A Proposal for International Monetary Reform"), arguing to "throw some sand in the well-greased wheels." The thread has been picked up by others, for example, Joseph Stiglitz, who argues for a broader financial transaction tax: "Using Tax Policy to Curb Speculative Short-Term Trading," *Journal of Financial Services Research* 3, nos. 2–3 (1989). Others have roundly criticized such tax proposals; see Stephen Ross, "Commentary: Using Tax Policy to Curb Speculative Short-Term Trading," *Journal of Financial Services Research* 3, nos. 2–3 (1989). I am with Keynes, Tobin, and Stiglitz on this one.

3. Oil Pollution Act of 1990, H.R. 1465. There has been much chatter in light of the BP Gulf oil spill disaster to raise the limit—alas, no such luck by the time this goes to press over a year later.

4. Jon Krosnick, "The Climate Majority," *New York Times*, Op-Ed, June 8, 2010. Other polls show greater American skepticism and, in particular, demonstrate a polarization along party lines: Democrats agree with the science; Republicans don't. Anthony Leiserowitz et al. have done careful polling, which they presented in "Global Warming's Six Americas" (2010); the attitudes range from "alarmed" to "cautious" and "disengaged" to "dismissive."

5. "Proposition 23: Backers Were Outspent, Out-organized," *Los Angeles Times, Greenspace* (blog), November 2, 2010.

6. His speech can be found at http://www.glaserfoundation.org/program_areas/ measuring_progress.asp. Kennedy, of course, was not the first. Simon Kuznets is commonly acknowledged as the father of GDP and won a Nobel Prize for his work. He has also acknowledged its shortcomings himself; see his "How to Judge Quality," *New Republic*, October 20, 1962. The latest review of GDP came from the Stiglitz-Sen-Fitoussi commission; see Joseph Stiglitz, Amartya Sen, and Jean-Paul Fitoussi, *Report by the Commission on the Measurement of Economic Performance and Social Progress*. Jon Gertner provides an accessible review of the topic in "The Rise and Fall of the GDP," *New York Times Magazine*, May 16, 2010.

7. Technically, most economists talk about GNP, gross national product, or, as it's officially known, gross national income, but GDP is the more accepted term. The distinction is largely unimportant here.

8. Ray Fair has written several influential papers on this topic, for example, "Econometrics and Presidential Elections," *Journal of Economic Perspectives* 10, no. 3 (1996).

9. Robert Repetto et al., *Wasting Assets: Natural Resources in the National Income Accounts* (World Resources Institute, 1989).

10. For an introduction to green accounting, see "Measuring Our Worth," a story I produced for National Public Radio's environmental news show *Living on Earth*, aired on April 9, 2004. Graham Davis from the Colorado School of Mines supplied the numbers for the NPR story, and he helped me update them here, reflecting a change in coal prices.

11. Larry Summers's paper—or at least this phrase—remains unpublished to this day. Several independent sources, however, confirm it. Among them is Justin Fox's *Myth of the Rational Market: A History of Risk, Reward, and Delusion on Wall Street* (Harper Business, 2009), which independently of the quotation is a good summary of the issues.

12. Martin Weitzman's *Share Economy* (Harvard University Press, 1984) argues that both the average worker and the overall economy would be better under a model where a significant portion of every worker's wage was directly linked to his or her company's performance. The *New York Times* editorial "The Best Idea Since Keynes," March 28, 1985, argues how such a system would change attitudes toward performance and hiring and shield employees against unemployment. Stock option schemes for managers and frequently also some employees represent a partial implementation of this idea. Weitzman's idea has sparked a rich academic debate. His so far final contribution on the issue is "Incentive Effects of Profit Sharing and Employee Share Ownership: Theory and Evidence," in *Trends in Business Organization*, edited by Horst Siebert (Tübingen: J. C. B. Mohr, 1995).

13. The Centers for Disease Control's *National Health Statistics Report* catalogs average height, weight, and other vital statistics. Height data here are from a survey conducted in the United States between 2003 and 2006.

14. David Warsh has the story on the always prescient *Economic Principals* blog: "The Flash Crash: A Cautionary Tale," October 3, 2010.

15. Even fat tails go to zero eventually, but they do so infinitely slower than normal distributions. That's the technical property that matters here: the ratio of a fat-tailed to a thin-tailed probability is infinity. It's not that hundred- or thousand-foot women are "likely." Technically, what distinguishes fat tails from the rest is that infinitely tall women are infinitely more likely.

16. Weitzman's latest papers include "Some Basic Economics of Extreme Climate Change" (February 19, 2009); "Reactions to the Nordhaus Critique" (March 17, 2009); "What Is the 'Damages Function' for Global Warming—and What Difference Might It Make?" (July 30, 2009); "Additive Damages, Fat-Tailed Climate Dynamics, and Uncertain Discounting" (August 1, 2009); "The Extreme Uncertainty of Extreme Climate Change: An Overview and Some Implications" (October 20, 2009); and "GHG Targets as Insurance Against Catastrophic Climate Damages" (June 3, 2010).

17. Cognitive dissonance ensures that the most comfortable thoughts and feelings prevail. It goes back to Leon Festinger's *Theory of Cognitive Dissonance* (1957). George Akerlof and William Dickens introduced the idea to economists with "The Economic Consequences of Cognitive Dissonance," *American Economic Review* 72, no. 3 (1982). I summarize this and other psychological problems with Richard Zeckhauser in "Climate Policy: Hard Problem, Soft Thinking" (*Climatic Change*, 2011). Carol Tavris and Elliot Aronson wrote the accessible version: *Mistakes Were Made (But Not by Me)* (Houghton Mifflin Harcourt, 2007).

18. Martin Weitzman's paper is titled "GHG Targets as Insurance Against Catastrophic Climate Damages" (June 3, 2010). The original source is Steven Sher-

wood and Matthew Huber, "An Adaptability Limit to Climate Change Due to Heat Stress," *Proceedings of the National Academy of Sciences* (2010).

19. Wolfram Schlenker and Michael Roberts, "Nonlinear Temperature Effects Indicate Severe Damages to U.S. Crop Yields Under Climate Change," *Proceedings of the National Academy of Sciences* (2009). Schlenker, Roberts, and others have published many more papers on this and similar topics.

20. Solomon M. Hsiang, "Temperatures and Cyclones Strongly Associated with Economic Production in the Caribbean and Central America," *Proceedings of the National Academy of Sciences* (2010). Hsiang also cites several further studies that consistently show productivity decreases with higher-than-usual temperatures.

21. Jean-Marie Robine et al., "Death Toll Exceeded 70,000 in Europe During the Summer of 2003," *Comptes Rendus Biologies* 331, no. 2 (2008).

22. Weitzman goes as far as to avoid citing his earlier estimates of a 5 percent chance of warming greater than 18°F (10°C) and a 1 percent chance of warming greater than 36°F (20°C) in his latest papers. He still calls the calculations correct but says, "The numbers come out so shocking that I wish I hadn't made this part so prominent—because it deflects attention from the main message [around the importance of fat tails] which is unnerving enough as is." That clearly speaks to his intellectual rigor and desire to avoid appearing too alarmist. However, alarmist may well be the appropriate attitude right about now.

23. Weitzman also was not the last. He has spawned an entire cottage industry of economists trying to make sense of extreme climate events. MIT's Robert Pindyck took his role as official discussant of Weitzman's presentation at a 2008 National Bureau of Economic Research summer conference particularly to heart. He experimented with different functional forms and concluded that taking extreme events seriously would justify spending anywhere between 1 and 6 percent of global GDP as insurance. He has since narrowed the range to 2 to 3 percent; see "Uncertain Outcomes and Climate Change Policy" (NBER Working Paper 15259, 2009). Gary Yohe and Richard Tol have argued a bit provocatively that Weitzman's results merit their own label: "Warning: Not to be taken to its logical extreme in application to real world problems"; see "Precaution and a Dismal Theorem: Implications for Climate Policy and Climate Research" (2007). Resources for the Future's Carolyn Kousky and Roger Cooke have taken Weitzman's prescriptions one step further and argue that there are three important implications of extreme events for climate policy: "The Unholy Trinity: Fat Tails, Tail Dependence, and Micro-correlations" (2009). In the realm of financial markets, Joseph Stiglitz has argued most forcefully that "the crisis was predictable and was predicted, and largely the result of deregulation and problems of corporate governance in the banking system." His *Freefall* (Norton, 2010) provides a

book-length account of that argument. Yale's Robert Shiller spells out some of the reasons in more detail in his short but authoritative account *The Subprime Solution* (Princeton University Press, 2008). *n+1's Diary of a Very Bad Year: Confessions of an Anonymous Hedge Fund Manager* (Harper Perennial, 2010) provides an insider's account.

24. Buffett's earthquake deal is less risky than most of his ordinary stock dealings. To be sure, Buffett's bet on the California earthquake insurance actually contradicts Nassim Nicholas Taleb's advice. Buffett bet that the earthquake would not happen. Taleb advises to never underestimate the chance of extreme events. The genius of Buffett's calculation is that he sees even the most extreme risk, a payout of "no more than $600 million," as imminently manageable: "less than 3% of our book value and 1.5% of our market value. To gain some perspective on this exposure . . . note the much greater volatility that security markets have delivered us."

25. Roger Lowenstein's *When Genius Failed* (Random House, 2000) tells the amazing story of John Meriwether and his partners' misguided attempts to rely on computer models of risk to explain inherently uncertain situations. Many books have been written about the global financial crisis. Andrew Ross Sorkin's *Too Big to Fail* (Viking, 2009) is the most comprehensive. John Cassidy's *How Markets Fail* (Farrar, Straus and Giroux, 2009) provides a sobering look at the role of misguided economic theories. Carmen Reinhart and Kenneth Rogoff's *This Time Is Different* (Princeton University Press, 2009) takes a long-term view of financial crises over eight hundred years, disproving the statement in its title: this time may not have been all that different after all. Bethany McLean and Joe Nocera's *All the Devils Are Here: The Hidden History of the Financial Crisis* (Portfolio/Penguin, 2010) assigns blame where blame is due. Raghuram Rajan's *Fault Lines: How Hidden Fractures Still Threaten the World Economy* (Princeton University Press, 2010) is a must-read for anyone wanting to understand the underlying causes. Robert Pozen's *Too Big to Save? How to Fix the U.S. Financial System* (Wiley, 2009) is a must-read for any would-be reformer.

26. *The Wall Street Journal* cites the $3 trillion number. Bloomberg's tally comes in at $13 trillion. *The New York Times* reports about the additional $1 trillion European bailout in 2010.

27. A handful of books discuss geoengineering in eloquent detail: Jeff Goodell's *How to Cool the Planet: Geoengineering and the Audacious Quest to Fix Earth's Climate* (Houghton Mifflin Harcourt, 2010); Eli Kintisch's *Hack the Planet: Science's Best Hope—or Worst Nightmare—for Averting Climate Catastrophe* (Wiley, 2010).

2: DOING NOTHING

1. A half ton of carbon dioxide emissions per year allows the bare minimum for cooking, transport, and electricity: one liquefied petroleum gas canister per month, around forty miles of travel by bus or motorbike, and around eight hundred kilowatt-hours of electricity *per year*. Those are direct emissions. Double it to account for indirect emissions embedded in foods, clothes, and other products. Massimo Tavoni and Shoibal Chakravarty collected these figures for a presentation titled "One Billion High Emitters: An Individual Perspective on Emissions and reductions" (Environmental Defense Fund, 2010).

2. For simplicity, this calculation only takes into account carbon dioxide emissions, which were at twenty-six billion tons globally in 2003, rather than all greenhouse gases. Data come from Shoibal Chakravarty, Ananth Chikkatur, Heleen de Coninck, Stephen Pacala, Robert Socolow, and Massimo Tavoni's "Sharing Global CO_2 Emission Reductions Among One Billion High Emitters," *Proceedings of the National Academy of Sciences* (2009); they have broken out the data by country and calculated per capita emissions. Emissions and population levels have gone up since 2003, but the orders of magnitudes are the same.

3. Total global greenhouse gas emissions need to decline to around twenty billion tons of carbon-dioxide-equivalent emissions by 2050 at the latest. See "Turn Toward Climate Safety" (Environmental Defense Fund, 2009), only one of hundreds of papers making that case.

4. The technical term for this process of putting value on nature is "contingent valuation," also commonly known as a "stated-preference" approach.

5. For those who do check appendixes, there is a subtle but important difference between *marginal* damages of one extra ton of carbon dioxide pollution released into the atmosphere and *average* damages of all tons already there. The $20 figure is the *marginal* damage. Hence it would be fine to add up numbers for a particular household and, to some approximation, even for Americans as a whole. We can't, however, add up marginal damages across all seven billion of us.

6. That number is based on several earlier academic estimates. Chief among the academics in that field is Bill Nordhaus, who started estimating the optimal carbon price in the early 1990s. In the 1994 iteration, that price was below $5 per ton of carbon dioxide for 2015. His numbers have increased ever since. They also get higher the more detailed the model. His latest Dynamic Integrated Model of Climate and the Economy (DICE) using one model for the world comes up with $12 per ton of carbon dioxide for 2015 (in 2009 dollars). His latest Regional Integrated Model of Climate and the Economy (RICE) estimates a price of $21 per ton of carbon dioxide for 2015, rising to above $50 by 2050 (in 2009 dollars). See "New Estimates of Efficient Approaches to the Control of Global Warming"

(Cowles Foundation Discussion Paper 1716, 2009) for a comparison of DICE and RICE models across the years, something Nordhaus himself calls "humbling."

7. I keep adding "in 2010" to these estimates because they, too, increase with time. Twenty dollars in 2010 grows to closer to $25 in 2015. By 2050, each ton of carbon dioxide released into the atmosphere will cost society around $45—once again with ranges attached to it, depending on how high we value our children and whether or not we consider the cost of surprise events. Add those, and the range for 2050 goes from a low of $15 to a high above $135 per ton.

8. The International Energy Agency estimates that global fossil fuel subsidies topped $500 billion in 2008. The Environmental Law Institute calculates fossil subsidies to the tune of $10 billion per year for the United States alone; see *Estimating U.S. Government Subsidies to Energy Sources: 2002–2008*.

3: ALL-OR-NOTHING CONSERVATION

1. For sticklers who insist that we start counting at 1 rather than 0, the decade, of course, ends with December 31, 1980. That lets two more acts sneak in, both with equally arcane official names and far-reaching implications: the Alaska National Interest Lands Conservation Act (1980), mostly known for pretty pictures of caribou and for barring drilling in the Arctic National Wildlife Refuge; and the Comprehensive Environmental Response, Compensation, and Liability Act (1980), a.k.a. Superfund.

2. Charles Wurster was intimately involved in banning DDT and wrote one of the first and still most authoritative histories: "The Decision to Ban DDT: A Case Study" (1975). Marion Lane Rogers retells the story of the founding of EDF in conjunction with the DDT case in *Acorn Days: The Environmental Defense Fund and How It Grew* (Environmental Defense Fund, 1990).

3. The Cornell Lab of Ornithology spearheaded the latest search effort (http://www.birds.cornell.edu/ivory/), which continued from 2004 through 2010. Jack Hitt summarized the search in a *New York Times Magazine* article, "13 Ways of Looking at an Ivory-Billed Woodpecker," May 7, 2006. The American Birding Association classifies the bird as "definitely or probably extinct." David Sibley has a drawing but does not include it in his published birding guide. He calls the bird "extremely rare, presumed extinct" and summarizes the history of the latest search efforts and his thoughts at http://www.sibleyguides.com/bird-info/ivory-billed-woodpecker/.

4. Stuart L. Pimm et al. provide a seminal survey in "The Future of Biodiversity," *Science*, July 21, 1995, estimating number of species and rates of extinction.

5. Martin Weitzman's first foray into species conservation came with "On Diver-

sity," *Quarterly Journal of Economics* 107, no. 2 (1992), followed by "What to Preserve? An Application of Diversity Theory to Crane Conservation," *Quarterly Journal of Economics* 108, no. 1 (1993).

6. Dean Lueck and Jeffrey A. Michael, "Preemptive Habitat Destruction Under the Endangered Species Act," *Journal of Law and Economics* 46, no. 1 (2003), and Daowei Zhang, "Endangered Species and Timber Harvesting: The Case of Red-Cockaded Woodpeckers," *Economic Inquiry* 42, no. 1 (2004), study the red-cockaded woodpecker's case in detail. Jonathan Adler retells the story in *Resources Magazine*, August 4, 2008; and Stephen J. Dubner and Steven D. Levitt popularize it in their Freakonomics column "Unintended Consequences," *New York Times*, January 20, 2008. Lueck and Michael compile estimates from various sources to show that a single woodpecker colony occupying two hundred acres of mature pine forest results in forgone timber harvest of between $30,000 and $200,000.

7. John List, Michael Margolis, and Daniel Osgood, "Is the Endangered Species Act Endangering Species?" (NBER Working Paper W12777, 2006).

8. Dale D. Goble, J. Michael Scott, and Frank W. Davis, eds., *The Endangered Species Act at Thirty* (Island Press, 2005).

9. The U.S. Fish and Wildlife Service Endangered Species Program provides the latest tally of listed as well as delisted species at http://www.fws.gov/endangered/.

10. See James Grier, "Ban of DDT and Subsequent Recovery of Reproduction in Bald Eagles," *Science*, December 17, 1982.

11. The Centers for Disease Control retells some of the history of malaria eradication in the United States (http://www.cdc.gov/malaria/history/index.htm). Internationally, DDT is still used to combat malaria. The World Health Organization has never banned it outright, although it did discourage its use in the past. A 2006 decision reinstated DDT as an important component in the fight against malaria, as long as it would be used for "indoor residual spraying." See http://malaria.who.int/docs/IRS-position.pdf for the WHO decision. A *New York Times* article explains the decision: "WHO Supports Wider Use of DDT vs. Malaria," September 16, 2006.

12. Weitzman isn't alone here. Katrina Wyman presents some stark implications in "Rethinking the ESA to Reflect Human Dominion over Nature" (New York University Law and Economics Research Paper Series, 2009). Wyman also cites Norman Myers et al., "Biodiversity Hotspots for Conservation Priorities," *Nature*, February 24, 2000, who calculate that 1.4 percent of the earth's land, split across twenty-five biodiversity hotspots, harbors "44% of all plant species" and 35 percent of all vertebrates. See note 5, page 226, for references to Martin Weitzman's work on diversity.

13. The technical term for these kinds of arrangements is "conservation banking"

(http://www.fws.gov/endangered/factsheets/conservation_banking.pdf). In the
Fort Hood case, the arrangement goes under the heading: "recovery credit system."

14. Short of outright trading, another system employed by the Department of the
Interior is the so-called safe-harbor agreements. Landowners enter into agreements with the department to protect species on their land and, in exchange, are
spared from legal challenges. This system, pioneered by Michael Bean while an
attorney at the Environmental Defense Fund, is employed on millions of acres
across the United States and adds a bit of flexibility and regulatory certainty to
the Endangered Species Act.

4: FEWER FISH, MORE DOUGH

1. The original *Science* article discussed in the next paragraph of the text barely
mentioned "2048," making sure to present it as an extrapolation of current
trends rather than a prediction; see Boris Worm et al., "Impacts of Biodiversity
Loss on Ocean Ecosystem Services," *Science*, November 3, 2006. Nevertheless,
several articles appeared around the time, mentioning the date: "World's Fish
Supply Running Out, Researchers Warn," *Washington Post*, November 3, 2006;
"Sayonara, Sushi . . . ," *Nature*, November 2, 2006; "Seafood May Be Gone by
2048, Study Says," *National Geographic News*, November 2, 2006. That coverage
has continued, in parts, for years: "'An Inconvenient Truth' for Fish," *Daily Beast*,
June 17, 2009.

2. Shrimp caught in the ocean get an "eco-best" or at least "eco-ok" designation in
the Environmental Defense Fund's Seafood Selector. Imported, farmed shrimp
fare much worse.

3. Food and Agriculture Organization (FAO) data show that the average person on
the planet consumed twenty-eight grams of fish and fishery products per day in
2002, up from seventeen grams in 1961 (http://earthtrends.wri.org). Citizens of
developing countries increased their consumption from nine to twenty-three
grams in the same period. Developed countries easily top that with forty-seven
grams consumed per person per day in 2002.

4. Exceptions prove the rule. Linda Greenlaw wrote *The Lobster Chronicles* (Hyperion, 2002), a compelling memoir of "life on a very small island," about her experience as a female lobsterperson in the local Lobstermen's Association.

5. James Acheson's *Lobster Gangs of Maine* (University Press of New England,
1988) and *Capturing the Commons* (University Press of New England, 2003) have
good histories of lobster fishing in New England. The first is a mystery novel
only insofar as some of the implications are concerned. It is, in fact, a serious schol-
arly book—with charts, tables, endnotes, and an appendix titled "Economic and

Biological Benefits of Territoriality." Greenlaw's *Lobster Chronicles* adds some more color. Dick Allen's site www.lobsterconservation.com provides terrific information.

6. Aristotle, *Politics* 2.

7. Thomas Friedman attributes the car quotation to Larry Summers in *Longitudes and Attitudes: The World in the Age of Terrorism* (Anchor Books, 2003). Others credit motivational speaker Stephen Covey, who has been cited as saying, "No one washes a rented car"; see Ralph Keyes, *The Quote Verifier* (St. Martin's Press, 2006). The original probably goes back much further, although we can safely exclude Aristotle from that list.

8. Garrett Hardin, "The Tragedy of the Commons," *Science*, December 13, 1968. Hardin wrote a follow-up piece thirty years later: "Extensions of 'The Tragedy of the Commons,'" *Science*, May 1, 1998.

9. Elinor Ostrom's *Governing the Commons* (Cambridge University Press, 1990) provides the seminal introduction and, in many ways, also culmination of her research. Her "Beyond Markets and States: Polycentric Governance of Complex Systems," *American Economic Review* 100, no. 3 (2010), is a more recent treatment.

10. Robert O. Keohane and Elinor Ostrom edited *Local Commons and Global Interdependence: Heterogeneity and Cooperation in Two Domains* (Sage, 1995), an eclectic mix of scholars studying local commons problems and international relations scholars. An important previous compendium is *Institutions for the Earth*, edited by Peter Haas, Robert O. Keohane, and Marc Levy (MIT Press, 1993). Scott Barrett's *Why Cooperate? The Incentive to Supply Global Public Goods* (Oxford University Press, 2007) provides a highly readable, more recent treatise.

11. Paragraph 23 of the Magna Carta decrees that all inland fish weirs in England be dismantled. Also see Richard Hoffman, "Economic Development and Aquatic Ecosystems in Medieval Europe," *American Historical Review* 101, no. 3 (1996).

12. Suzanne Iudicello, Michael Weber, and Robert Wieland's *Fish, Markets, and Fishermen* (Island Press, 1999) provides an accessible introduction to "the economics of overfishing," which also happens to be the book's subtitle.

13. Several good studies detail this case. One is Elisia Barlow and Andrew Bakker, "Managing Alaska's Halibut: Observations from the Fishery." Also see http://www.edf.org/page.cfm?tagid=48874 for a good overview.

14. Christopher Costello, Steven D. Gaines, and John Lynham cite the sobering collapse statistics and show the power of catch shares in "Can Catch Shares Prevent Fisheries Collapse?" *Science*, September 19, 2008.

5: CURIOUS COMPANY KEPT

1. Richard Newell and Kristian Rogers analyze the lead market in "The Market-Based Lead Phasedown" (RFF Discussion Paper 03-37, 2003). Herbert Needleman reviews the science and politics of the phaseout in "The Removal of Lead from Gasoline: Historical and Personal Reflections," *Environmental Research* 84, no. 1 (2000). David Harrison surveys the policy landscape in "Tradable Permits for Air Pollution Control: The United States Experience" (NERA working paper, 1998).

2. Eric Pooley's *Climate War: True Believers, Power Brokers, and the Fight to Save the Earth* (Hyperion, 2010) provides a terrific journalistic account of this and many other steps in the early environmental history that eventually led to the political fights around climate policy.

3. For a thorough comparison of U.S. and EU environmental laws, pick up a copy of Winston Harrington, Richard Morgenstern, and Thomas Sterner, eds., *Choosing Environmental Policy: Comparing Instruments and Outcomes in the United States and Europe* (RFF Press, 2004).

4. Once again, Pooley's *Climate War* has the best account of the events.

5. A. Denny Ellerman, Frank Convery, and Christian de Perthuis produced the most comprehensive account of the EU's trading system to date: *Pricing Carbon: The European Union Emissions Trading Scheme* (Cambridge University Press, 2010).

6. In theory, you would, in fact, get the exact same outcome if there were no transaction costs involved. With these costs, distributional issues do matter, but they are at best a second-order phenomenon.

7. The U.K.-based NGO Sandbag has produced some good reports on the allocation mechanism and resulting overallocation of allowances in the EU. Again, though, for the most comprehensive look at the EU's emissions-trading system, read Ellerman, Convery, and de Perthuis's *Pricing Carbon*.

8. Thomas Sterner and Gunnar Köhlin's "Environmental Taxes in Europe," *Public Finance and Management* 1 (2003), offers a comprehensive survey. Ian W. H. Parry and Kenneth Small answer the question "Does Britain or the United States have the right gasoline tax?" with neither (Resources for the Future Discussion Paper 02-12, 2004): U.S. taxes are much too low; the U.K.'s may be too high.

9. Lucas Davis and Lutz Kilian, "Estimating the Effect of a Gasoline Tax on Carbon Emissions," *Journal of Applied Econometrics* (2010), estimate the effect of tax increases on carbon emissions based on state-level differences across the United States to derive short-run effects. Thomas Sterner shows that long-run effects are at least three times as high, owing to larger adjustments that can only

be made over time; see his "Fuel Taxes: An Important Instrument for Climate Policy," *Energy Policy* 35, no. 6 (2007). Wait for Chapter 7 for much more on driving (and flying).

10. "Happiness" economists may create an additional wrinkle here. Some, such as Lord Richard Layard, author of *Happiness: Lessons from a New Science* (Penguin, 2005), argue that taxing labor may actually be appropriate to *dis*courage "excess" work.

11. The Norwegians Annegrete Bruvoll and Bodil Merethe Larsen study their country's case in statistical detail: "Greenhouse Gas Emissions in Norway: Do Carbon Taxes Work?" *Energy Policy* 32, no. 4 (2004). They do, but only up to a point.

12. Ryan Lizza, "As the World Burns: How the Senate and the White House Missed Their Best Chance to Deal with Climate Change," *New Yorker*, October 11, 2010.

13. George Packer, "The Empty Chamber: Just How Broken Is the Senate?" *New Yorker*, August 9, 2010.

6: MIND VERSUS MATTER

1. The Global Footprint Network has among the best statistics on this topic. The World Resources Institute and Earth Policy Institute compile similarly prescient numbers.

2. The United Nations Department of Economic and Social Affairs publishes *World Population Prospects: The 2010 Revision* (2011). Hans Rosling puts global population growth into context in a short TED talk, "On Global Population Growth" (June 2010).

3. Robert Solow's observation appeared in a short article, "To Grow or Not to Grow," *Newsweek*, March 13, 1972. For the latest by a subset of the original authors, see Donella Meadows, Jørgen Randers, and Dennis Meadows, *The Limits to Growth: The 30-Year Update* (Chelsea Green Publishing, 2004).

4. Jared Diamond's *Collapse* (Viking, 2005) provides the door-stopping, authoritative account.

5. Matt Ridley's *Rational Optimist* (Harper, 2010) has the last word on the subject. Martin Weitzman's "Recombinant Growth," *Quarterly Journal of Economics* 113, no. 2 (1998), has the mathematical version.

6. See Kenneth Arrow, Partha Dasgupta, Lawrence Goulder, Kevin Mumford, and Kirsten Oleson, "Sustainability and the Measurement of Wealth" (NBER Working Paper 16599, 2010), which presents the latest and one of the best efforts of trying to come to terms with this issue.

7. Ray Kurzweil, *The Singularity Is Near: When Humans Transcend Biology* (Viking, 2005).

8. Gwynne Dyer's *Climate Wars* (Oneworld, 2010) is a particularly powerful example in the genre of war scenario planning.

9. Cited by John Tierney, who tells the whole story in "Betting on the Planet," *New York Times Magazine*, December 2, 1990.

10. In "Burning Buried Sunshine: Human Consumption of Ancient Solar Energy," *Climate Change* 61, nos. 1–2 (2003), Jeffrey Dukes calculates that every gallon of gasoline "required approximately 90 metric tons of ancient plant matter as precursor material," making it one of the more inefficient fuels: "The formation of oil and gas from phytoplankton is less than 0.01% efficient." (By contrast, current solar panels achieve approximately 15 percent efficiency.) William Broad provides a short, comprehensive account of the formation of oil in "Tracing Oil Reserves to Their Tiny Origins," *New York Times*, August 3, 2010.

11. See Weitzman's "Recombinant Growth."

12. Jane Brox's *Brilliant: The Evolution of Artificial Light* (Houghton Mifflin Harcourt, 2010) recounts this tale as part of the evolution of artificial light.

13. Ugo Bardi details whale oil extraction and prices in "Prices and Production over a Complete Hubbert Cycle: The Case of the American Whale Fisheries in 19th Century" (Association for the Study of Peak Oil and Gas, November 24, 2004), largely based on numbers collected by Alexander Starbuck in his self-published *History of the American Whale Fishery from Its Earliest Inception to the Year 1876* (Waltham, Mass., 1878). Brox retells the story in *Brilliant*. Ugo Bardi and Alessandro Lavacchi show data on whale oil and the size of the fleet in "A Simple Interpretation of Hubbert's Model of Resource Exploitation," *Energies* 2, no. 3 (2009). Note that the label in figure 5 of that paper should read "year 0 = 1818," not "1804," a typo confirmed with the authors.

14. The horse manure story has been told many times, most comprehensively by Eric Morris in "From Horse Power to Horsepower," *Access*, no. 30 (2007); most prominently by Steven D. Levitt and Stephen J. Dubner in *Superfreakonomics* (William Morrow, 2009); and most convincingly by Elizabeth Kolbert in a *New Yorker* review of the book's climate section ("Hosed," November 16, 2009). Kolbert thankfully also clears up some of the misconceptions propagated by *Superfreakonomics*.

15. See James Flink, *The Automobile Age* (MIT Press, 1988); and Glenn Yago, *The Decline of Transit* (Cambridge University Press, 1984).

16. Eyal Dvir and Kenneth Rogoff provide oil price data from 1861 to 2008 in "The Three Epochs of Oil" (Boston College Working Paper in Economics 706, April 13, 2009).

17. James Hamilton's "Why New Oil Price Highs?" (April 17, 2008), provides a unifying explanation. Michael Masters is a particularly outspoken proponent of the theory that much of the price spike was a bubble akin to that in the housing

market (talk at MIT's Center for Energy and Environmental Policy Research conference, November 2008).

18. James Hamilton put the Chinese increase at 860,000 barrels a day between 2005 and 2007 at a talk at an MIT Center for Energy and Environmental Policy Research conference in November 2008. He also showed that consumption by countries that are part of the Organization for Economic Cooperation and Development actually decreased during that time, albeit by a smaller amount, exacerbating the power shift.

19. A. F. Alhajji and David Huettner provide the most convincing evidence around Saudi Arabia's domination of world oil markets. Their article "OPEC and Other Commodity Cartels: A Comparison," *Energy Policy* 28, no. 15 (2000), provides good background information, and their article "The Target Revenue Model and the World Oil Market: Empirical Evidence from 1971 to 1994," *Energy Journal*, April 1, 2000, lays out the case for Saudi Arabia as the dominant player. Bassam Fattouh surveys the latest evidence in "OPEC Pricing Power: The Need for a New Perspective" (Oxford Institute for Energy Studies WPM 31, 2007).

20. Jon Stewart took on the issue on *The Daily Show* with characteristic aplomb ("An Energy Independent Future," June 16, 2010).

21. In "The End of Cheap Oil," *Scientific American*, March 1998, Colin Campbell and Jean Laherrère support their title's declaration with good evidence, and that before the latest price rally. There is still plenty of controversy and active debate around this issue. Google "peak oil" for the latest, although most respected institutes in the prediction business (the likes of the International Energy Agency, the U.S. Energy Information Administration, and others) agree with the basic tenets that the era of cheap oil is over.

22. Cynthia Lin and I published these results in "Steady-State Growth in a Hotelling Model of Resource Extraction," *Journal of Environmental Economics and Management* 54, no. 1 (2007). The Handbook of Natural Resource and Energy Economics, edited by James Sweeney and Lonfe Allen Kneese (1993), provides a comprehensive earlier survey of many of the theoretical issues.

23. Richard Carson, Maria Damon, Leigh Johnson, and Jamie Gonzalez, "Conceptual Issues in Designing a Policy to Phase Out Metal-Based Antifouling Paints on Recreational Boats in San Diego Bay," *Journal of Environmental Management* 90, no. 8 (2009). Damon and Carson go one step further and highlight the features of two-part technology standards in "A New Approach to Environmental Technology Standards" (draft, March 2010).

24. Arthur van Benthem, Kenneth Gillingham, and James Sweeney come to this conclusion in "Learning-by-Doing and the Optimal Solar Policy in California," *Energy Journal* 29, no. 3 (2008). In "Analyzing Historical Cost Trends in California's Market for Customer-Sited Photovoltaics," *Progress in Photovoltaics: Research*

and Applications 15, no. 1 (2007), Ryan Wiser, Mark Bolinger, Peter Cappers, and Robert Margolis conclude that installation costs, independent of module costs for solar panels, have declined significantly.

25. The Stanford team's research, of course, comes with plenty of caveats and special extensions. One is that it focuses on learning by doing on the installer and contractor side rather than at the level of solar panel manufacturers. That means the results are much more universally applicable, and not just for renewables. See Kenneth Gillingham and James Sweeney, "Market Failure and the Structure of Externalities," in *Harnessing Renewable Energy in Electric Power Systems: Theory, Practice, Policy,* edited by Boaz Moselle, Jorge Padilla, and Richard Schmalensee (RFF Press, 2010). The topic is still very much an area of active research. Gillingham is analyzing a new set of data that may provide a more detailed look.

26. Daron Acemoglu, Philippe Aghion, Leonardo Bursztyn, and David Hemous's "Environment and Directed Technical Change" (working paper, April 28, 2010) summarizes many of the issues and lays out a comprehensive model addressing negative environmental and positive technical externalities. See also Adam Jaffe, Richard Newell, and Robert Stavins, "A Tale of Two Market Failures: Technology and Environmental Policy," *Ecological Economics* 54, nos. 2–3 (2005).

27. Your fridge would notice if the sun suddenly didn't shine or the wind didn't blow. This kind of "intermittency" is a real issue for some renewable energy sources. But it, too, has a ready solution: advancing energy storage facilities— from something as simple as a flywheel to pumping water uphill.

7: CARS (AND PLANES)

1. Daniel Sperling and Deborah Gordon present a wealth of statistics and policy solutions in *Two Billion Cars* (Oxford University Press, 2009).

2. Several lists have similar rankings. This one is taken from "10 Countries with Cheapest Gas Prices in the World," http://current.com//19cae4c.

3. Redefining Progress cites some of the prominent studies adding up total externalities from driving ("Beyond Gas Taxes: Linking Driving Fees to Externalities," 2010). Later notes throughout this chapter point to other studies focused on tallying externalities.

4. Aaron Edlin and Pinar Karaca-Mandic provide the requisite statistics and much more in "The Accident Externality from Driving," *Journal of Political Economy* 114, no. 5 (2006). They also make a crucial mistake in the original publication, since corrected in "Erratum: 'The Accident Externality from Driving,'" *Journal of Political Economy* 115, no. 4 (2007). Everything presented here reflects the correction. The error, by the way, was discovered by Roy Mill, then a student at

Hebrew University. Mill started his Ph.D. at Stanford a year after the correction was published. Attention to detail pays.

5. For math aficionados, here's what I did: National costs are around $400 billion. Americans drive around three trillion miles a year. That gives you an unaccounted accident cost of ten to fifteen cents a mile. At an average of twenty miles a gallon, that leads to a per-gallon cost of $2 to $3.

6. "Giffen goods," or rather "Giffen behavior," provides one major exception to the law of demand. Robert Jensen and Nolan Miller wrote the seminal paper identifying this property for rice in poor, rural southern China: If the price of rice goes up, the poor may no longer be able to afford meat, but they will still have to eat. They now buy more of the more expensive rice and less of the still much more expensive meat to keep their calories up and their food budget in check. See their "Giffen Behavior and Subsistence Consumption," *American Economic Review* 98, no. 4 (2008).

7. Molly Espey provides an early survey of related studies in "Explaining the Variation in Elasticity Estimates of Gasoline Demand in the United States: A Meta-Analysis," *Energy Journal* 17, no. 3 (1996), two years later updated and internationalized in "Gasoline Demand Revisited: An International Meta-Analysis of Elasticities," *Energy Economics* 20, no. 3 (1998). Ian W. H. Parry, Margaret Walls, and Winston Harrington have one of the latest and most comprehensive surveys, including a discussion of externalities more generally: "Automobile Externalities and Policies," *Journal of Economic Literature* 45, no. 2 (2007). Also see Jonathan E. Hughes, Christopher R. Knittel, and Daniel Sperling, "Evidence of a Shift in the Short-Run Price Elasticity of Gasoline Demand," *Energy Journal* 29, no. 1 (2008). Daniel J. Graham and Stephen Glaister zero in on how people react to higher gas prices and survey the international literature: "The Demand for Automobile Fuel: A Survey of Elasticities," *Journal of Transport Economics and Policy* 36, no. 1 (2002). Also see Kenneth Gillingham, "Identifying the Elasticity of Driving: Evidence from a Gasoline Price Shock in California" (2010).

8. Toyota says to call more than one Prius "Prius." Some Prius owners take pride in calling their possessions "Prii." That's not exactly right, as the Latin plural would be "Prioria," which (*a*) sounds odd and (*b*) is medieval Latin for "priories." See Jan Freeman, "The Plurals of 'Prius,'" *Boston Globe*, March 12, 2007. "Priuses" it is: "And while Prius drivers are a devout lot, they probably don't think of their cars as nunneries and monasteries."

9. See note 7, above, for studies looking at the topic. The upshot is that for a 10 percent increase in gas prices, drivers use around 1 to 3 percent less gas immediately, mostly by driving less. (In "Evidence of a Shift in the Short-Run Price Elasticity of Gasoline Demand," Hughes, Knittel, and Sperling get numbers below 1 percent for recent years.) After months and years with higher gas prices,

they shift to more fuel-efficient cars and drive fewer miles in them. The overall effect is then around 5 to 8 percent lower gas use for any 10 percent long-term increase in price. The biggest impact comes from driving more fuel-efficient cars; the rest comes from driving fewer miles.

10. Hunt Allcott and Nathan Wozny's paper on the topic is "Gasoline Prices, Fuel Economy, and the Energy Paradox" (latest working paper version: March 29, 2010, presented at the NBER Summer Institute, July 29, 2010).

11. Kenneth Small and Kurt van Dender have one of the latest studies on the rebound effect: "The Effect of Improved Fuel Economy on Vehicle Miles Traveled: Estimating the Rebound Effect Using U.S. State Data, 1966–2001" (*Energy Policy and Economics* 14, September 2005). Small and van Dender have a follow-up study showing even smaller effects: "Fuel Efficiency and Motor Vehicle Travel: The Declining Rebound Effect," *Energy Journal* 28, no. 1 (2007).

12. John DeCicco assesses CAFE standards in the context of the wider transportation policy web in "Vehicle Standards in a Climate Policy Framework" (chapter 7 in Daniel Sperling and James S. Cannon, eds., *Climate and Transportation Solutions: Findings from the 2009 Asilomar Conference on Transportation and Energy Policy*, Davis, CA: University of California, Davis, Institute of Transportation Studies).

13. David Greene surveys the literature in "How Consumers Value Fuel Economy" (EPA, 2010) and finds that of twenty-five distinct studies, twelve say consumers undervalue fuel economy and five say consumers overvalue it. The CAFE debate is also very active. Carolyn Fischer, Winston Harrington, and Ian W. H. Parry answer the question in their title, "Should Automobile Fuel Economy Standards Be Tightened?" *Energy Journal* 28, no. 4 (2007), with a "maybe." Mark R. Jacobsen, one of the brightest young lights focused on CAFE, calculates that gas taxes are over twice as cost-effective in achieving emissions reductions relative to CAFE standards ("Evaluating U.S. Fuel Economy Standards in a Model with Producer and Household Heterogeneity," working paper, September 2010). A National Research Council committee on the "Effectiveness and Impact of Corporate Average Fuel Economy (CAFE) Standards" (2002) is more positive.

14. One particularly striking result is that the introduction of E-ZPass, which allows drivers to pay their tolls without stopping and handing over cash, created significant improvements in infant health for mothers living close to tollbooths; see Janet Currie and Reed Walker, "Traffic Congestion and Infant Health: Evidence from E-ZPass," *American Economic Journal: Applied Economics* 3, no. 1 (2011).

15. Martin Wachs comments on the effects in "When Fuel Taxes No Longer Get the Job Done," *Resources* (Summer 2010).

16. Another version is insure-as-you-go. Insurance companies make little distinction between the safe, slow, occasional driver and those who feel the need for speed on every turn. With some few exceptions for age and past accident history, almost everyone pays the same rate regardless of how many miles they drive. The solution: link insurance premiums to how much and how fast drivers actually go. Average premiums wouldn't change by much, but now it quickly becomes much fairer. Slow, careful, occasional drivers would see their premiums drop dramatically. Those who live behind the wheel would pay more. Search for "pay-as-you-go" or "insure-as-you-go" to find some of the few companies already offering this service.

17. See http://www.tfl.gov.uk/roadusers/congestioncharging/ for more on the London system. Todd Alexander Litman details implications for emulators: "London Congestion Pricing: Implications for Other Cities" (http://vtpi.org/london.pdf). A *New York Times* article of March 16, 2008, lists some of the more cumbersome aspects of the system: "Costly to Drive, Painful to Pay." Bruce Schaller recounts the New York experience: "New York City's Congestion Pricing Experience and Implications for Road Pricing Acceptance in the United States," *Transport Policy* 17, no. 4 (2010). Charles Komanoff has been one outspoken advocate for New York congestion pricing. He also has a host of other proposals to improve traffic in New York: http://www.komanoff.net/cars_II/.

18. Donald Shoup penned a comprehensive account titled *The High Cost of Free Parking* (Planners Press, 2005). If reading 750 pages is not your thing, Shoup has also written many an article, including "The Price of Parking on Great Streets," in *Planetizen Contemporary Debates in Urban Planning*, edited by Abhijeet Chaven, Christian Peralta, and Christopher Steins (Island Press, 2007); "Cruising for Parking," *Access*, no. 30 (Spring 2007); and, with Douglas Kolozsvari, "Turning Small Change into Big Changes," *Access*, no. 23 (Fall 2003).

19. "Modern Cargo Ships Slow to the Speed of the Sailing Clippers," *Guardian*, July 25, 2010.

20. An eye-opening report looks at the costs of suburban living in and around Boston. The Urban Land Institute published both the report, *The Boston Regional Challenge,* and a website with a cost calculator, http://bostonregionalchallenge.org.

21. Andres Duany, Elizabeth Plater-Zyberk, and Jeff Speck have written a terrific guide in *Suburban Nation: The Rise of Sprawl and the Decline of the American Dream* (North Point Press, 2000). Harvard economist and dean of urban economics Edward Glaeser provides a riveting account in *Triumph of the City* (Penguin, 2011). He passionately argues against subsidizing suburban landscapes and against restricting the growth and renewal of cities.

8: BRIGHT IDEA

1. Jane Brox describes the birth of electric light in *Brilliant: The Evolution of Artificial Light* (Houghton Mifflin Harcourt, 2010).
2. See Roger Fouquet and Peter J. G. Pearson, "Seven Centuries of Energy Services: The Price and Use of Light in the United Kingdom (1300–2000)," *Energy Journal* 27, no. 1 (2006).
3. Matthew Eckelman, Paul Anastas, and Julie Zimmerman come to this conclusion in "Spatial Assessment of Net Mercury Emissions from the Use of Fluorescent Bulbs," *Environmental Science and Technology* 42, no. 22 (2008).
4. The EPA guidelines for CFL cleanups are available at www.epa.gov/cfl/cflcleanup.pdf.
5. Jeff Tsao et al. describe the cost evolution of LEDs in "Solid-State Lighting: An Energy-Economics Perspective," *Journal of Physics D: Applied Physics* 43, no. 35 (2010), and go on to describe the implications of cheaper light on the demand for lighting and its effects on productivity. *The Economist*, August 26, 2010, summarizes the results (and overplays them a bit) in "Not Such a Bright Idea." Tsao et al. correct the record in a letter to the editor, *Economist*, September 9, 2010.
6. See Tsao et al., "Solid-State Lighting." See also Bill Nordhaus, "Quality Changes in Price Indexes," *Journal of Economic Perspectives* (Winter 1998).
7. The negative link between mercury and cognitive development is increasingly well understood, especially in fetuses and in children. See Joshua Cohen et al., "A Quantitative Analysis of Prenatal Methyl Mercury Exposure and Cognitive Development," *American Journal of Preventive Medicine* 29, no. 4 (2005), for a recent survey. Carmen Freire et al., "Hair Mercury Levels, Fish Consumption, and Cognitive Development in Preschool Children from Granada, Spain," *Environmental Research* 10, no. 1 (2010), conclude that "higher mercury exposure in children . . . was associated with cognitive development delay." Kyrre Sundseth et al., "Economic Benefits from Decreased Mercury Emissions: Projections for 2020," *Journal of Cleaner Production* 18, no. 4 (2010), see "large economic benefits" on the order of $2 billion a year in 2020 through "reducing global mercury emissions."
8. The National Cancer Institute contains a wealth of information, including the latest report of the President's Cancer Panel: pcp.cancer.gov. Nicholas Kristof draws attention to the report in "New Alarm Bells About Chemicals and Cancer," *New York Times*, May 6, 2010.

9: A BILLION POLLUTERS

1. These numbers are for carbon dioxide only. See the first notes in chapter 2.
2. See Shoibal Chakravarty, Ananth Chikkatur, Heleen de Coninck, Stephen Pacala, Robert Socolow, and Massimo Tavoni, "Sharing Global CO_2 Emission

Reductions Among One Billion High Emitters," *Proceedings of the National Academy of Sciences* (2009). Also see Shoibal Chakravarty, Robert Socolow, and Massimo Tavoni, "A Focus on Individuals Can Guide Nations Towards a Low Carbon World," *Climate Science and Policy*, November 13, 2009. Some data come from a talk by Massimo Tavoni and discussions with Tavoni and Shoibal Chakravarty at the Environmental Defense Fund's Climate Economics Seminar (February 11, 2010). Most other data are available at http://cmi.princeton.edu/co2emissions.

3. Carbon intensity figures come from the International Energy Agency's report *CO_2 Emissions from Fuel Combustion* (2009). Focus on the table starting on page 88. The numbers show CO_2 emissions per dollar of GDP, using the purchasing power parity figure, which adjusts for how much a dollar is truly worth in your country. That makes China and other poor countries, where $1 buys more than in rich Europe or America, look better than without the adjustment, but it's fundamentally the right way to look at the numbers. For a counterexample, see the table starting on page 85, where the GDP numbers aren't adjusted and the picture looks much worse for poor countries, including China.

4. Keith Bradsher documents China's energy policies in a series of *New York Times* articles, including "China's Energy Use Threatens Goals on Warming," May 6, 2010, and "In Crackdown on Energy Use, China to Shut 2,000 Factories," August 9, 2010.

5. Milton and his wife, Rose, wrote many classics. My quotations come from *Free to Choose: A Personal Statement* (Houghton Mifflin Harcourt, 1990).

6. For a more technical discussion of this idea, see Alan Krupnick, Ian W. H. Parry, Margaret Walls, Tony Knowles, and Kristin Hayes, *Toward a New Energy Policy: Assessing the Options* (National Energy Policy Institute and Resources for the Future, 2010).

7. McKinsey has published a slew of reports on its cost-curve work, all available at http://www.mckinsey.com/clientservice/sustainability/Costcurves.asp. The U.S. energy-efficiency data come from *Unlocking Energy Efficiency in the U.S. Economy* (July 2009) and focus on 2020. The most recent global cost curve was published in *Impact of the Financial Crisis on Carbon Economics: Version 2.1 of the Global Greenhouse Gas Abatement Cost Curve* (August 2010), which provides a post-crisis update to the more comprehensive report, *Pathways to a Low-Carbon Economy: Version 2 of the Global Greenhouse Gas Abatement Cost Curve* (January 2009). These global reports focus on 2030. Hence the difference in years in the text.

8. I use $50 per ton of CO_2 or five cents per kilowatt-hour in 2030 as "reasonable cost"; $50 per ton corresponds to a social cost of carbon at a 2.5 percent discount rate. (See appendix 15A referenced in chapter 2.) China accounts for over 2.5

billion tons in possible emissions reductions by 2030 that all come in as net savings, and over 7 billion tons if we stick to under $50 each.

9. The subsidy number comes from the International Energy Agency, "Energy Subsidies: Getting the Prices Right" (June 7, 2010). The other cost estimates are from the McKinsey reports. (See prior notes.)

10. The UN Secretary-General's High-Level Advisory Group on Climate Change Financing is only the latest to say as much (final report published in November 2010).

11. Gernot Wagner, Nathaniel Keohane, Annie Petsonk, and James Wang, "Docking into a Global Carbon Market: Clean Investment Budgets to Finance Low-Carbon Economic Development," in *The Economics and Politics of Climate Change*, edited by Dieter Helm and Cameron Hepburn (Oxford University Press, 2009), has more detail. Jeffrey Frankel proposed a similar concept: "An Elaborated Proposal for Global Climate Policy Architecture: Specific Formulas and Emission Targets for All Countries in All Decades" (Harvard Project on International Climate Agreements Discussion Paper 08-08, 2008). See also Jonathan Wiener, "Climate Change Policy and Policy Change in China," *UCLA Law Review* 55 (2008).

12. The report *China's Green Revolution* (2009) dives deeper into these numbers.

13. Simon Kuznets's original article appeared in 1955: "Economic Growth and Income Inequality." Many have tested his hypothesis, initially with great success. More careful analyses have since poked holes into the theory. Gary Fields summarizes the latest evidence and disputes the existence of a Kuznets curve for income inequality: *Distribution and Development: A New Look at the Developing World* (MIT Press, 2001).

14. The Frenchman Emmanuel Saez has become the go-to expert on income inequality in the United States. See the book he co-wrote with Thomas Piketty, *Income Inequality in the United States, 1913–1998* (National Bureau of Economic Research, 2001). More accessible and updated: "Striking It Richer: The Evolution of Top Incomes in the United States" (working paper, 2010).

15. Two of the first and most significant papers in this series were Thomas Selden and Daqing Song's "Environmental Quality and Development: Is There a Kuznets Curve for Air Pollution Emissions?" *Journal of Environmental Economics and Management* 27, no. 2 (1994), and especially Gene Grossman and Alan Krueger's "Economic Growth and the Environment," *Quarterly Journal of Economics* 110, no. 2 (1995). William Harbaugh, Arik Levinson, and David Molloy Wilson cast doubt on the general conclusions in "Reexamining the Empirical Evidence for an Environmental Kuznets Curve," *Review of Economics and Statistics* 84, no. 3 (2002). William Brock and Scott Taylor's "Green Solow Model" (NBER Working Paper 10557, 2004) provides a well-grounded theoretical explanation for the environmental Kuznets curve and successfully tests the predicted convergence

in pollution across Organization for Economic Cooperation and Development countries. Joe Aldy adds trade to an analysis of pollution in U.S. states: "An Environmental Kuznets Curve Analysis of U.S. State-Level Carbon Dioxide Emissions," *Journal of Environment and Development* 14, no. 1 (2005); and "Energy and Carbon Dynamics at Advanced Stages of Development: An Analysis of the U.S. States, 1960–1999," *Energy Journal* 28, no. 1 (2007). One of my own papers, "Energy Content of World Trade," *Energy Policy* 38, no. 12 (2010), combines trade with the environmental Kuznets curve and finds the relationship for production but not consumption.

16. Werner Antweiler, Brian Copeland, and Scott Taylor wrote the authoritative study on the topic and answer the title question affirmatively: "Is Free Trade Good for the Environment?" *American Economic Review* 91, no. 4 (2001). Copeland and Taylor summarize a good portion of the literature in "Trade, Growth, and the Environment," *Journal of Economic Literature* 42, no. 1 (2004). Carolyn Fischer paints a more complicated picture in "Does Trade Help or Hinder the Conservation of Natural Resources?" *Review of Environmental Economics and Policy* 4, no. 1 (2010).

17. Glen Peters has assembled the largest body of work of anyone looking at production versus consumption-based emissions accounting. One of his latest is: Glen Peters, Jan Minx, Christopher Weber, and Ottmar Edenhofer, "Growth in emission transfers via international trade from 1990 to 2008," *Proceedings of the National Academy of Sciences* (2001).

18. Timothy Deal provides a good summary of options in "WTO Rules and Procedures and Their Implication for the Kyoto Protocol" (U.S. Council for International Business, 2008).

10: MARKET MORALS

1. Loren Eiseley's original story appeared in *The Unexpected Universe* (Harcourt, Brace & World, 1969), posthumously reprinted in *The Star Thrower* (Times Books, 1978).

2. That twist, I am happy to say, does not come from an economist. It comes courtesy of Tim and Wendy, two foster parents who grew tired of hearing the starfish story "justify any action to help people, no matter how ineffective or inefficient it is" (Foster Parenting Podcast, episode 90, "A New Starfish Story," http://fosterpodcast.com/episode-90-starfish-story/).

3. For one of the latest and best accounts of how to channel the profit motive to do good, see Ha-Joon Chang's *23 Things They Don't Tell You About Capitalism* (Bloomsbury Press, 2011): "My criticism is of free-market capitalism, and not all kinds of capitalism. The profit motive is still the most powerful and effective fuel

to power our economy and we should exploit it to the full. But we must remember that letting it loose without any restraint is not the best way to make the most of it, as we have learned at great cost over the last three decades."

4. For some terrific, recent expositions of the general ideas, pick up Dan Ariely's *Predictably Irrational* (Harper Perennial, 2010) and Barry Schwartz and Kenneth Sharpe's *Practical Wisdom* (Riverhead Books, 2010).

5. David Cutler, Edward Glaeser, and Jesse Shapiro provide a comprehensive answer in "Why Have Americans Become More Obese?" *Journal of Economic Perspectives* 17, no. 3 (2003).

6. Michael Sandel first made this argument in a *New York Times* Op-Ed shortly after the Kyoto climate talks: "It's Immoral to Buy the Right to Pollute" (December 15, 1997). He has since repeated and refined his argument in discussions of his book *Justice* (Farrar, Straus and Giroux, 2009), which does not address the issue directly but has given me the libertarianism/utilitarianism distinction in the previous section. For a different take on business ethics and the ethics of business, see Martin Sandbu's *Just Business: Arguments in Business Ethics* (Pearson Education, 2011).

7. The WTO states this flat out as part of its effort to counter misinformation "found on websites." Good luck, but here's a start: http://www.wto.org/english/thewto _e/minist_e/min99_e/english/misinf_e/03lab_e.htm.

THANK YOU

To Rob Stavins and Marty Weitzman, both of whom have been not just recurring guides throughout this book but also central characters in my own life ever since I set foot in their offices during my first week of freshman year in college. This book would not have been possible without them.

To Dale Jorgenson, who opened his office door to me before I knew what econometrics meant and who introduced me to the world of green accounting and many an idea throughout this book.

To Bill Hogan and Richard Zeckhauser, whose magnetic orbits I was fortunate to enter when I returned to Cambridge for graduate school.

To Nolan Miller, who opened my eyes to the values of teaching and turning perfectly well-adjusted students into economists.

To Glenn Adelson, Larry Buell, Steve Curwood, Bill Pannapacker, Ingrid Schwarzenbacher, and Don Wolter, who taught me to tell my first (English) stories.

To Nat Keohane, who guided me through my first environmental economics classes and made it an easy decision for me to join him at the Environmental Defense Fund when he called ten years later.

To Peter Goldmark for his unending support, criticism, encouragement, mentorship, and joie de vivre.

To Peter Edidin for his early enthusiasm for this book and for standing by me every step along the way.

To Tom Olson, for a lifetime of irreverent quips and a level of enthusiasm and attention to detail for this project that remain unmatched.

To Richard Davies and Judy Stoeven, who were there from beginning to end with editing tips for my book proposal and a quiet place to read final page proofs wedged between a beach and a fireplace.

To Cynthia Hampton, Miriam Horn, Joel Plagenz, Gail Ross, Anna Sproul, and Howard Yoon, for helping me channel my nebulous idea into a book and for having last names that let me list them in both alphabetical and chronological order.

To Thomas LeBien and his team at Farrar, Straus and Giroux and Hill and Wang, whose love of books turned this into one.

To Ryan Chapman, Dan Crissman, Kathy Daneman, Meredith Kessler, Amanda Schoonmaker, Jeff Seroy, Sarita Varma, and the entire publicity team at FSG, who will no doubt make sure the planet notices this book, never mind that it hits shelves some time between the latest offerings by the thrice-Pulitzered Tom Friedman and the Pulitzer-winning novelist Jeffrey Eugenides. (The relevant economic concept is diminishing marginal returns. Their books sell themselves. Every minute you spend on mine makes a real difference.)

To Christina Baute, Nayon Cho, Jason Das, Jonathan Fetter-Vorm, Abby Kagan, and Yuki Kokubo for lending their artistic talents, respectively, to jacket suggestions, jacket design, illustrations throughout the book, my website, book design, and my mug shot.

To Fred Krupp, David Yarnold, and Marcia Aronoff for helping me take on this five-to-nine project on top of my nine-to-five job.

To Delia Barrack, Diahan Walker-Sealy, and especially Miriam

Chaum for making my day job anything but, and who still found time to help me with this book in every way imaginable.

To L. A. Burdick for providing a writing home away from home, a place to hide from the office, and the best hot chocolate between Cambridge and New York.

To Fahad Huq, Thomas Hwang, Jared Schor, Ben Spar, Sasha Vartelskaya, and in particular Lily Kelly for researching and checking entire story lines based on my vague recollections of odd facts and factual oddities.

To Daron Acemoglu, Martin Ådahl, Jonathan Adler, Richie Ahuja, Joe Aldy, Hunt Allcott, Dick Allen, Jon Anda, Ugo Bardi, Scott Barrett, Michael Bean, Ruth Greenspan Bell, Emma Berndt, Mark Brownstein, Barbara Buchner, Eric Budish, Jing Cao, Shoibal Chakravarty, James Crabtree, Maria Damon, Steve Davis, Antoine Dechezleprêtre, John DeCicco, Richard Denison, Dan Dudek, Denny Ellerman, Michael Faye, Jamie Fine, Tim Fitzgerald, Meredith Fowlie, Rod Fujita, Keith Gaby, Ken Gillingham, Sasha Golub, Kevin Gorman, Larry Goulder, Rod Griffin, Steve Hamburg, Ayelet Haran, Jennifer Haverkamp, Liza Henshaw, Cameron Hepburn, Mun Ho, Sol Hsiang, Alan Iny, Mark Jacobsen, Scott Kaufman, Peter Klebnikov, Matt Kotchen, Carolyn Kousky, Alan Krupnick, Mike Levi, Ian Lloyd, Karl-Gustaf Löfgren, Måns Lönnroth, Frank Loy, Ruben Lubowski, Oleg Lugovoy, Emily Maynard, Joe Mazor, Kyle Meng, Roy Mill, Lisa Moore, Naki Nakićenović, Michael Oppenheimer, Cindy Paladines, Jisung Park, Sandeep Patel, Annie Petsonk, Eric Pooley, Patira Puttharuksa, Doug Rader, Michael Regan, Jack Riggs, Kate Sims, Thomas Sterner, Dick Stewart, Ian Sue Wing, Max Tavoni, Jim Tripp, Derek Walker, Rohit Wanchoo, James Wang, Michael Wara, Dave Witzel, David Wolfe, Katrina Wyman, and many others for enlightening discussions, insights, and comments along the way.

To Oma, Opa, Mutti, Vati, Michael, and Robert, who taught me to live.

To Siripanth Nippita, who taught me to love.

INDEX